The Reminiscences

of

CAPTAIN WALTER C. CAPRON

U. S. Coast Guard (Retired)

U. S. Naval Institute
Annapolis, Maryland
1971

This manuscript is the result of a series of tape-recorded interviews with Captain Walter C. Capron, USCG (Retired) at this home in Arlington, Virginia, during 1969 and 1970. These interviews were conducted by Mr. Peter Spectre for the Oral History Office in the U. S. Naval Institute.

Only minor emendations and corrections have been made by Captain Capron. Therefore the reader is asked to bear in mind that he is reading a transcript of the spoken word rather than the written one.

DECLARATION OF TRUST

The undersigned does hereby appoint and designate as his (her) Trustee herein, the Secretary-Treasurer and Publisher of the United States Naval Institute to perform and discharge the following duties, powers, and privileges in connection with the possession and use of a certain taped interview between the undersigned and the Oral History Department of the United States Naval Institute.

1. Classification of Transcript.

    ( )a. If classified OPEN, the transcript(s) may be read or the recording(s) audited by the qualified personnel upon presentation of proper credentials, as determined by the Secretary-Treasurer of the U. S. Naval Institute.

    (X)b. If classified PERMISSION REQUIRED TO CITE OR QUOTE, the user will be required to obtain permission in writing from the interviewee prior to quoting or citing from either the transcript(s) or the recording(s).

    ( )c. If classified PERMISSION REQUIRED, permission must be obtained in writing from the interviewee before the transcribed interview(s) can be examined or the tape recording(s) audited.

    ( )d. If classified CLOSED, the transcribed interview(s) and the tape recording(s) will be sealed until a time specified by the interviewee. This may be until the death of the interviewee or for any specified number of years.

2. It is expressly understood that in giving this authorization, I am in no way precluded from placing such restrictions as I may desire upon use of the interview at any time during my lifetime, nor does this authorization in any way affect my rights to the copyright of my literary expressions that may be contained in the interview.

Witness my hand and seal this 2nd day of August 1970

Walter C Capron

I hereby accept and consent to the foregoing Declaration of Trust and the powers therein conferred upon me as Trustee:

R E Bowler J

Public Information Division
U. S. Coast Guard
Washington 25, D. C.

RECEIVED SEP 18 1969

Biographical Sketch

CAPTAIN WALTER C. CAPRON, U. S. COAST GUARD (Ret.)

Walter Clark Capron was born in Elmira, N. Y., on September 25, 1904, son of the Rev. Harold S. Capron and Mrs. Mattie C. Capron. He attended Hannibal Hamlin Grammar School and Bangor High School of Bangor, Me., and was graduated from Rogers High School at Newport, Rhode Island in 1923.

He was appointed a cadet at the U. S. Coast Guard Academy, New London, Conn., on April 14, 1925, and was graduated and commissioned an Ensign on May 15, 1928. Subsequently he advanced in rank to Lieutenant (jg), May 15, 1930; Lieutenant, May 15, 1932; Lieutenant Commander, May 23, 1941; Commander, September 15, 1942; Captain, August 11, 1945.

During his first assignment he served aboard the Destroyer CONYNGHAM of the Boston Division of the old Destroyer Force (operated by the Coast Guard between 1924 and 1934 to suppress smuggling). He then served with the Cutter SENECA of the New York Division in the North Atlantic and at Puerto Rico, from March 1931 to January 1934. After a tour of duty as Communications Officer and Public Relations Officer at Boston, he returned to sea in March 1937 as executive officer of the Cutter THETIS of Boston. In November of that year he was assigned as executive officer of the Cutter COMANCHE, stationed in New York. He commanded the cutter from November 1938 to August 1939.

Transferred to Baltimore, Md., he served as commanding officer of the Cutter CALYPSO and had the additional duties of Captain-of-the-Port of Baltimore, and nearby ports of Maryland, Virginia, and Washington, D. C.

In May 1941 he was assigned to the staff of the Transports Commander, Atlantic Fleet, and served afloat alternately aboard the USS BARNETT, USS McCAULEY, USS HARRY LEE, USS MT. VERNON and USS LEONARD WOOD. During this tour of duty, his group took the first U. S. troops (34th Division) to Ireland. A year later, after the United States had entered World War II, he joined the staff of the Engineer Amphibian Command, U. S. Army, at Camp Edwards, Mass., where he commanded a Coast Guard Detachment and directed the Army's first school of instruction for troops in beach landing craft operations. In August 1942 he was assigned to the staff of Commander, Amphibious Force, Atlantic Fleet. He conducted training in beach landings for most divisions, engineer regiments, and naval beach battalions used in the Atlantic battle. Captain Capron himself was Officer-in-Charge, Beach Party School and Commanding Officer of First Naval Beach Battalion. (Much of the training took place off Norfolk, Va., and Fort Pierce, Fla.)

(more)

CAPT Walter C. Capron, USCG - (Cont'd)

Relieved of amphibious training operations with the other services in May 1943, Captain Capron commanded the Coast Guard Cutter SPENCER on convoy escort operations between United States and Mediterranean ports, and Caribbean ports. He received a Navy Commendation Ribbon with Combat Distinguishing Device for this service.

Reassigned in August 1944, to Coast Guard Headquarters, Washington, D. C., he served first as Assistant Operations Officer until March 1946, then as Chief, Enlisted Personnel Division, until September 1950. He then commanded the Cutter SPENCER out of New York on North Atlantic Ocean Station (Weather) Patrol until January 1951, when designated Law Enforcement Officer on the staff of the Commander, Third Coast Guard District in New York City.

After attending the National War College in Washington, D. C., from August 1951 to July 1952, he became Chief, Program Analysis Division at Coast Guard Headquarters. In March 1955, he became Operations Officer on the staff of the Commander, 12th Coast Guard District in San Francisco, later becoming Chief of Staff.

In July 1957, Captain Capron returned to Coast Guard Headquarters to assume the duties of Deputy Chief of Staff. He held that post until his retirement on September 1, 1962. As a climax to his 34 years in the Service, Captain Capron was awarded the LEGION OF MERIT "For exceptionally meritorious conduct in the performance of outstanding services as Deputy Chief of Staff..." The accompanying citation which he received praised his constant interest, broad vision, and skillful interpretation of mariti legislative, and military trends, and his unsparing personal diligence which produced accomplishments of great value to the Service and the American people.

For his work with the Amphibious Forces and command of a group of escort ships during World War II, Captain Capron was awarded Army and Navy Commendation Ribbons with Combat "V". In addition he received the following World War II campaign service medals and ribbons: American Defense with fleet clasp, American Area, European-African-Middle Eastern Area, World War II Victory. He also has the Expert Rifle and Pistol Marksman Medals.

Captain Capron married the former Gertrude Louise Booth of Newport, R.I. He has three children, all married: a son, Walter C., Jr., who served as a Corporal in Korea where he received a Purple Heart for service with the 35th Infantry Regiment of the 25th Division; and two daughters, Marilyn and Patricia. Captain Capron's present address is 4912 16th Road North, Arlington, Va. 22207

Rev.
MAY 1959-eas

Interview # 1

Captain Walter C. Capron, USCG, Ret.　　by Peter Spectre
Arlington, Virginia　　November 1, 1969

Mr. Spectre: I wonder Captain if you could tell me a little about your early life, where you were born, something about your parents, and this type of information.

Captain Capron: My father was a congregational minister whose family originally had come from New England. My mother had been a school teacher. Her family had originally been in New England, and subsequently went to New Jersey. Father was a Brown University graduate, and Union Theological Seminary and with a Master's degree from Columbia.

I was born in Elmira, New York; which was his first pastorate. At about one or two years of age, the family moved to Rochester, New York.

Q: Could you give me the date of your birth?

Capron: September 25th, 1904.
We lived in Rochester, and one of the suburbs, until I was twelve, 1916; at which time we went to Bangor, Maine.

Q: Did you attend public schools in Rochester?

Capron - 2

Capron: I attended public schools in Rochester and the suburb, which was then Irondequoit. Then, in Bangor, I attended the public schools; first the grammar school and later on Bangor High School.

Q: Did your father move to Bangor because of his pastorate?

Capron: Yes.

Q: Do you remember the name of the Church?

Capron: The church in Bangor was the Hammond Street Congregational Church.

In 1921, we moved to Newport, Rhode Island where my father was pastor of the United Congregational Church.

Q: You went to schools both in Bangor and Newport?

Capron: (Then again) Yes In Newport. I attended Rogers High School, which was the only public high school in Newport, and graduated in 1923.

Q: When was the first time that you became interested in the Coast Guard: Was it while you were in Maine or in Newport? Did you come in contact with --

Capron - 3

Capron: Frankly I don't know exactly where. In Maine, I had never heard of the Coast Guard. In Newport, in the early part of the time that I was there, all I knew about the Coast Guard was the fact that there was a Lifeboat Station at Brenton Reef.

However, at that time, in the rather early days of prohibition; the Coast Guard was coming in to more and more prominence in the newspapers. I had, what you might call, a slight interest in it at that time. However, after graduating from high school I was somewhat foot-loose with the intention of ultimately going to college, with no thought of what I would do after I graduated from college. And frankly, no idea of how I was going to finance the college education.

Q: What did your father have to say: Was he interested in you following the ministry, like himself?

Capron: I think he actually was, but he never once to my recollection ever tried to slant me in any way toward any profession. After graduating from high school, I worked for a couple of years. I drove a delivery truck for one of the local meat markets for almost a year.

Q: You continued to live in Newport?

Capron - 4

Capron: I continued to live in Newport with my family. Then, I got a job for part of the summer on a large sea-going yacht. The name of it was the NARADA. It's owner was Henry Walters, the railroad man who claimed Baltimore as his home.

Q: He had a summer house in Newport?

Capron: He had a summer home in Newport. Most of his business was in New York, but he still had his Baltimore connections. It was while I was on that yacht, that I really became interested in going to sea.

Q: Did you have any experience with the sea, or boats, or anything before that?

Capron: Small boats that any boy who grows up on the sea coast has. I could row a boat, yes, that was about the extent of it.

Q: What did you do on the NARADA?

Capron: I started out in the exalted position of fourth steward. I guess I was the youngest kid on the ship. She carried a crew of around 37 or 38 people.

Q: How big was it?

Capron - 5

Capron: 230 odd feet long, she was a big yacht.

Q: About as big as some of the Coast Guard Cutters.

Capron: They permitted me to change to quartermaster. I acted as one of the quartermasters for a few weeks until the end of the season. Both the Captain and the Chief Engineer, shall I say, took a shine to me or they were interested. They first talked to me about the Coast Guard Academy. They thought with my background, that I was foolish if I wanted to go to sea and be only a seaman or what have you; and that if I didn't want to go to sea, I should try something. They suggested the Coast Guard Academy.

So, after being paid off from that, I went back home. My next job was as a roofer's helper. Meanwhile, about this time, my father began to worry just a little bit. I was talking very seriously of enlisting in the Coast Guard. So, he arranged an interview for me with a friend of his, a Lieutenant Colonel in the Marine Corps.

Q: Was this to join the Marines?

Capron: Not so much as join the Marines as to do something rather than what he thought was kind of a waste of education. Another thing, which I haven't mentioned, is that I attended for three years in the summers the CMTC camp (Citizens Military

Capron - 6

Training Camp); which were throughout the country. The one I attended was Camp Devon, Massachusetts. At the end of that time, just as soon as I reached 21, I would have been qualified for second Lieutenant in the organized reserves.

Q: This was a government program?

Capron: A government program which was established under the National Defense Act of 1921. The same act established ROTC in high schools and colleges. (Re-established in colleges.)
With that background, plus my high school diploma, they all thought that I would be wasted if I enlisted. So, this Colonel talked to me and offered several alternatives; including them was an appointment to the Naval Academy. He happened to be in a nephew of the then Secretary of the Navy, Denby, I believe. The upshot of that was, that I decided I would try in the Coast Guard Academy.

Q: During this time, did you give any thought to a civilian career? You did mention, thinking about going to college.

Capron: I never could think of anything I wanted to do. The closest thing was talking about being an electrical engineer. I was a little interested in amateur radio, solely from the kids standpoint of building receivers and small transmittors and so on. But, at that time, I actually decided that I wanted to try for the Coast Guard Academy.

By this time, I had been out of school for nearly two years. So, I was involved in a lot of study catching up. I was working a pretty full six day week as a roofer, except when it rained. I applied to take the examination, and took them in Boston.

Q: When you were studying, did you study on your own, or did you go to ---

Capron: Strictly on my own.

Q: Do you know if the Coast Guard Academy had programs such as preparatory programs? At the Naval Academy, there are always a lot of prep schools.

Capron: At that time, there were none. The closest thing to it would have been what we had in Rogers High School, what was called a Naval Academy prep course; which basically would have taken care of preparation for the Coast Guard Academy.

Q: Was the exam the type of exam it is now, a competetive exam without appointments?

Capron: Yes. The exam was strictly competetive examination. If you had the right credits from high school, you took an examination in three subjects - English, History and Math. If you did not have those credits, you had to take qualifying examinations in addition; which would establish what you might call the equivalent of your high school education.

I took my exams, St. Patrick's day was the first day, in Boston, March 17th. Frankly, until I saw all the numbers that were taking the exam up there at that time; it never occured to me that I might fail. After I saw the number that were taking it, I almost lost courage.

Q: These were boys from all over New England?

Capron: These were boys from all over New England. A number of them were from the Massachusetts Nautical School, the old Nantucket. When I saw them, I began to be frightened. However, it turned out I passed. I ended up to be tendered an appointment as a Cadet, and actually reported at New London on the 4th of May, 1925.

Q: Do you remember about how many people competed nation-wide?

Capron: Approximately 650 is what we were told. My entering class was 41. I don't mean necessarily that only 41 were high enough. There are always some people that are tendered appointments that just don't accept them. The top 41 that accepted were in my class.

Q: Was there an interview conducted also?

Capron: The interview was conducted at the time you took the examination. As a result of that interview, plus the various recomendations that you had submitted, and any other documents that might have influence; from that you were given a mark in adaptability. So, that your final mark consisted of actually four points - Mathematics, English, History, and general adaptability. Each one weighing equally.

At that time, the Academy of course was three years. We entered in May and the first of June we sailed on the Cadet cruise.

Q: The Academy was in New London?

Capron: In New London at Fort Trumbull.

Q: Do you remeber if there were any people who entered the Academy with you who hadn't taken the exam, but had gotten appointments because of pull that they might have had?

Capron: Everybody that was there had taken the examination and had passed high enough to be selected. As an example, that summer there was a young yeoman made the cruise. At the end of the cruise, he was discharged. Then, we found out that

Capron - 10

he was a nephew of either the Assistant Secretary of the Treasurey or under Secretary of the Treasury. The following year, he had taken the examination, and entered the class behind me. Having gone to a full thrown exam and everything else So, I am convinced that if he had to go through that, that everybody did.

Q: You mentioned that he was a yeoman. Were there other Coast Guard enlisted men who got into your Academy class?

Capron: In my class, there was one Cadet who had been a Warrant Officer in the Coast Guard, a Warrant Machinist. There were several who had been enlisted in the Navy. I don't remember any that had been enlisted in the Coast Guard.

Q: After you had been at the Academy only a month, you went on a cruise?

Capron: Right.

Q: Do you remember the ship?

Capron: It was the old ALEXANDER HAMILTON, which had been the Navy gunboat VICKSBURG. A three-master barkentine with a triple-expansion steam engine, originally built in

1898. One of three or four of very similar class; she had been the Cadet training ship since about 1918.

Q: Can you tell me something about the cruise? What you did on it? What your duties were? About your instruction.

Capron: It's the summer practice cruise. Needless to say we worked like the devil.

Basically, the third class, which was my class; would be the apprentices seaman recruits or what have you. The second class acted as Petty Officers, and the first class acted as commissioned officers. There was a small enlisted crew on board, and of course, quite a few Academy officers.

We did all the work practically that you do aboard ship. Being a coal burner, we shoveled a lot of coal down in the fire room. When there was enough wind, we sailed. Quite often, they'd disconnect the propeller shaft and just sail along. There was always plenty to do in setting sail, turning sail, and so forth and so on.

Which I might say, parenthetically, is one excellent reason for having a sailing ship as a practice ship. In that there's a lot of work that will keep a Cadet busy, without it being obviously "made work," to keep him out of mischief. At the same time, after handling some nine months of intensive classroom work; you can't have him studying all summer. So, that the sailing ship is the ideal, to my mind, practice ship.

Capron - 12

By giving him work to do that is not obviously just "made work;" like scrubbing paint work, or chipping paint or something like that.

Q: Did you have any classes on board?

Capron: We had seamanship classes, very elementary courses in navigation and astronomy. By elementary I mean, we were taught the formulas, the working of sights; and how to use a sextant.

Q: But you weren't taught any theory?

Capron: We weren't taught any theory. We could work out a sight yes, having been given the formula and knowing how to take a sight and how to use a nautical almanac and that's about it. But we didn't know why we were doing that. That came much later in the course.

Q: Did you find that difficult, Not knowing what it was about, but still doing it, or the reasons why you were doing it?

Capron: I didn't know. Probably some of them did. My short tour of a couple of months on board this yacht had given me enough of a knowledge of a ship, so I felt, at least, that I was practically an old timer.

Capron - 13

Q: Something I forgot to ask you before - Was the yacht a sailing yacht?

Capron: It was strictly steam. We still had wooden decks, but she was a steel ship.

Port and starboard, and forward and aft and all of that, which the other boys were learning; had become second nature to me to use those terms.

Q: You were pretty lucky.

Capron: Oh, I was. In addition, I was a little more lucky than that. One of my classmates was a graduate of the Nantucket, Schoolship in Boston. He was rather a close friend and helped me a lot in various things. He also taught me how to do a little fancy goldbricking.

As an example, the foremast was square rigged. So, when we were to furl sail, the first ones up were the ones that went all the way up to topgallant - a long ways up, an awful small sail. If you were smart, you were one of the first ones up. You went up there and when you got your sail furled, the boys down below were still sweating it out on the larger sails. That little thing saved me an awful lot of work by just being the first one up.

Capron - 14

Q: I would imagine, knowing a lot about it before you get there really would help.

Capron: It helped a lot. It so happened, in this boy's case, he knew too much. He ended up by being dropped at the end of the Cadet cruise, for a number of things. Basically, he knew too many tricks.

Q: Were you learning both Deck Seamanship and engineering at the time?

Capron: Yes. Basically, we were divided into engineer and line Cadets. Let me go back --

Up until the 1st of July, 1926; Coast Guard officers were in separate corps. There was a line officer and an engineer officer. Cadets were the same way, line Cadets and engineer Cadets.

I was a line Cadet. On that first Cadet cruise, the third class line Cadets made the cruise. The third class engineers stayed back at Fort Trumbull.

Q: How did they decide who was going to be a line officer and who was going to be an engineer officer?

Capron - 15

Capron: You could make a choice on your standings in the examinations. You might got your choice on that. Basically, and probably very improperly, the line Cadet was rated above the engineer Cadet.

Q: Did you want to be a --

Capron: I wanted to be a line. So, on my first Cadet cruise I did not work in the engine room. But, on the 1st of July, 1926; when the official nomination [amalgamation] took place, we all became the same. We worked both on deck and in the engine room, and fireroom.

Q: So, the ones that had been left behind the year before, also went on the cruise?

Capron: They also went on the cruise. From then on, we all took the same subjects. However, the engineers had had to have a little more engineering than we had. We had a little more navigation than they had. There was a year of adjustment, wherein each group had to catch up with the other group.

Q: Do you know the reason why they made this change? Do you have any idea what the background was to that?

Capron: There'd been a lot of agitation for many many years to amalgamate. Many of the engineers actually resented the fact that they never could command. An engineer could never command a ship, or command anything other than a shipyard. I guess it was just generally felt that it would be better to have everybody all around, rather than have this group of specialists. There actually was considerable feeling.

Q: Was there rivalry between the groups?

Capron: There was rivalry and occasionally animosity. Where you would find it, would be on board ship, I'd say. The executive officer, a line officer succeeds to the command of the ship. The Chief Engineer could very easily be senior to the exec, as far as the list of seniority is concerned. But no matter what happened, that engineer could never command a ship. Quite often, if the Captain went on leave, the Chief Engineer would take leave too. Just so he wouldn't have to be under an officer much junior to himself.

Q: They had different insignia?

Capron: Yes. The engineers had a purple background under their stripes, whereas the line officer had no background.

Capron - 17

Q: But they both had the shield?

Capron: Both had the shield. But it was just the background under the stripes. At the same time, we also had a construction corps made up of four to six officers only. And the former life-saving officers, who were a separate corps. They also had a different background under their stripes.

Q: So that in 1926, everybody became the same?

Capron: Everybody, except engineers above the rank of Lieutenant Commander. They sill remained engineers. From Lieutenant Commander on down, they all became the same. They also had to qualify, essentially by taking the promotion examinations.

Q: They must have had a lot of studying to do.

Capron: Some of them had an awful lot of studying to do.

Q: What was the reason for the men above Lieutenant Commander? Was this because they thought they were beyond the point --

Capron: I think probably it was because it was felt that they had sufficient rank that (1) there was still enough jobs for

Capron - 18

them to do and (2) that it would be rather unfair to take an officer who had say already 20 years service and make him start all over again. And particular, to put him in the kind of position that he might be in, as an inexperienced line officer over a very experienced line officer. Which could be quite embarrassing.

Q: So, you see that as a good thing?

Capron: I see it as a good thing. I felt so at the time. As a matter of fact, prior to the passing of that legislation; in our English classes several times we had to write themes taking the stand pro or con as the case might be toward the amalgamation.

Q: To get back to your summer cruise, where did you go on your cruises? Were they just in the local area or --

Capron: The first cruise we stopped at the Azores at Horta. From there to Graves End, England; then to Cherburg, France; Cherburg to Gibraltar; Gilbraltar to Cadiz, Spain; then Bermuda and back home.

Q: Did you get time for yourself in port?

Capron: We had liberty in every port. At that time, it was relatively unsupervised liberty. By that, I mean there were no excursions organized and we were strictly on our own, when we went ashore.

Some years later, that was changed. Whether it was for better or worse, I don't know. It was changed so that a lot of the Cadets had it laid out for them. That is a trip to go see this or to do that or whatever it might be. Educationally, it undoubtedly was good. But it wasn't anywhere near as much fun.

Q: When you look back, do you think that the cruise was a good thing, in light of the fact that you had only been at the Academy a month? Would you rather have had a longer period of time to prepare for it?

Capron: I think it had both its good points and its bad points. The bad point particularly, we had only been at the Academy 25 days, we had no indoctrination as to what was expected of a Cadet. We went on a Cadet cruise and had liberty in all kinds of ports and everything else. I think perhaps that some of my class that were dropped at the end of that first cruise, solely on the basis of behavior. I don't mean misbehavior in the sense of jumping ship or anything like that. I mean merely being heard cussing all the time, a lot of obscene language or something like that. He was just quietly dropped.

I think if he'd been there six months or a year, he'd have learned that those things aren't done. And, there were cases where they were strictly bad habits and nothing else. He'd have overcome it. So, on that basis, I think probably they lost some good people. Because we didn't have a good indoctrination period before we made the Cadet cruise.

Q: Can you remember how many Cadets left at the end of the cruise?

Capron: Counting the engineer Cadet who left, all told I would say pretty close to 20; pretty close to half of them left.

Q: About how many of them resigned?

Capron: Technically, they all resigned.

Q: How many left on their own free-will, because they wanted to?

Capron: I would make a guess of about half of that 20, 10. Some of the engineers left during the summer, because they were right there.

Essentially a lot of the Cadets that came there didn't know a thing about the Coast Guard. They knew nothing what-

Capron - 21

soever about going to sea. When they came, they saw Fort Trumbull; which consisted of World War I wooden barracks and some pretty awful looking terrain. A couple working around there were just completely fed-up. It took considerable desire on the part of anybody to stay.

Q: What were the engineering Cadets doing while you were gone? Did they have ships that they practiced on or --

Capron: One thing they did was a lot of manual labor, but they also had classes in Heat Engines and so forth. Not having experienced it myself, about all I can do is try to remember what they told us that they had done that summer. They emphasized the fact that they did an awful lot of manual labor.

Q: They must have had a pretty dull time compared to what yours was.

Capron: It was, it was very dull. That's the last time they ever did that. As a matter of fact, we were the last class to enter just before the cruise.

From then on, they varied the entering time. Sometime it might be September, sometime it might be July. Now, it's about the 1st of July. In no case, do they make a real cruise until

Capron - 22

after they'd had an academic year. They do take them out, for instance, for a week maybe or something like that. But it's not a real cruise. Then, they also have that indoctrination during the summer. Which, as I said, I think makes an awful lot of difference.

Q: So, you came back in September from your cruise?

Capron: We came back about the 1st of September or the 29th of August, and immediately went on three weeks leave. Which was the first chance we had to show off our uniforms back home.

Q: You went back to Newport?

Capron: I went back to Newport.
   Our academic year started about the 22nd of September. The only other leave we had during the year, was ten days at Christmas time.

Q: Did you get the same amount of leave that a commissioned officer got?

Capron: Thirty days.

Q: Also, in the matter of seniority, did your time for seniority begin when you entered the Academy or when you were commissioned?

Capron - 23

Capron: It changed all the time you were at the Academy. It depended on your average marks for the year. What you graduated with, was what you kept the rest of your life.

Q: What I mean is, for pay purposes. When did you Coast Guard career begin?

Capron: Cadet service does not count for longevity or for retirement. We were Cadets in the Coast Guard. As an odd situation, a Cadet who leaves the Academy and enlists gets Cadet time counted, if he's an elisted man. But if he's an officer, it didn't count.

Q: That's odd. What were the courses that you took in your first year?

Capron: English, Astronomy, Math - which consisted of Algebra and Spherical Trigonometry,--

Q: Did you have courses in Gunnery or --

Capron: Yes, we had courses in Gunnery. Which, at that stage of the game, were more or less do it yourself courses. That is, we were actually working on guns and so forth. No theory, that came later on.

Capron - 24

Q: Did you have any particular difficulty in any of the courses that first year?

Capron: The first year, the thing that almost all of us had difficulty with was Physics. I think it tripped up more people than any other study that we had.

Q: Had you taken Physics in high school?

Capron: I had Physics in high school, but it was an entirely different subject than what I had at the Academy. I know a number of us, just before mid-years, the instructor told us that we were failing. He offered to give us special classes, for those of us who wanted to. Four or five of us took advantage of it. I'm quite sure if it hadn't been for those special tutoring classes that he ran strictly on his own time and on our own time, we would have failed at mid-year. At that time, if you failed a major subject, you went out.

Q: Just one?

Capron: Just one. You could fail a minor subject, like Signals for instance. There were a few minor subjects. You could fail one of those, and make it up later. But one major, and out you went.

Capron - 25

A little later on, in some cases, at the end of the year they would turn a Cadet back. One of my class was turned back at the end of his third class year. As far as I know, he was the first one that they had ever done that with.

Q: If you failed a minor subject, how could you make it up?

Capron: You'd have to make it up by, ultimately, passing the term examination on that part of the subject that you had failed.

Q: You had to study independently?

Capron: You'd have to do that on your own.

Q: What about the instructors that you had there? Were they civilians or commissioned officers?

Capron: At that time, there was one civilian - Professor Chester H. Dimmock, who was in Mathametics. He didn't teach all the Mathametics, but he taught the higher Math. Who, incidentally was finally retired right after World War II. One of the finest men, and one of the finest instructors I've ever seen.

Captron - 26

The rest of the instructors were all regular officers. Some of there were very good, and let's face it, some of them were lousy.

Q: How did they decide on who was going to be an instructor?

Capron: I was never in high enough position at that time to have any idea.

Q: Did they send officers who had specialized in their subject?

Capron: As a general rule, yes. Certainly, they never would send a line officer to teach an engineering subject. And vice versa.

I know that subsequently the instructor that I had in Ordnance, for instance, and Gunnery was a gunnery expert. I know our instructor we had in Navigation was very much of an expert in Navigation. But when you got to some subjects, like Physics and Chemistry and certain subjects which were basic to your education, which were not actually used very much in the day to day work in the service; in those quite often the individual wouldn't be strong enough.

Q: Did they have a permanent instructor corps there, as they do now?

Capron: No, not at that time.

Q: This was just a regular assignment?

Capron: They were carefully selected. That selection may have hurt more than it helped, in that almost invariably an instructor would have been one of the top men in his class. Therefore, things probably had come easy to him. He had a little difficulty understanding some of us dumb johns who were down at the bottom.

Q: What was your relationship with the other two classes that were there? Was it precarious in the sense that there was a lot of hazing?

Capron: Using the definition of hazing that was used then, there was no such thing as hazing. There was running, and I suppose that nowadays you might call it hazing. No upperclassman ever laid a finger on an underclassman. As far as physically was concerned, never. If the individual had refused to do any of the things, he probably would have ended up by being ostracized; not only by the upperclassmen, but by his own class. And one or two did. After a month or so, they quietly submitted their resignations. With the exception of an occasional sadist, which you get in any group of people, there was nothing vicious or personal about the running. Once in a while, you'd get somebody who was. He would single out one individual, and make his

Capron - 28

life miserable. On the whole, it was a group affair. That is, they'd get the whole third class, all of us, out at once. We'd just do calisthenics or things like that. It wouldn't be a question of just picking on one man and saying - okay, you're a bum, and so on.

Q: It was probably a lot easier to bear if all of you were involved.

Capron: Oh, it was.

Q: What about the discipline, as far as the commissioned officers go? Was it very strong discipline?

Capron: I think it was, yes. There isn't any question that it was stronger then, than it is now. I'm not making any determination as to whether it was better then, than it is now. But it was stronger then, than it is now.

The internal discipline of the Cadet Corps was actually maintained by the first class, under the supervision of the faculty. They, in turn, exercised that to a certain extent through the second class but not entirely. They were the ones that you came in contact with. They were the ones that would put you on report for minor violations of discipline and being late for formation, and things like that.

The demerits were very carefully delineated in the regulation book - a specific violation might be three demerits. The upper classman didn't have any choice as to whether he'd give you five or fifty or what have you. Of course, you always had the right to, what we called, belly-ache, protest. In which case, the exec would more or less hold a mast or what have you and hear your side of the story and the upper classman who put you on report - his side of the story.

Q: What was your batting average - on something like that?

Capron: On protesting?

Q: Right.

Capron: Damn near zero.

Q: What about at the end of that year - how were you doing in your studies and ---

Capron: I was holding on by the skin of my teeth.

Q: There were only about 20 Cadets left in the class?

Capron - 30

Capron: There were only about 20 left. We had an exodus of several at mid-years, that third class year. After our second class cruise, which was an Atlantic coast cruise, several more. I think probably by the time we entered our second class year, there were 16 in my class. And one of them went out at the end of that cruise. (first class cruise)

Q: Was this enough officers for the service?

Capron: No.

Q: Were they trying to do anything about it?

Capron: They were bringing in officers as temporary officers without anything like Officer's Candidate School, who had sufficient background. In many cases merchant service, and in some cases Navy - they were bringing them in as temporary officers. After awhile those that they thought were more or less shaping up, they were offered permanent ~~positions~~ commissions and were integrated.

There was a period then of eight to ten years when there was a rather strong feeling between the Academy officer and the non-Academy officer. It practically disappeared around 1933, at a time when the new President decided that he was going to use his executive powers to put the Coast Guard in the Navy.

Capron - 31

We heard about it, and practically every officer in the service wrote to his Congressman. In those days, that was a court martial offense. They wrote to the Congressmen, Senators, and so on, with every bit of possible aid outside that we could.

Actually, the end result was that a committee of maritime Congressmen and Senators, regardless of party, called on Roosevelt and said, "Leave them alone."

That was might you call the beginning of the Alumni Association as an influential group. Prior to that, it had been nothing but a social group that met once a year when you paid your dues of 50¢ and so on. The dues went up. The ex-temporary officers were all invited to join.

That was just about the beginning of the end of that feeling between the two groups of officers. It had been bitter in many cases. It never came out again. Even later, when the Lighthouse Service came in the Coast Guard and the BMIN came in.
(Note: BMIN was Bureau of Marine Inspection and Navigation.)

Q: If so many Cadets dropped out or resigned, say for instance in your class, you started out with some 40 odd. After your second year, you were down to 10 or 11. Why was it that they didn't start out with a larger class? You said there were about 650 applicants.

Capron: I don't know exactly if I can answer that, anymore than I can say why they were bilging people who were much better than those they were bringing in from the outside and commissioning them. Now I can't answer that question. I don't know why. It was an anachronism that is very difficult to understand.

Q: Could it have been money? They just didn't have enough money?

Capron: I don't think so, no, it wasn't. At that particular time, from about 1921 when the Coast Guard began to get into the prohibition business, up until 1933; the Coast Guard never had to worry about money. As a matter of fact, that was one big reason that the Navy wanted the Coast Guard; because we were getting money and they weren't.

Q: That sounds a lot like the situation now -- juggling agencies.

Capron: Specifically, on that one, I don't know. Except that I think that there was a feeling that they still wanted to keep the Academy officer at a very very high level. That's the only reason that I can see, but I wouldn't mention it publicly.

Ten of my class graduated. Two died within eight or ten years. Of the other eight, the first one to go out had 28½ years service when he went. So, that is a good argument for very strict discipline at the Academy. Because they had the eight of us for 28½ years.

Q: Did the two die in the line of duty, or for other reasons?

Capron: Technically, no, line of duty, yes. Dale Carrol was killed, he was driving from one station to another somewhere out in Arizona. A drunken driver coming the other way crossed over the center line, and he had a head-on collison.

The other one died over here in ~~Walter Reed~~ Baltimore Maine Hospital with some service incurred sickness of some kind.

Q: The last time we talked about - you had said at the end of the year that you were experiencing difficulty; you were just barely hanging on. Did they help you in any way to bring up your grades?

Capron: I don't think they did anything in particular, no. When I said that I was just barely hanging on, I was like almost everybody else. You might have some subjects where you just sailed through, but you had one or two that were pretty rough. In my case, Physics had been one that was really rough.

Some of them had trouble with English. I never did. It was probably because at home, I heard nothing but good English all the time I grew up. For me, it was a subject that was very easy.

I do think any in my class who had been in the position toward the end of the year, that I had been in in the middle of the year with Physics; probably had offers from the instruc-

Capron - 34

tor of that subject to give him extra time. I'm quite sure they did. Even the instructors that I characterize now as being rather poor, were really sincere and dedicated. They didn't know how, maybe; but they felt that it was almost an insult to themselves if they had to fail people.

Then of course there were other things too. This is really rambling -- I had a classmate whose name was Chadwick, whose father had been a Navy Captain. Chadwick had gone there, to the Academy, mostly because his father wanted him to. A very likable chap, but he didn't care about staying. He did a minimum amount of studying. I'm quite sure that solely on the basis of his personality a couple of times, a 69 might have been boosted to a 70 or something like that.

Then along about a month before mid-years of second class year, all of a sudden Chadwick changed. He decided that he liked it there and wanted to remain. He really started to work, but he couldn't in one month undo the damage of a year and a half. So, come mid-years, he just flunked about everything. Thereby, the Coast Guard lost what I think would have been an outstanding officer.

Q: So, the real desire to stay in was one of the key elements?

Capron: The desire to stay was THE key element; because with those competetive examinations that you had to take, unless

you had an individual who already had a lot of education
to begin with - several of my classmates had had one, two,
or three years in college - his passing of that examination
was evidence of his having the mental capacity of getting
through.. Unless, there was a case of cheating or something
like that. He had the mental capacity or he wouldn't have
gotten there in the firstplace.

From then on, as least as far as studies were concerned,
it was incentive. If he hadenough incentive and would work
over time and so forth, he'd make it.

My biggest trouble was the fact that (1) high school
was easy. I never learned how to study in high school. And
(2) I was out of school for two years before I went back.
That whole first year that I was there, I was learning how
to study and basically to be a student.

Q: Did they give you time, did you have ample time to study?

Capron: That of course, was strictly a matter of opinion.
We had basically, classes in the morning from eight to ten.
Then study period from ten to eleven, class eleven to twelve;
classes one to three three days a week; and military from three
to four two days a week. The other two days, there would be
classes, which were usually laboratory, from one to four.
Compulsory athletics were from four to five, unless you were

on one of the athletic teams. In which case, you spent the whole time from four to six really.

Then we had chow at six. Study period from seven until nine-thirty, and lights out at ten. The next morning, you got up at six. You'd be out on the parade grounds doing calisthenics at six-fifteen. So that, I'd say, it's really a matter of opinion.

Some of those that got things easily, they had a lot of time to waste. Others didn't have too much time.

Q: Did you play athletics?

Capron: I tried. I weighed about 135 pounds dripping wet. I played basketball all three years I was there. I never made the first team, but was always on the second team. I went out for football without any success. We had so few, they never cut anybody. We only had 60 Cadets there, one year that I was there. We didn't have any real organized baseball. But we used to play a lot of baseball with local teams and so forth. The last year, I was Captain of this unorganized baseball team.

Q: What other colleges did you play in intercollegiate?

Capron: The first time we ever played Norwich was in my last year, first class year. We used to play, what was then the Connecticut Aggies, which is now the University of Connecticut.

And Trinity. We only played basketball with Rhode Island State. I happened to remember that particularly well because I had played basketball at Rogers. In our first five at Rogers, four of them went to Rhode Island State and I went up to the Coast Guard Academy. I ended up playing against them. We had Providence College, which was pretty good basketball, up there at that time, we played them. There was another boy at Providence College who had been on this same team at Newport.

At that time, our real intercollegiate sport was basketball. My first year, we had no football team at all. They only started it in my second class year. We played with Rhode Island State, I remember. We were building up at that time. Not only trying to build up a reputation but trying to build up a schedule starting from scratch. The basketball team was the one really with intercollegiate calibre.

Q: We were talking about your first couple of years at the Academy. Do you remember anything unusual that happened while you were there? Anthing out of the ordinary that might be of interest?

Capron: Actually about the only thing that was out of the ordinary -- Our last Cadet cruise, we started out from New London. It was to be a European cruise. We started out on the ALEXANDER HAMILTON. We had been out about five days and we lost our propeller.

I had the 8 to 12 engine room watch. Throttle watch in the engine room. I came off at 10 of 12 when a classmate of mine relieved me. Within half an hour of that time, there was this heavy thump and the engine started

This classmate of mine had quickness of thought enough to immediately close the throttle. Subsequently, it was learned that the propeller had broken right off at the hull.

Parenthetically, I was rather glad that it didn't happen during my watch because I don't know whether I'd have had sense enough to close the throttle or not.

Anyway, we turned around and had to sail back to New London. We sailed for a couple of days. About the time we began to get adverse winds, the Coast Guard destroyer ERICSSON came out and cast us a tow line and towed us in to New London.

They then brought the MOJAVE, which was one of the very modern cutters of that day; and transferred all of the Cadets and all the Academy officers from the HAMILTON over to the MOJAVE leaving a few of the MOJAVE's crew and few of their officers aboard. We started out again.

MOJAVE being an electric-drive ship capable of 15 knots or more, We were able to catch up and make about the same schedule as far as the ports were concerned, that we would have made if we'd stayed on the HAMILTON. That, of course, was kind of an interesting experience.

Q: It was probably beneficial to get to see --

Capron: It was beneficial, but at the same time, that was what gave me the original objection to being on a steamship. They made work to keep you busy. On the sailing ship there was enough work to sail the ship to keep you busy.

Q: When you went on the Cadet cruises, there wasn't any other Coast Guard cutter with you as they do now?

Capron: No, just the one.
A year or so later, I think the year after I graduated; when the number of Cadets were greater, they sent two ships. They sent the ALEXANDER HAMILTON and the destroyer SHAW. One third of the Cadets would be on the SHAW, and the other two-thirds on the HAMILTON. They rotated them during the cruise. That probably was one of the best ways of doing it because you got experience on both types of vessels.

Q: Were the destroyers - the ERICSSON and the SHAW - four-stackers from the Navy?

Capron: The Coast Guard obtained from the Navy in 1924 and '25, 25 of the old broken-deck destroyers. The first 60 or 65 destroyers that the Navy ever had were broken-deckers, raised fo'cle and just aft of the bridge a drop down of eight feet maybe, and then flush deck from there aft.

Q: They weren't the new flush-deckers?

Capron: They were not the new flush-deckers. They were the first 60 or 65 destroyers they ever had. Most of them were broken down into two rough classes, the so-called 740s (740 tons) and the 1,000 tonners. We actually had 13 of the 740s and 12 of the 1,000 tonners.

The broken deckers preceeded the World War I type of flush decker. That World War I type was built during World War I. They built several hundred of them. When we went into World War I, we didn't have any of those.

It so happened, my first ship was the destroyer CONYNGHAM. It had been a Navy Destroyer DD 58. She was CG-2.

So, we had these 25 ships relatively fast that were turned over to us strictly for our prohibition work, anti-smuggling. They were organized into four divisions, six ships each; the 25th one being a training ship for destroyer men. In all those divisions; one was stationed in New York, two divisions in New London, and one division in Boston, Those are the ones I'm speaking of. They were older, although mine, the 58, the CG-2;

was only maybe a year or so older than the Flush Deckers. There were only roughly classes of vessels.

For instance, there were often only two alike. The one I remember was the PORTER and the CONYNGHAM. They were both built by Bath Iron Works. Basically, that's the way they ran. There would be one or two that would be just alike.

Then the next ones that were built some months later, in a different yard, would be somehwat different. And the power plants were different. A few of them had three screws, some of them had two screws.

Q: I'd like to get back to these, later on, when we talk about prohibition. Just one quick question about them. Were they in fairly good condition when the Coast Guard got them, or were they really surplus?

Capron: They had been laid up in the back channel at Philadelphia from around 1919 until 1924. Our people got a chance to go over and pick out the ones that they thought were in the best shape. They had not been moth-balled in the sense of the word that they do nowadays. Nobody ever heard of it then. All they did was put cosmoline grease on everything they possibly could, put covers on the guns, and that was it. They were in rather tough shape in many ways. Their machinery was probably fairly good. Their boilers were lousy, and the condensers were lousy.

Capron - 42

A short time after we got them, we had to practically re-tube all the boilers and all the condensers. That brings up something that I mentioned in my book that might be of interest later on, in that they spoke of putting those ships in commission as the First and Second Battles of Philadelphia.

The first ship to go out was in wonderful shape. They stole from ever other ship that was there. Finally, when they got toward the end of it, the got to the point where they didn't even have any port hole rims for some of the ships. So, they ended up getting new equipment.

Q: Maybe we ought to put in the record the name of your book.

Capron: U. S. COAST GUARD.

Q: Who is it published by?

Capron: Franklin Watts, Inc.

Q: And what was the date of publication?

Capron: I think it's '66. I'll have to look at the copyright date. You know your manuscript like that gets there about a year before the book itself comes out. (copyright 1965)

Q: So, when we left off in our narrative; you were on the MOJAVE on your Cadet cruise.

Capron: On the MOJAVE, there was another incident which was extremely tragic. On the 4th of July, 1926; we had been in very rough seas. The Cadets as usual had fallen in in two ranks back on the quarterdeck for 8 o'clock formation, made colors and so on. The ship took a very very heavy lurch one way and then another way and took aboard a heavy sea; and one Cadet was washed overboard. He was seen some 50 yards astern of the ship, when he came up and he waved. Numerous life rings were thrown over. We went through the standard man overboard procedures, went around in a circle hoping to come back in the same place. We could never see him again.

Q: Was he in your class?

Capron: He was in the class behind me.

As a matter of fact, I had just been relieved on the bridge. I was Cadet officer of the deck on the four to eight and I had just been relieved and was on the way down the ladder when this happened.

He was never heard from again. We stayed there for about 24 hours. With the heavy seas, the doctors said they didn't

Capron - 44

believe anybody could survive in those seas even with a life jacket more than about 20 minutes.

This is the boy that the present Academy football field is named for - Jones Field.

Q: What was his full name? Do you remember?

Capron: I should, but I don't.

Q: So, on that cruise, you went ~~out~~ to Europe.

Capron: We went over to Europe. We went into London docks, we actually got the ship into London this time. From there to Le Havre; from Le Havre to La Corunna, Spain; then Casablanca; Canary Islands; Bermuda; and then back home to New London.

Q: While you were on these cruise, I forgot to ask, did you ever get an opportunity to meet Cadets from European service academies?

Capron: No. We did a couple to times, arrive in the same port as one of the other American school ships. I remember, once or twice, we were in at the same time the Pennsylvania school ship, the ANNAPOLIS, was in. We saw them. If I remember

Capron - 45

rightly, we ran across the NANTUCKET one time. As far as any foreign school ships, no.

Q: How did you fair in your academic career in your last two years? What other subjects did you cover during that time?

Capron: As far as subjects were concerned, we had quite a few of the engineering subjects. Some were thermodynamics, marine engineering, and in the math line - calculus, both integral and differential. Although, I've been told since, we didn't go very far with them. At the time, I was sure we did. Quite a few, what you might call, trade school -- marine surveying, compass compensation, ordnance and gunnery, international law, and plenty of customs and navigation laws.

Q: Did they give you any special training to prepare you for what most of you were eventually involved in - the prohibition --

Capron: As far as the theory was concerned, the study of customs and navigation laws. We covered that.

Q: How about actual practice, more of less enforcement, did you get any training for that?

Capron = 46

Capron: The only thing along that line you could say we got was -- At that time, there were a number of 75 foot patrol boats operating out of New London. They used to go out anywhere from 24 to 48 hours. They were skippered by either a Chief Boatswain's mate or a Warrant Boatswain. It was possible for a Cadet to make arrangements through the base to go aboard one of these -- say on noon time Saturday, make a trip out with them and come back Sunday night. You went strictly on your own. It wasn't a part of the curriculum but I think they were glad to see that you had that much interest. I made several trips that way and really enjoyed it very much.

Q: Did you have any activity during that time?

Capron: No. I've got a strong hunch that they'd put us on a 75 footer where we wouldn't have too much activity. Because in the case where there was shooting and so on, I think probably the adverse publicity of a Cadet being involved on one of them would have been such that they wouldn't care for it.

Q: Also, on that similar line; was there any talk or training or anything concerning aviation? Did they encourage any of you

Capron - 47

Capron: At that particular time, Coast Guard aviation was dead; literally, there wasn't any.

Probably just about 1928, give or take a year, there was a revitalization you might say of Coast Guard aviation. Several officers, Von Paulson was one of them, had got some interest around in Washington, particularly up on the hill; in aviation. They managed to borrow a couple of old airplanes, seaplanes from the Navy; and a tent hanger from the Army. The hanger was installed on Ten Pound Island in Gloucester Harbor. They flew these two crates out of Gloucester on scouting missions for prohibition - anti-smuggling.

Here again, parenthetically; we were never enforcing prohibition. We were enforcing the smuggling laws, which said you could not introduce liquor into the United States, without going through customs. The mere fact that another law said that the customs wouldn't pass it through, didn't alter this. As far as we were concerned, it was the anti-smuggling angle rather than the anti-prohibition. The reason I make that point was that I don't believe too many of us believed in prohibition as such. But it was a question of smuggling. I think most of us would have wanted to take a poke at somebody if they had called us prohibition agents, or something like that.

Q: Getting back to the Academy, there was really nothing to do with aviation at all?

Capron: Nothing at all.

Q: When did you graduate from the Academy?

Capron: May 15th, 1928.

Q: Did you get a degree as well as a commission?

Capron: At that time, we did not get degrees. At that time, there was no provision for any of the service Academys to give degrees. We got a commission.

As an interesting side line here, practically every University Club in the United States which required members to have degrees accepted our diploma as a degree. But it was some time later that Congress authorized first the Military Academy and the Naval Academy; and later on the Coast Guard Academy to issue degrees. They also authorized them to be made retroactively.

So, my degree is dated '46, going back to '28.

Q: You got a B.S.?

Capron A B.S., yes.

Q: You were commissioned Ensign?

Capron: As an Ensign, right.

Interview # 2

Captain Walter C. Capron, USCG, Ret. by Peter Spectre
Arlington, Virginia November 8, 1969

Mr. Spectre: Captain, you graduated from the Coast Guard Academy in 1928. Could you tell me something about your first assignment? Did you have any choice in your assignment?

Captain Capron: Yes. Prior to graduation, as much as six weeks before; we were asked to give a number of choices both as to type of duty - by that, I mean destroyer or cutter, and as to location.

Now in my case, I had been quite interested in destroyers. My family lived near Boston. So, I asked as my first assignment, to be assigned to a destroyer in Boston. The destroyers were not the most popular stations, by a long shot and neither was Boston. So, that I had no difficulty whatsoever in getting my choice.

There were a couple of interesting things from the historical standpoint that were involved immediately following my graduation. The Coast Guard had just completed a War Memorail in Arlington Cemetery.

Q: This is Arlington, Virginia Cemetery?

Capron: Arlington, Virginia. At that time, it was the World War Memorial. World War II wasn't even dreamed of.

Instead of our going on leave immediately upon graduation, we remained at the Academy two or three days as brand new Ensigns. Then, we were brought down with the Cadet Corps to Washington; for the dedication of the War Memorial, which took place somewhere around the 25th of May, 1928.

I think probably that headquarters had a slight difficulty trying to figure out what to do with ten brand new Ensigns. Obviously, we couldn't march with rifles with the Cadet Corps. So, we ended up by acting as ushers and carrying the floral tribute up to the War Memorial. Which is still in Arlington and occupies a rather prominent place, in the heights just overlooking the Navy Annex.

We went on leave from Washington, if we so desired. Otherwise, we could go back to New London.

As a personal aside, my fiance, at our graduation, had been stricken with appendicitus. Two or three days after graduation had had to go back from New London to a hospital in which she was training, Truesdale Hospital in Fall River.

Q: She was studying to be a nurse?

Capron: Yes, to be a nurse.

She had this emergency appendectomy while we were actually on route from New London to Washington. So, I elected to leave

Capron - 51

right from Washington and go back up to Fall River to see her. And see how she was progressing.

I reported in to my first duty about the 20th of June, 1928. I found that the ship I was reporting to was a little bit unique in that the Commanding Officer was a bachelor, the Executive Officer was a bachelor, the Engineer was a bachelor, and the one Watch Officer was the only married officer on board.

Q: You were going to be the second watch officer?

Capron: I was to be the second watch officer. I might point out that that was one of the reason that destroyers were very unpopular, in that they only had two watch officers. The exec took one watch at sea, but in port these two watch officers rotated the days' duty. Which actually meant, that you had, with the schedule we were on then, ten days liberty a month, anywhere from 2 o'clock until 4:30 until 9 the next morning.

Of course, there were just as many departments on a destroyer as there were on the cutters. So that, the watch officers ended up with several departments, rather than just one.

Q: What did you get?

Capron: I went aboard and became Gunnery Officer and Commissary Officer right away.

Capron - 52

To get back to these bachelors, the Captain who was Lieutenant Commander J. A. Starr (known throughout the service as Jerry Star) did not approve of junior officers being married.

Ten days after I reported aboard, on the 30th of June, I was married. And I was faced on the morning of July 1st with the problem of telling the Captain that, even knowing his antipathy of married junior officers, I had become married. I enlisted the assistance of the engineer to break the news, which he did, at the dinner table. I can still remember the Captain's remark, "Huh, we'll have to get rid of him then."

Within a day or so, we went out on our first patrol. At that time the destroyers were operating on a five days out, ten days in cycle. I ended up with the 8 to 12 watch and had that watch as soon as we went to sea. I didn't have quite enough sense to be scared and thought that I was pretty much of a veteran.

Q: When you reported aboard then, they didn't have a junior watch officer program at all?

Capron: We didn't have enough officers in the Coast Guard to have any such thing. It's true the cutters, as a general rule, had three watch officers. They were on a different schedule and were usually out longer at any given time. They were commanded by much more senior officers than the destroyers. For quite a while at least, if not for the whole time we had destroyers, we were almost the orphans.

Q: Weren't destroyers bigger than the cutters?

Capron: It's all a question of how you classify bigness. They were longer, yes. They were essentially 300 or 310 feet long. Tonnage wise, some were of the 740 class, some were of the so-called 1,000 class.

Most of the cutters would be in the neighborhood of 1,500 to 2,000 tons. Lengthwise, the cutters were much shorter and broader of beam and much slower. The older cutters made 10 knots, maybe 12 knots. The newer ones, which were just comeing out at that time, so-called Lake Class, had a maximum speed of about 16 to 17 knots with reasonable cruising speed of 12 to 15.

Our destroyers were capable of 22 to 24 knots on one fire room and 27 to 29 on two fire rooms. We normally cruised with only one fire room.

Horse-power wise, we were much more powerful than any of the cutters. As I remember my destroyer, the CONYNGHAM, was in the neighborhood of 27,000 horsepower, compared to the cutters that might range anywhere from 1,000 up to 2,000 horsepower.

Our normal cruising speed during daylight hours, would be 15 to 18 knots. Night time we usually slowed to 7 to 7½ knots. At night, we normally ran dark, completely dark.

So that years later, when World War II came along; those of us who grew up on destroyers were well prepared for two things - high speed and running dark at night.

Of course, as you well know, radar had never even been heard of or dreamed of at that time. Everything that we did, depended completely on eyesight even on the blackest of nights.

The basic operating principles at that time consisted of relatively high speed scouting and searches off shore by the destroyers.

Q: What were you searching for?

Capron: For, what we called, off-shore rummies.

The principle, that the rummies at that time were using, foreign vessels - most of them under the British flag, but many under the French - ranging from 100 feet long to maybe 150; usually of the offshore diesel fishermen type had the capability of carrying roughly 3,000 cases of liquor or alcohol. All of them were done up in sacks.

These vessels would load out of a Canadian port quite often at St. Pierre Miquelon or down in some of the West Indies ports, which the town of Barbados sticks in my memory as one place. They would then proceed to off the coast of the United States, where they would drift anywhere from 15 to 30 or 40 miles off shore.

Q: Were these sail or power vessels?

Capron: They were auxiliary with the capability of sail. Usually not sail, in the sense of going anywhere, but a steadying sail or just loafing along at one or two knots. They were mostly diesel powered. As I remember, most of them had the speed capability of anywhere from 10 to 13 or 14 knots.

They would then, under cover of darkness, come in fairly close to shore, in many cases come in right close to the beach; and rendevouz with high speed motor boats operated by Americans. Who would take aboard their limit of cargo, possibly 500 cases and then run it in to whatever port, or small harbor, or what have you that had been arranged.

Q: In your operations, what particular area did you cover?

Capron: We covered the area off shore.

Capron - 56

Q: How far south and north did you go?

Capron: From Nova Scotia as far as Delaware Bay entrance, that was the area that the destroyers covered. Usually, the area that we were assigned to would be from Nova Scotia down as far as Long Island, Montauk Point.

Q: Before we go any further, you mentioned, we were talking about the destroyers versus the cutters in the size and so forth. You mentioned your first assignment, you didn't have any trouble getting what you wanted because destroyers were not considered great duty. Could you give me a reason why this is so?

Capron: The basic reason, I think I have already touched on. The destroyers had a very limited number of officers on board How much of this was poor assignment by Coast Guard headquarters and how much of it was due to the limited quarters on board; I don't know.

My ship, for instance, had five staterooms, of which one always had two officers assigned. The other quite often had two. So, that basically, the maximum number of watch officers you could have was three.

As a result, the individual had to work much harder because you had several departments. You had in port day and day duty. Whereas, in cutters, they had either one in three or even one in four.

In addition, the minimum you could get by with at sea on watches was four on, eight off. Quite often as on my ship, the first year I was on board; the other junior officer and myself alternated taking the first DOG watch -- four to six. So that one day we'd have ten hours on watch, the next day we'd have eight hours on watch. The executive officer would have six. His other duty kept him going pretty much.

I think probably the fact that there was so much more work for the individual to do, probably had as much to do with the less popularity of destroyers than anything else.

As far as Boston was concerned, during prohibition days, the Coast Guard was very very unpopular. More than once in the so-called St. Patrick's Day Parade, which was always called Evacuation Day I believe, always was through South Boston; our contingent quite often would be the recipient of not only rocks but rotten eggs and fruit. So much so that finally, the Coast Guard refused to march in those parades.

On the duty at sea, we in the destroyers would scout well off shore for the foreign rummies. Upon finding one, you would then picket him until relieved usually by a smaller vessel.

Q: Would this be one of the cutters?

Capron: One of the 125 foot patrol boats, of which there were 33. I believe the very last one of those, just went out of commission, within the last six months.

Q: When you were searching for these rummies, did you have any idea where they were, or were you just going out and patroling an area hoping to come upon them?

Capron: At that time, just about that. Patroling and knowing generally where they might be found.

The accuracy of their naviagtion was extremely important. Because if they were going to make a contact that night with a speed boat coming out from shore, all of this without any lights, they had to be extremely accurate. So, therefore, they would be in some position wherein they could get good radio bearings from light ships and light house, and so forth. So, that gave you certain areas wherein you were more apt to find these rummies than not.

On finding them, then, the destroyer would have to picket them until you could be relieved. Sometimes it would be two or three days before you could be relived by one of these 125 foot patrol boats.

We seemed to have a knack at that time, with the exception of our _____ destroyers, of building patrol boats which invariably turned out to be one knot slower than the vessel they were supposed to catch.

I think probably from the excitement angle, we had more excitement picketing these rummies than in anything else.

It was necessary to again operate without running lights to stay close enough to this rummie so that he couldn't make off after darkness, and get away. Being small craft, they would have a turning circle of possibly 25, 30 yards. Our destroyers had a turning circle of around 600 yards. So, the experienced rummy would try getting underway at a relatively low speed to get you circling. If he could get you circling, he then would shoot down your side in the opposite direction and be lost in the darkness, long before you could ever turn around.

As I said, we had no such thing as radar. On a very dark night, as soon as he got out of your searchlight beam; he was gone.

Q: Did you have many get away that way?

Capron: Oh, yes. It's hard to come up with any kind of a percentage because quite often one would get away and then four or five hours we would pick him up again. Of course, it was a battle of wits. One trying to guess where he would go so that come daybreak, you'd be close enough to see him.

Then, of course, there was a different degree of skill in the rummies themselves; as there was in the people in the destroyers. And, there was this fact that we were always working in international waters.

If you did have a collision, for instance, the 'International Rules of the Road' prevailed. So, you had to be careful that whatever you did, even though it might be outside the law as far as 'International Rules of the Road' was concerned; it had to be something that you could defend subsequently, if you had a collision and you had to go to court.

Q: When you were picketing them, what were you trying to prevent? They were in international waters, so they had every right to be there. What were you trying to stop?

Capron: By keeping in contact with him, he could not unload into any American vessel.

Q: Any American vessel?

Capron: That's right. All of the speedboats were American vessels. As long as we were in sight of that rummie, no American vessel could go alongside; because we could seize him. By doing it long enough, and that happened often enough to make it worth the attempt, you could keep him from making contact so long that ultimately he'd run out of fuel and supplies and would have to go back home or go into a foreign port.

Q: It was like a seige.

Capron: Very definitely.

At that time, they used to go to Bermuda quite often. Subsequently, the United States - this was several years later - worked a treaty with Great Britain, under which any vessel sailing from a British port with a cargo of liquor had to post a bond that he would go to the port to which he had cleared.

Obviously, they didn't clear officially for any United States port. Normally, they would clear for a Central American port of the French. I'm speaking of the West Indies now. And, of course, they'd never go there.

After this treaty had been consumated; the vessel, if he did get in trouble and needed supplies, had to go to the port to which he was cleared. Otherwise, he would forfeit his bond that he had had to post.

Q: Was it a high enough bond to matter?

Capron: It was, yes. This was the reason for picketing in later days of smuggling, and I'm not too sure if it was before the end of prohibition or not, because liquor smuggling continued several years after prohibition. It was still a very

Capron - 62

profitable deal for a long long time.

Q: We started out by talking about your first trip out on the CONYNGHAM. Could you tell me a little bit about that?

Capron: I don't particularly remember too much about it, except that being off the New England coast we were fog bound most of the time, operating in fog. I didn't know for many months, the fact that all the time I was on watch the Captain was down below in the emergency cabin with his eyes glued to the port hole. I felt that I was up there all alone, which probably was very excellent training in that as far as I knew the Captain reposed strict confidence in me. It was a long long time before I learned that, when I was on watch, he'd always been where he could see and if necessary, get up on the bridge.

Q: Did you find your training at the Academy useful for what you were doing then?

Capron: Oh, yes. The training at the Academy, of course -- I'm speaking now of the actual training as differentiated from the purely educational angle - on the Cadet Cruises and occasionaly trips on other ships, plus the theoretical classes in seamanship, navigation, gunnery and so forth; all of those

Capron - 63

operated to give me the necessary know-how at least, to be an efficient officer-of-the-deck. Any failures that any of us may have had could have been laid to inexperience or carelessness, rather than a failure in our training at the Academy.

Q: You mentioned gunnery - what type of guns did the CONYNGHAM carry?

Capron: We had three ~~large~~ Inch 50 caliber broadside guns and several 30 caliber Lewis machineguns, 1 one-pounder, and the usual small arms necessary for a 40-50 man landing force.

Q: Was the crew proficient in handling guns?

Capron: I don't think there's much question about that they were proficient. The fact that very seldom did you ever have occasion to use the 4 inch gun, and we were pretty strictly ~~bombed~~ bound by regulations as far as using guns was concerned; they were aboard actually mostly as a part of the war-time armament, rather than law-enforcement. The one-pounder and the machineguns were law-enforcement.

Actually, the destroyers used to go south for six weeks each year for small arms target practice and for other practice. We used the modified navy battle practice manouevers - modified in that we had no torpedo tubes. Other than that, we used strictly

Capron - 64

the training procedures and requirements that the Navy had for their own destroyers.

Q: You say you went south - did you go to Guantanamo?

Capron: The first year, we operated out of Charleston, South Carolina on the old so-called Southern Drill Grounds. We had our small arms practice at Parris Island with the Marines.

From then on, we went to St. Petersburg, Florida. We had our small arms practice at Egmont Key and our battle practice in the Gulf off of St. Petersburg.

Appropo of using the large guns, there was one case in the very early days of destroyers wherein a destroyer did shoot at a rummie American with his big gun, and hit him. Inasmuch as all of our projectiles were either explosive or Star shell, when he hit him, he just blew him all to pieces. After that, we were practically forbidden to ever use the large guns, for law enforcement.

Q: How about the Commanding Officer of your ship - was he well qualified for the type of duty that you were doing? Was he specially trained in any way?

Capron: In answer to the first part of your question, my first Commanding Officer was and is in my opinion one of the best Commanding Officers I ever had. He had this antipathy to married junior officers. I might add that I lived it down and later on, admitting the disparity in rank and age, I think we became fairly good friends.

Q: This is Lieutenant Commander Starr?

Capron: Starr. I served under him some seven or eight years later, when he was Chief of Staff in Boston and I was the Communications Officer. He was very cordial and very easy to work with.

His objection, essentially was based on (1) an Ensign didn't get enough money to marry on to live. Including my allowances, my monthly income was $183 a month. After the first pay raise, which came after three years, you went to $271 a month. On $271 you could live reasonably comfortably - a young officer. As an Ensign you were scratching all the time. The Captain's idea was that you would be so worried over your finances that you couldn't devote your time to your job. That's a point well taken.

In addition, a lot of the wives would be down on the dock when the ship came in. He had another ship that had an experience with one particular wife; who would march on board and into the Wardroom and practically take over - which he, understandably, didn't like at all. So, he had the rule that no ~~one~~ woman was permitted on board that ship.

After I'd been on there about eight months, the Captain called the other married officer and myself in and compliemnted us on the fact that we had never taken advantage in that our wives were not the kind that came down and waited on the dock for us and all that sort of thing. He relaxed his rule, and said that anytime on weekends when he was not aboard, we could have our wives down when we had the duty for dinner or what have you. Which, to him, was a very great concession.

Back to your other questions, actually Starr was a highly efficient officer. As far as training for the job was concerned, the only way anybody could learn that was on the job training. Basically it was a matter of having a good grounding of seamanship and a fairly level head.

Q: What about the law enforcement in, for instance, the complicated customs regulations and the off-shore limits, and so forth?

Capron: We did not, ourselves, in the destroyers do very much boarding. Our boat capacity was very limited. The boarding was normally done by patrol boats and so forth who had the capability actually of going alongside usually the particular vessel that we were going to board.

So, it got so in the destroyers; we did not ourselves do too much boarding. As a matter of fact, if we caught someone, we would normally radio for a smaller vessel to come out and do the actual boarding.

Q: Were there enough small craft available for this type of work?

Capron: Yes and no. We never had enough, but you could depend on getting assistance within a reasonable length of time.

To go back a little bit -- The Coast Guard had 25 destroyers, 33 125-foot patrol boats, roughly 300 of the 75-foot patrol boats - a wooden vessel of originally top speed of about 15 knots. When they got older, of course, they slowed down. They were powered with gasoline engines - actually they were called Sterling Coast Guard engines. They were built especially for the Coast Guard by Sterling. They performed the inshore work.

In addition, we were able to get quite a few seized rummies turned over by the courts to us and we kept the ones that we thought were suitable. At that time, we didn't have anything around that was really fast; but the seized rummies would do anything up to 35-40 knots. Most of them probably had a top speed when loaded of 30.

Capron - 68

Q: You were very fortunate to get those.

Capron: We were very fortunate to get those. The BLACK DUCK, which was one of the rather persistant rummies that we caught off Newport about 1930, we converted to our own use. She was very valuable. We had quite a few others that we were able to catch.

Their value to us, was their capability of speed. To us this was quite valuable because we didn't carry a cargo. Whereas, the rummies when they'd load them down; they would knock off 5 or 10 knots off their top speed in order to carry the cargo. In fact, that would be the main reason that we could catch them.

Plus the fact that, as a general rule, you'd catch them when they were trying to sneak into shore or in the act of unloading or something like that. You'd start a chase, and unless you shot them up, you didn't have too much of a chance to catch them.

At this time, the time that I was actively engaged in the anti-smuggling business; which was three years in the destroyers, most of the American boats were owned and operated by syndicates. The crews were practically gangsters.

In the very early days of rum running, the early '20s, possibly the middle '20s; most of these speedboats were operated by realtively honest and decent men, who'd take this on as a side line, maybe. But, by the late '20s, they were frozen out; almost completely frozen out by the gangster element. So, that the people that we were dealing with in these speedboats were scum. The newspapers and a lot of the public had a lot of sympathy for them and everything else. But they were gangsters.

The people that were operating the off-shore boats, the foreign boats; were relatively decent people who were trying to violate our customs laws - yes. But, they were certainly not gangster, or anything like that.

Q: When you picketed these rummies, did you ever communicate with them?

Capron: Well, yes, shall I say there was considerable yelling back and forth. It depended on the ship and the Commanding Officer and so forth. There were cases of harrassment and so forth.

One thing - if you came across him and he was cruising, the very first thing you did was cut across his stern close aboard. If possible, you cut his log line
It was standard procedure with these rummines; if you were bearing down on them, they'd get that log line in fast.

Later on, when we had some different types of vessels and much younger Commanding Officers; there was a lot of harrassment. Technically, I expect you might say that none of it was legal. At the same time, it did make things a little more difficult, for these off-shore people.

Q: What other type of harrassment did you engage in, other than cutting their log line?

Capron: That question that you just asked, I think you have to qualify when you say 'you'. Some Coast Guard vessels, it never occured on the ones I was on, for instance would hold a fire drill and would turn the hoses on the people on board the runner.

Later on, when we had 165-foot patrol boats replacing the destroyers; sometimes they would tow a three or four inch line, with their short turning radius, just circle the rummie and try, at least, to foul up his propeller.

There were stories, none of which I can substantiate one way or the other, where there would actually be the type of fight where potatoes and nuts and bolts were thrown back and forth. I never saw it happen.

Q: Captain, what other type of duty did you engage in the CONYNGHAM, other than anti-smuggling activity?

Capron: As an individual, I was detached temporarily from my ship when Sir Thomas Lipton's yacht SHAMROCK V raced against the American yacht ENTERPRISE off Newport for the America's Cup. I was one of several officers that was detached from our regular duties. In my case, I was given command of four 75-footers. Our particular job, which maybe was not quite so interesting as some of the others, was to precede the racers along the course warning any yachts or other vessels that might wander on the course to get out of the way for the racers.

At that time, the racing was on either a 15 mile windward leeward course or a 10 mile triangular course, 10 mile on a side. Actually, they alternated between the two types. My job was to go ahead of them. So that, as far as the racers were concerned, we could see them in our binoculars and that was about it. However, even so, it was interesting.

I had one case where I had to exercise judgement and discretion. One afternoon, after we had come in from a race; I was approached by a reporter from the New York HERALD TRIBUNE. Ev Morris was his name, whose last job I know of was with MOTORBOATING, as editor. This then relatively young cub reporter, asked me about coming out and seeing the race from the standpoint of a vessel on patrol.

In addition to our patrol boats, there were some destroyers and some large cutters involved in the actual patrol of the races. We had been forbidden to take any passengers, and I told him so.

He said, "Supposing you didn't know anybody was aboard until you got out to the races. What would you do?" I said, "Obviously I wouldn't turn around and come back in to put him ashore. I'd be kind of stuck with the situation." He said, "Okay."

The next day, it happened to be a very rough nasty day; after we got out near the starting line, who should show up but Ev Morris.

Q: On your boat?

Capron: On the boat. I, of course, was not too surprised; although I had exercised as much caution as I could that nobody did come aboard. I'm quite sure the crew knew all about it. So, Morris stayed with us. I did exact from him a promise that he would not in his article name the patrol boat he was on, or use any names which could identify me or any of us with where he'd been.

As I said, it was a very rough day. Morris really prided himself on being a salty sailor, having originally been a fisherman in New Bedford. But, that day, the cook choøse to serve pørk chop sandwiches. A nice greasy port chop between two hunks of bread, when you're on a 75-footer bouncing all over and hanging on for dear life, is not conducive to a strong stomach. And Morris took about three bites, and promptly pitched his cookies for all he was worth.

He did write up a very very fine story for the HERALD TRIBUNE, which he gave from the viewpoint of the patrol boats. We actually were not close enough to the race to know what was really going on, but we were still working very hard to make it a success. To me, that was very very interesting. No ill effect ever came from it that I know of.

One other thing that occured during the time I was on the CONYNGHAM, the ship itself was assigned the job of patrolling the Fisherman's Race off Gloucester in 1931.

Q: Is this the one that the BLUENOSE ---

Capron: This was between the BLUENOSE and the GERTRUDE L. THIBAUD. The BLUENOSE being the Nova Scotian one, and the GERTRUDE L. THIBAUD being the Gloucester one. The THIBAUD was skippered by a Gloucester fisherman named Ben Pine, with a crew of all Gloucester fishermen; mostly skippers of their own boats. The BLUENOSE was skippered by the regular Captain, Angus Walters; who was her regular skipper.

Ultimately the THIBAUD won. Not that I think she was the fastest vessel, but I do think she was better handled.

Walters did make some navigational mistakes; which cost him at least one, if not two races.

Q: How long was the series?

Capron: I think it was three out of five, I'm really not too sure.

Q: Do you remember how long the course was?

Capron: As I remember it, it was roughly seven miles on the side on a triangular course and something like ten miles on a windward leeward course.

The finish line was the line between the Gloucester Harbor Lighthouse at the end of the breakwater and a point on the beach, so that they actually had to come into the harbor to cross the finish line.

The thing that I remember most about that particular tour, aside from the fact that there was such wrangling between the committee and the Captains of the two vessels, and so forth, that any international friendship that might have been generated by the races was completely lost in animosity; was the fact that after we had gotten underway one day, we discovered we had a woman on board.

Q: On the CONYNGHAM?

Capron: On the CONYNGHAM, a reporter.

The Captain had been rather firm that, because of the fact that we didn't have any toilet facilities for women (in the Wardroom, we had only one) and so forth, and inasmuch as it was at least a twelve hour trip each day and possibly overnight; that we couldn't have any women on board.

So, this gal,- I've forgotten who she was a reporter for - we had some 75 reporters on board, came aboard dressed as a man. Once you saw her, there wasn't any question about her being a woman. But, when a group of some 75 or 80 strangers come on board over the side and so forth; nobody even noticed her until we got out to sea. There was nothing that anyone could do. She got away with it, in that sense of the word. I don't even remember anything about the article that she might have written. I do remember that the old man was really quite put out.

Q: You mentioned the animosity between the Captains of the two racers. Do you remember what they were arguing about?

Capron: They were arguing about a number of things. One thing that concerned us. That is, one very foggy day; we acted as committee boat and patrol for the race and so on. So that, what we tried to do was keep in sight of the races as much as we could and prevent anyone from interfering with the race. As far as navigation was concerned, the only navigation we did was enough to keep ourselves out of trouble and paid no attention as to whether it was part of the race course or not. The BLUENOSE saw us through the fog, and decided that we were running along their racecourse. Actually we were staying near the BLUENOSE so that she didn't get into trouble with spectators.

The upshot of it was, that as he'd try to get a little bit closer to us, we'd pull a little bit down here; and he never did find the finish line. He claimed it was deliberate on our part to mislead him. There was a lot of unpleasantness in that way.

Other than the accusations of petty violations about the rules covering the races and so on, I can't remember any particular details. Those meetings that were held after the races were quite acrimonious.

Q: What other type of thing did you do on the CONYNGHAM?

Capron: We, as any Coast Guard vessel was, were available for any type of rescue work. Our primary mission was, as I said, anti-smuggling. If you were the nearest vessel to any kind of a distress case, you proceeded and did the job, or tried to do the job. Destroyers are not very maneuverable, except at high speeds; so that towing a disabled vessel with a destroyer is pretty much of a job. If you've got a lot of sea room, there's nothing to it. If you're pretty close to a beach, or operating in a harbor, or something like that; a destroyer is rather difficult to manouver with somebody behind you on the end of a tow line.

I cannot, at this moment, remember any particular distress incidents that we had while I was on the CONYNGHAM. Although I know there must have been a number of relatively minor cases of towing in a fisherman who's engine had broken down, or possibly got his screw fouled in a net or something like that.

Q: What happens if you were picketing a rummie, and there was a distress case? Which had precedent?

Capron: It depended entirely on the degree of severity of the distress case, the availability of other help, and so on.

Q: Did you have rescue coordination centers then?

Capron: Not as such. Each district office had a communication center, which operated in much the same way as the present day RCCs.

However, there's one point that I should make clear. The destroyer force and the section bases, which operated the 75-footers; and the off-shore patrol force which consisted of the 125-footers - all operated under their own command, not under their districts. I'm speaking entirely of the Atlantic coast. So that, the destroyer force for anti-smuggling had the responsibility for the waters from Nova Scotia, south as far as the Delaware breakwater which crossed over at least two districts.

At that time, they were called divisions; but they are now districts. In other words, the present first and third districts, were the Boston and New York Divisions.

It was a complete separate command. I think there was an awful lot of difficulty up at the top. You had a district commander who had all search and rescue responsibility, under whom all the cutters and lifeboat stations came. And yet, superimposed on him or on his territory you had this independent command over which he had no authority or responsibility.

Q: So that really, your next line of authority in the Chain of command was Coast Guard headquarters?

Capron: Coast Guard headquarters, the Commandant.

There were incidents of poor coordination, particularly between the section bases operating the patrol boats and life boat stations that might be nearby. Certainly those incidents should never have occured.

Whether, if there had been a more unified command at the top; they would have been eliminated or not, that's purely guess work.

Capron - 79

We did have cases where a patrol boat from the section base shot up a picket boat from the lifeboat station. Each one thinking the other guy was a rummie. There'd be no centralized authority to disseminate the information to the lifeboat station that a patrol boat was in that area, and vice versa.

Q: So, you should get it from the chain of command?

Capron: Oh, yes.

Q: So then you remained on the CONYNGHAM for three years, and then you went on to a new assignment. Did you do any particular manouevring to get your new assignment? Did anybody ever ask you --

Capron: No one ever asked you. In those days, even on your fitness report, I do not remember there being any place where you could indicate a preference for assignment. You took what came.

My next assignment after that was about the first of March, 1931 to the cutter SENECA in New York.

That was an entirely differenty type of duty. Our primary mission was, what is now called search and rescue. We did considerable patroling with the idea of preventing smuggling and so forth.

Capron - 80

Q: You were a Watch Officer?

Capron: I was a Watch Officer and Navigator on the SENECA. The SENECA was actually an old vessel at that time. It had been built in 1908 and was relatively slow. Originally it had been built as a special purpose vessel, as a derelict destroyer, under a special act of Congress.

For me, this was a change from a vessel which always traveled at 15 knots or better to a vessel whose top speed was probably 10 knots. It was 204 feet long instead of 310; relatively wide and relatively deep-draft. Destroyers, for instance, were a 10 foot draft and the SENECA was 17 feet. So, for me, it was quite a change in type of duty.

We operated under the district commander whose headquarters were in New York. Our basic limits were from Montauk Point to the Delaware-Virginia line off Fenwick Island, below Delaware breakwater.

Q: How far out did you go?

Capron: On normal cruising, we probably didn't go out further than 15 to 25 miles. If you had a distress case, that was an entirely different proposition. Many case, you'd go 100 miles off shore, or even more.

Capron - 81

Q: How much time did you spend in port, versus sea time?

Capron: Roughly the same that we had in destroyers. Our schedule most of the time was seven out and fourteen in.

There was one decided difference between the duty on destroyers and duty on cutters. In the destroyers, when you were in; your ship was in until the schedule said patrol.

On cutters, three cutters would rotate. One at sea, one in port on a strictly maintenance status, and the other one in port on a two hour stand-by. So, the one that was on the two hour stand-by had to be ready to go out with two hours notice. Which meant that you had to keep enough crew on board, plus those you could get hold of in a hurry, to be able to go out with two hours notice. Generally, that's what cutters have always been doing and probably still do; other than those that are assigned to ocean stations.

Q: When you patroled, what did you do on patrol? Stictly waiting for a case?

Capron: Essentially, you would more or less cover your area once during the time. Quite often, you'd go into the various small harbors and so forth. Mainly to improve your knowledge of the coast line, in case you did have a distress case. Apropos of that, every duty officer was required to keep a notebook, which he had to present to the Commanding Officer once every

Capron - 82

six months. In that notebook, among other things, he had diagrams of the various harbors within the district and other points of interest that would more or less prove that he had been keeping up his professional interest and professional knowledge of the area in which he was operating.

Q: So, you were writing your own coastpilot more or less.

Capron: To All intentional purposes, yes, we were writing our own coast pilot; particularly pointing out dangers and so forth that you might run into going in.

I particularly remember Cape May, for instance. It's not simple to go in and out of in any kind of easterly weather. There's a very narrow entrance between jetties. If you go in there on a following sea, you could ground on the way in.

Q: Do you remember any memorable distress cases?

Capron: I think probably the one that stands out the most in my memory, and certainly the one in which we accomplished the most was one that took place in late winter of 1932. We were anchored in Delaware breakwater, behind the breakwater, under gale conditions - which afterwards was called an extra-tropical hurricane. Among other things, we had our own trouble. We started to drag anchor with a shift of wind on my watch. It was the six to eight at night. The first intimation I had that we were dragging was when a pilot boat came over near us and looking over our stern I saw the breakwater light awfully close.

We couldn't have been dragging more than two or three minutes as we were checking cross bearings at least every five minutes. We tried to get underway and at this particular moment our anchor engine decided to act up. By going ahead we had taken the slack out of our anchor chain, but when it came time to actually pick up the anchor, it refused to work.

So, being in a rather dangerous position, we steamed outside of the breakwater with the winds sweeping the whole length of Delaware Bay, dragging this anchor. Fortunately, it didn't catch on anything, not even the submarine cable that went across there. We were able to anchor on the outside, which was still in the lee of the breakwater.

The engineers, after working some hours in 115-120 mile wind, managed to correct the difficulty of the anchor engine. So, we hoisted the anchor.

About that time, we got word that a 75-footer had left Rehobeth Beach bound for Cape May and was unheard of.

Q: This was a 75-foot Coast Guard patrol?

Capron: Yes. We got underway at daybreak and went out looking for them, plotting what we assumed would be his position from the wind and the Gulf Stream flowing out there. We got out aways and we came across a coastal oil barge drifting, just coated with ice, and wondered a little bit where it had come from.

We had no word at all of any vessel being in distress. Then, suddenly, from one of the portholes in the deckhouse of this oil barge, we saw an arm come out and frantically wave a shirt, which before we got to it, indicated there were two men on board.

The seas were breaking over and the oil barge was really in a pretty sad state as far as seas were concerned. No danger of foundering, or anything like that; for oil being lighter than water, you would practically have had to rupture everything for it to sink. Certainly it was too rough for anybody to get out on deck.

So, we stayed there and sent a message in that we couldn't look for the 75-footer anymore because we had another job. Subsequently, we learned that the oil barge had been anchored not far from where we'd been, behind Delaware breakwater.

It had torn loose from its tug and drifted out to sea. Before it got through, it drifted about 125 miles. So, we stayed near them, as I remember it from about noon one day until eight o'clock the second day following. At night, we steamed up and down slowly keeping them in the searchlight. We had no radar, or anything like that.

I had the personal misfortune, about five or six a.m., as we turned around to steam past this oil barge, of having the young quartermaster who was operating the searchlight, lose it.

Q: Lose the barge?

Capron: Lose the barge, and unable to pick it up again. Of course, there was only one thing to do and that's stop. With the visibility conditions, you wouldn't see it until you were within maybe 100 feet of it. You were too close under those conditions and we had to stop.

I had the unpleasant job of calling the old man and letting him know, that I, the most experienced watch officer was the one who had lost the barge.

With a certain amount of plotting the drift - of course, the barge was not affected as much by wind the way we were - we plotted his expected drift and so on. In the daylight, we ran down the line and there he was, about a half a mile away. The two individuals aboard were awfully glad to see us too.

The next morning it had calmed down enough for us to get a line on. We went near enough to put a heaving line over. They were able to get out on deck, even though it was icy, haul the heaving line and messenger on board, then finally the 10-inch hawser.

We started towing them into the Delaware breakwater. It was still blowing 50-55 miles an hour, nothing like it had been earlier.

Q: How were the men on the barge doing?

Capron: I suspect they were praying. They just had to stay all that time in the deckhouse, which was there living quarters. As soon as they got a line made fast, they went back in.

We started towing about nine or ten o'clock in the morning, and towed them all that night. The next day, I went off watch at eight o'clock, we could just barely see Five Fathom Bank Lightship which was a little off Delaware Bay. We could just barely see it's light.

I went on watch again at four o'clock, and we were just about abeam. That's how slow we were going. This lightship, as I remember it, was just about seven or eight miles off Delaware breakwater. So, that sometime later that day, we finally reached the shelter of Delaware breakwater in Delaware Bay.

The tug, which had originally been towing the barge, showed up and took over our tow.

I have a copy of a letter that we received, which I might point out that I cited this incidence in my book; but not in such detail. This letter came to us from the Captain of the oil barge, which made us all feel pretty good. There isn't much question that weather conditions being what they were, if we hadn't stumbled on that barge, they would never have been heard from.

To button up this story, the 75-footer for which massive search was instituted, particularly after we had taken over the responsibility of the oil barge, was found drifting about 75 miles southeast of Nantucket Lightship. She was picked up by a British tramp steamer, who took her in tow until a Coast Guard cutter could get there and take over. In this hurricane with a following sea, they had taken water through their stern exhaust which completely drowned out their engines. By the time they could work the water out of the engines, their starting batteries were completely gone. They were in good health, but awful hungry. The vessel herself was in good shape, nice and tight, and so forth.

Q: They drifted all that way.

Captain, do you remember any other particular interesting cases?

Capron: One particular one that I remember that had a number of slightly humorous facets, to use that word.

We were coming in from patrol one time up Ambrose Channel in New York in the fog. We sighted this large ocean liner over on the port bow. We wondered at the moment very much about it, because if we were where we were supposed to be in Ambrose

Channel, she had to be out of the channel. And furthermore, according to our charts, there wasn't enough water for her.

If you're familiar at all with New York harbor, this was just below what is called Rohmer Shoal in lower New York harbor, New York Bay.

We headed over that way and realized that she was aground. They identified her as the BERENGARIA, which was a large British ocean liner. I think she was White Star Line, but she might have been Cunard.

She was hard and fast aground. We put a line on her astern, and tried to pull her off. In so doing, we ended up many times being right across the channel. We had our radio going continuously, warning any ships not to come down near Ambrose Channel. Because, if one of them had and hit our tow line; you can just picture what would have happened with the BERENGARIA over here with all of her thousands of tons aground, and our little ship of 1500 tons over here, with a 12 inch tow line between us. We'd have wrapped around like nobody's business.

A little later on, other tugs came down - commercial tugs. Then, all of us pulled, and eventually got her off.

The humorous part about it was, during part of this operation we parted our tow line. So that there was possibly as much as 5 or 10 fathoms of our tow line on the BERENGARIA. Then, we passed another bight over there, and so on.

Later on, they very carefully sent down to us from their pier in North River the remnant of our 12-inch tow line.

Then, at that time as now, assistance reports are supposed to place a value of the vessel that you assist and the value on the cargo. The officials of the steamship line absolutely refused to give us any kind of a figure, and told us postively they were afraid to for fear there might be salvage charges or otherwise. Even though we explained the Coast Guard didn't do those things and couldn't; it made no difference, they just never would.

For people like us, relatively uninformed Coast Guard officers to try to place a value on an ocean liner like the BERENGARIA so that we could make out our assistance report, you can imagine how far off the final figure probably was.

We had a lot of minor cases, you might say. I remember one particular case. We came across a fisherman on fire. He was down off of Barnegat. He was hopelessly on fire. We took the crew aboard. After watching him burn for awhile, the master who was also the owner, authorized us to sink it. We used a four-inch projectile and fired a couple of them in there, and he went down. As a matter of fact, I've got a series of pictures I took at the time. Just about as fast as I could take them, the first one he was well above the water and the last one just the tip of the mast as he went down. That again, is a relatively minor one that you talk about in reminiscing and so forth. And that's about it.

Capron - 90

To go on with the SENECA, in the spring of 1932, it was decided by the Coast Guard headquarters that the Coast Guard would again station a vessel in San Juan, Puerto Rico. I say again, because there had been one there prior to World War I. It had been taken out at that time. Although, later on, there was a 75-footer there; there were no cutters in that area at all.

The SENECA was selected to be the vessel. We got the word somewhere during the later part of May that we were going to go to the Coast Guard yard in Baltimore for overhaul and refitting and whathaveyou. We would not return to New York, but would go directly from Baltimore to San Juan.

We arrived in Baltimore just prior to the first of July, 1932. Actually this was one of those fiscal deals of the government, in that we were to have work started on this the very first day of the fiscal year, July 1st. We remained there for the summer.

Incidentially, we were there when the very serious hurricane hit Puerto Rico. I've forgotten the name, for the moment. When we finally did sail in the latter part of September, we got down there and helped in some of the rehabilitation that was still going on. Many of the tin shacks had been flattened, and it was pretty generally a mess.

That was our new station in late summer, early fall of 1932.

Interview # 3

Captain Walter C. Capron, USCG, Ret. by Peter Spectre
Arlington, Virginia November 15, 1969

Mr. Spectre: Captain, in our last interview you talked a little about your duty on the Coast Guard cutter SENECA. You gave a brief description of the SENECA and mentioned that it was built originally as a derelict destroyer. Could you tell me something about that?

Captain Capron: The SENECA was originally appropriated for by Congress about 1907 to be a derelict destroyer. At that time, most of the coastal marine traffic was in schooners and auxiliary schooners; nearly all of which were of wooden construction. As a result, whenever any one of them got into trouble, which involved foundering or being abandoned, the hulk would float either just at the surface of the water or in a few cases submerged by a few feet.

These hulks, known as derelicts, were of course very very dangerous; inasmuch as they normally would originate at least in the main traffic lanes, would be unlighted and almost invisible from any distance greater than one-half to three-quarters of a mile. A collision between one of these derelicts and a steamer almost invariably resulted in, at least serious damage, if not sinking of the steamer.

So, that Congress determined that there was need for a vessel so constructed so as to be able to cruise distances, to operate under extreme weather conditions, with relatively good stability in rough seas. The SENECA was designed to answer these questions and was completed and commissioned in 1908.

I think it's of interest at this point to actually quote the original orders for the vessel which directed that she; "patrol the area to the eastward of the United States bounded by a line from Portland, Maine to Sable Island, Nova Scotia, thence to the Bermuda Islands and then to Charleston, South Carolina."

You can see that this was not only an extremely large area, but also covered most of the steamer lanes to the east coast of the United States.

The vessel herself was relatively slow with very powerful engines, so that with a tow she could handle a relatively large vessel at fairly good speed. However, even without a tow, her hull construction was such that she couldn't go much faster.

Q: Was that the only derelict destroyer that was every built?

Capron: As far as I know that was the only derelict destroyer that was ever built. She was originally painted in such a way that her mast and her funnel had green and white stripes to distinguish her as a derelict destroyer.

I can't at this moment say whether that was an international agreement as to painting, or whether it was strictly a United States idea. As far as water tight integrity is concerned, from the standpoint of post World War II standards, she had none. She had two collision bulkheads, one forward, separating the forepeak from the main hold; one aft, separating the steering engine compartment from the after hold. She had no complete water tight deck, so that is she were holed seriously anywhere between those two bulkheads, if her pumps could not control the flooding, she was bound to sink.

Q: How long did derelict destroyers activities last? Was it still going on when you were on that?

Capron: From the standpoint of covering the area originally names, I believe it ended with probably the beginning of World War I.

We still did destroy derelicts, even while I was aboard but the menace had become considerably less. However, we did carry, as did most other cutters, a great number of TNT mines and necessary equipment so that if you did have a derelict, these mines could be placed in or on the derelict and then exploded to blow the derelict up. Occasionally, that was quite a job because with a wooden vessel floating upside down or bottom side up; it would be necessary to chop a hole in the bottom, lower the TNT mine into the vessel, and then with a small boat pull off some distance from the derelict and by electrical contact explode the mine.

Among the early Warrant Gunners of the Coast Guard and Revenue Cutter Service, the mark of the Gunner was a missing finger or fingers; when the charge may have exploded prematurely.

Q: Sounds like dangerous work.

Capron: It was. Invaribly, you used a pulling boat. Then again power boats, even though they were quite reliable; weren't quite reliable enough to risk the failure of the engine at just about the time you were blowing the mine. Manpower was a little more dependable.

Q: You mentioned that after World War I the dangerof derelicts decreased. Can you tell me why?

Capron: I think probably, and this is conjecture on my part; that first an awful lot of the coastwise schooners, wooden vessels, were destroyed during World War I. Secondly, many of them laid up for fear of being attacked by German U-boats. There were many steamers that had been built during World War I, notably the Hog Islanders which were available for coastwise traffic at relatively low cost.

Q: In other words, the steamers were taking the place of the schooners?

Capron: The Hog Islanders were to World War I what the Liberty and Victory ships were to World War II.

Q: To get out of that subject - Could you tell me a little bit about your duty on the SENECA in Puerto Rico?

Capron: I believe I mentioned last week, we arrived in Puerto Rico very shortly after one of the more devastating hurricanes that had hit in recent years in the West Indies.

We were a little too late to actually participate in any of the rehabilitation work but we were able to see much of the result of the hurricane and suffer somewhat from the fact that many aides to navigation had been destroyed and still were not in place.

Our arrival at San Juan was somewhat interesting to those of us aboard the ship, inasmuch as about dawn we sighted land ahead and slightly on the bow what we determined to be two of the mountain peaks on the center of the island. Taking visual bearings on these mountain peaks, we were able to fix our position; and realized that we were still 60 or 70 miles away from the island.

With that as a starter, we picked up El Moro at the entrance to San Juan Harbor what you might say right on the nose, and came into the harbor there and anchored. To all of us aboard it was really quite a new experience.

At that time, Puerto Rico was relatively unknown to mainland Americans, long before anyone had ever dreamed of it being a winter resort. And at that time, it was suffering from the effects of the beginning of the depression. Puerto Rico was practically destitute, as far as it's own finances were concerned and unemployment was very high.

One of the aftermaths of any hurricane is destruction of many fields of sugar cane. At that time, the economy of Puerto Rico was based essentially on sugar, some coffee, and some tobacco. With the destruction of the sugar cane fields, unemployment was high and would remain so for several years before the cane fields could be restored.

Much of the interest that we had when we arrived was personal. We learned, for instance, that Spanish was the universal language. Most of the stores, including the large departments stores, would have only one or two clerks that could speak English. The insular police, which would correspond to state police and local police as well, in continental U.S. mostly spoke Spanish. Although theoretically every policeman had to know English.

Q: What kind of reception did you get?

Capron: We received a rather nice reception. At that time the Army had a fairly large, for those days, force consisting of the 65th infantry; which was basically Puerto Rican as far as it's enlisted. Officer-wise, the majority being continental Americans with a few Puert Rican officers. One battalion was located at El Moro in San Juan. The other battalion was in a post some 40 miles up in the hills called Cayez.

The Navy had a radio station, receivers being located in San Juan and the transmitters being located in the mountains near Cayez; with probably some 40 odd people assigned.

Q: Was the SENECA the only Coast Guard cutter there?

Capron: The SENECA was the only Coast Guard cutter there and was the first cutter to be assigned to Puerto Rico since 1917 at the outbreak of World War I. That is the entrance of the United States into World War I.

There had been a 75-footer stationed there, which was lost in the entrance to San Juan Harbor in a rather heavy storm several years previous.

Q: Were there any port personnel there? For instance, something comparable to a captain of the port.

Capron: There was no port personnel there. And as a matter of fact; with the exception of New York harbor, the port of New York and the port of Charleston, South Carolina; there was no such thing as a captain of the port anywhere in the United States. Nor where there any, of what we think of as, port security personnel.

Q: How were you supplied? Were you supplied by the Coast Guard or through the Navy or the Army?

Capron: We were supplied almost entirely by the Army commissary, with quite a few purchases being purchased from local dealers. I'm speaking now strictly of commissary supplies.

Shipboard supplies were purchased in the United States and shipped down to us, in almost every case.

The SENECA, as I believe I mentioned before, obviously from her type of construction was a coal burner. Of course, coal was shipped there from one of the local maritime coal dealers. Actually it was Berwind Coal Company, which you still hear of in the United States.

Q: Did the Navy have any ships there?

Capron: The Navy had nothing there, other than the two radio stations.

Our arrival was actually heralded by the local people. The largest newspaper in San Juan EL MUNDO, which is still being published, entirely in Spanish; gave us quite a few front-page articles and very many columns, not only giving the ships history but also giving more or less of a warm welcome.

Our main job developed into being essentially distress work.

To go back a moment to your welcome question -- At that time the Governor of Puerto Rico was Governor Beverly. He and his wife were particularly nice to us. The officers of the SENECA were almost invaribly on the invitation list to any function held in the governor's house, known as Fortaleza.

To get back -- Our main purpose was a certain amount of law enforcement, from the standpoint of equipment on board motor boats, power boats, and inter-island vessels; and the stand-by for distress work.

Q: What kind of equipment were you concerned with?

Capron: The essential safety items which all vessels were supposed to carry; life jackets, simple things like foghorns, fire extinguishers, and such items which were more or less accepted as a general practice throughout the continental United States. There was very seldom any fog in that part of the world, but they do have very heavy rain storms, particularly during the winter time in the rainy season, and of course during the hurricane season.

Whereas prolonged fog such as is off the Atlantic coast many times was unheard of. However, the visibility would be just as poor in one of these rain storms, even though it didn't last very long. There were quite a few collisions and small vessels lost, because they had no way of making their presence known.

Q: Did you have any smuggling problems?

Capron: The basic smuggling problem that we had was the smuggling of coffee from Santo Domingo into Puerto Rico.

Puerto Rican coffee, at that time and I presume still, was a very high grade coffee which was highly prized in many of the northern European countries; Scandinavian countries particularly, but also Holland, Germany, and so forth. It was relatively expensive.

Santo Domingo coffee, which in appearance in the bean is almost identical with Puerto Rican coffee, was a very inferior grade as far as taste was concerned.

So that, there was a lot of smuggling of coffee from Santo Domingo into Puerto Rico. Where it would then be mixed with the Puerto Rican coffee and exported as Puerto Rican coffee.

The only thing wich we actually did along that line was patrol off the west and southwest coast of Puerto Rico at times when the customs gave information that there were to be loads of coffee smuggled in.

Q: How about your search and rescue work load?

Capron: We had a few cases of small vessels, nearly all of them sailing, overdue and in some cases dismasted and so forth that we would tow in.

Capron - 102

We did have, during my stay there, several large cases. Our success in solving them was not complete but I feel we did pretty well.

(Old spelling) The first case that comes to mind was the case of the steamship ~~PUERTO~~ Porto RICO. She was one of the vessels, a freighter, of the New York - Puerto Rico Line. One night, just before midnight, with her sailing just as she came to a bend in the channel going out her steering gear fouled up.

Q: Was this in San Juan?

Capron: This was in San Juan. And so, making essentially what was a 90° turn to the right, she made part of a turn and headed right onto a reef.

We had been cruising earlier that day and had gotten in some time just before dark, so that our boilers were still hot. Being coal-burning with Scotch boilers, from the normal in port watch, there was only auxiliarys running. For us to get steam up, we normally took at least four hours. Having been underway that day, we were able to get underway if my memory is correct, a half an hour. We were able to get our crew back, by the simple expedient of blowing the whistle many many times. In a relatively small city, it could be heard all over, and the crew all came back. So, we got under way and headed out.

The PORTO RICO could be seen without too much difficulty, well outside of the channel. So, the decision was made to try to pull her off exactly in the opposite direction in which she had gone on. To place ourselves in that position it was necessary for us to continue on out to sea, turn around, come back in, pass inside the channel buoys, and pass close to the stern of the PORTO RICO so that we could pass a line from our stern to her stern. Which we did.

I was navigator and therefore, responsible for the piloting that was necessary. All of this being at night and being outside of the channel, I found it a rather hairy experience. I'm sure the Captain did too.

We did fasten the line and start pulling and got nowhere. Finally, anchored, still with the line to the PORTO RICO and waited for daylight and for high tide.

We pulled intermittently for several days with the assistance of a couple of harbor tugs there. Later on, inspection indicated that the PUERTO RICO was badly holed forward under her main holds. And that if she would be pulled off, she'd undoubtedly sink.

The end of the story of the PORTO RICO was that Merritt-Chapman-Scott came down and performed a salvage job on her. She was then towed back up to continental United States and scrapped.

Capron - 104

The next job of any size that I can remember was a Gulf Oil tanker, the NEW JERSEY, which went aground on a sandbar in one of the small harbors on the southwest end of Puerto Rico. This was Guyanilla, where Gulf Oil Company had a large tank farm.

The vessel was in no immediate danger, but very well grounded. So that, with the nearest commercial salvage some 1500 miles away, indicated that we'd try to pull her off.

We worked with the lighthouse tender, ACACIA; and ultimately were able to free the NEW JERSEY without any apparent damage; so she could go on about her business.

Q: The ACACIA was a Coast Guard ship?

Capron: She was a lighthouse tender. That was about seven years before the Light House Service became a part of the Coast Guard. At that time, we were two separate agencies. This was strictly a cooperative deal between us locally.

Q: Did the Light House Service have many lighthouses in Puerto Rico?

Capron: Off hand I would say in the neighborhood of a dozen lighthouses. Of course, all harbors were buoyed with many day beacons and so forth. There was enough to keep one tender busy.

Capron - 105

This ACADIA, as an aside, was the one that was shelled and sunk by the Germans in World War II; after she became a part of the Coast Guard, and still in that area.

Q: How were your relations with the Light House service at that time?

Capron: Our relations there were very good. As a matter of fact, they were very good everywhere. There was a rather general respect between the two services. In many places the Coast Guard did furnish certain logistic support for the Light House Serivce.

We had another job which was of possible interest. Another large freighter, the GOLDEN MOUNTAIN went on a reef off of Mayaguez and was stuck hard and fast. In that case, much of her cargo had to be lightered off and we were then able to pull her free, without too much damage.

There was an interesting case that took place about that time which didn't involve much active work on our part, other than escorting the vessel. I do not even remember her name, but she was a large tanker, Cities Service I believe, that was steaming down through Mona Passage.

Mona Passage is the body of water between Puerto Rico and the island of Haiti, now called Hispaniola. In the middle of this passage is a large island called Mona, which is United

States property, with a lighthouse. Nearby is a smaller island called Monita, or little Mona. Under normal conditions, it causes no navigational difficulty.

It seems that this tanker in steaming down through Mona Passage had a rather inexperienced 3rd mate on watch, who saw the loom of a light over the horizon. He reported to his Captain that he had sighted a light on the northwest coast of Puerto Rico. On the basis of that report, the vessel changed course; and suddenly found Monita Island - little Mona - dead ahead of them in the darkness. The vessel backed full speed, but not soon enough to prevent the bow from striking the island which was rocky and almost mushroom shape; caving in the upper part of the bow.

How much pandamonium existed is difficult to say, but they never stopped backing. So, she backed around in a circle and hit the same island with the stern. Again not damaging the underwater part of the vessel; but seriously damaging the upper stern.

She then came in to San Juan, we went out and met her and escorted her in. The incident certainly had its humorous incidents.

I do think from the personal standpoint, to go back to our first arrival there, the housing difficulty for those of us on the ship was extreme.

The Army had housing for all of their personnel, dependent housing for all of their officers. The small Navy contingent had housing. There was no other housing of any kind. So, it was necessary for us to all find rentals in the San Juan area.

Q: You brought your wife with you?

Capron: They came down later on an Army transport, some month and a half or so later. Most of us ended up living in Santurce, which at that time was a separate municipality from San Juan proper. Now I believe, it is more or less called New San Juan.

It was quite an experience for our families, as well as for us in a foreign-speaking country. For instance, on my street there was only one other family that could be called continental Americans. I use that expression 'continental Americans' because if you spoke of yourself as an American, as opposed to a Puerto Rican; they became very much incensed. They were Americans as much as we were.

So that, my boy who was about two, was much more fluent in Spanish than he was in English. Unfortunately, he outgrew that in later years.

Q: Tell me, did your duty involve cooperative work with other Carribean Islands or countries in the area, in search and rescue or any other type of activity?

Capron - 108

Capron: For one thing, our cruising area, area responsibility; was the American Virgin Islands and Puerto Rico. We had to cruise our station, so-called, at least once a month. So that we were visiting St. Thomas; this was at the time that both the island and the city had the same name, St. Thomas (the city now being Charlotte Amalie); St. Croix; and St. Johns'.

The other islands in that area – shall we say, seldom had any distress cases and they had no forces whatsoever to cope with them, if they had. The island of Haiti being just to the westward of us, occasionally would have trouble in the entrance to Santo Domingo City; but we never had occasion to go over there.

There was one incident, or series of incidents; again with which we had no immediate concern. There was a Cuban revolution during 1933, in which a number of Coast Guard destroyers were ordered to go to Key West and to a couple of Cuban ports with Navy destroyers; to more or less protect American interest. With us being so close, we always expected actually to get orders to go over ourselves. And although we did have standby orders, nothing else ever came of it. Ultimately, that revolution – whether it died a natural death I can't say. I think it was in that revolution which Batista first came into power.

Capron - 109

As a commentary, as a result of the various disarmament treaties and so forth, and a certain amount of ecomony; the Navy did not have enough destroyers in the Atlantic. That was why Coast Guard destroyers were assigned to the Navy, for that purpose.

Q: Do you know if there were any landing parties?

Capron: There were a number of landing parties, particularly around certain areas where sugar centrals were located and where there were quite a few American personnel living.

I know of no cases where any shots were exchanged. Of course, all this is hearsay, as far as I am concerned.

Q: Captain, maybe this time would be a good time to talk about the state of the Coast Guard in general.

Capron: At this particular time, in March 1933; the administration of Franklin D. Roosevelt came into office. He came in on a governmental economy program, which ultimately ended up with many of us being cut initially cut 15% in pay. Which was not finally restored for some three years. There was involved a cut in the Coast Guard of very high percentage in money, particularly personnel money. The Coast Guard was more or less forced to de-commission a number of ships.

Capron - 110

Among other things, during the later part of the Hoover administration, a new series of vessels had been built - the 165 foot patrol boat, of which the last had just gone into service. These vessels became active in 1933 and '34 and were used ultimately to displace all of the destroyers.

Q: What was their main purpose of being built?

Capron: Strictly anti-smuggling. They were a smaller vessel, of course, than destroyers. They carried a crew in the neighborhood of 37 men. They were twin diesel, highly manouevrable, and relatively fast. At that time, when first built, a top speed of 16 or 17 knots. Because of their low personnel requirements, their low fuel requirements; they were an extremely economical replacement for the destroyers; and probably overall as efficient in their particular phase of anti-smuggling work.

Q: Were they used for picketing or seizures?

Capron: They were used basically in the same way the destroyers had been. However, there had been a gradual build up in the Coast Guard intelligence area, with particular reference to intercepting rummie radio traffic and getting direction finder bearings. This was the first use of high frequency direction finders. In fact, they were developed at that time by and for the Coast Guard.

Q: These are the ones that were used very successfully during the second World War.

Capron: These were forerunners. To have these effective, they had to be practically on a wooden ship. We had a number of 75 foot patrol boats equipped with these direction finders, which were spotted around the coast in small harbors and so on. They would obtain direction finder bearings and either a 165 foot patrole boat or a destroyer would be sent to run down the line of bearing obtained from the direction finder. In most cases, you'd get down to the end of it, and you'd find an offshore rummie.

Later on Intelligence, and this was particularly true working with customs and the Alcohol Tax Unit of Treasury, became pretty efficient decoding and deciphering messages.

Q: Did the rummies know that you were doing this?

Capron: They, ultimately, knew it. It undoubtedly became obvious after a number times when after a radio transmission, within a few hours that one of our vessels would show up. They adapted various methods of countering, such as -- getting under way and moving to another location as soon as they finished a radio transmission. It's warfare in miniature.

Every action, there was a counter-reaction by the opponent. Then you'd come up with something new, and he'd come up with something new.

Q: This was good experience then for anti-submarine work during the second World War.

Capron: I feel that the training that most of our officers of the period had was almost irreplacable, when World War II came and we began manning naval patrol vessels - DEs, PCs, and our own 327-footers.

I know that, as far as I was concerned, my junior officer training on a high speed vessel and the fact that we indulged in manouevres as groups and divisions; was invaluable to me later on during World War II when I commanded the SPENCER, and operated with a task force that had 12 Navy destroyers. I would have had a lot more to learn, if I hadn't had that basic experience as a junior officer.

To get back to the way things were going. — This is something that is very little known at this time. —

At the end of World War I, Franklin Roosevelt was Assistant Secretary of the Navy. At this time, the Coast Guard had been in existance as such for only three or four years; as an independent service for only a couple of years - from 1915 to April 6, 1917.

Capron - 113

As Assistant Secretary of the Navy, Mr. Roosevelt felt very strongly that the Coast Guard, particularly the ships from the old Revenue Cutter Service, belonged in the Navy. As Assistant Secretary of the Navy, he did everything he could to prevent the return of the Coast Guard to the Treasury Department.

During one of his absences from Washington, (this is strictly hearsay,) the executive order returning the Coast Gurad to the Treasury Department was placed on the President's desk - President Wilson, who as you know was in very poor health at about that time - and was signed. And the Coast Guard again became a part of the Treasurey Department.

Some years later, after Franklin Roosevelt became President, it became rather evident that he had never forgotten his original idea that the Coast Guard belonged in the Navy. It was his intention to sign an executive order, under the Coast Guard Act of Establishment, transferring temporarily the Coast Guard to the Navy. Then seeking legislation, to make it permanent.

This was all soon after his innauguration in 1933. The Coast Guard, represented by most of it's officers, let us say, felt that we very definitely should not in the Navy. We were quite sure if such a thing took place that within not too many years, the service would disappear. We had as a precedent

Capron - 114

what happened to the old Naval Auxiliary Service, immediately following World War I when it was militarized from being a civilian supporting organization. Within not too years, all of the personnel who had been civilian officers in the Auxiliary Service found themselves retired or anyway out of the Navy.

Q: What was the Naval Auxiliary Service? What was their function?

Capron: They operated all the *Collieus*, all the support ships for the fleet.

Q: Similar to the MSTS.

Capron: Only similar in the sense that it was civilian manned.

Q: So, they were strictly Merchant Marine officers.

Capron: By this amalgamation they became naval officers, but didn't remain very long.

We thought the same thing would happen to us, whether rightly or wrongly, is strictly guess work.

Capron - 115

However, at that time there was a considerable feeling between the Navy and the Coast Guard. To understand much better - the Navy had been pinched for appropriations for some ten years or so; whereas the Coast Guard had had almost anything it had asked for.

About this time, the Navy had been in a position where they could not even commission all their Annapolis graduates. The lower ones were graduated, but not commissioned.

So, that, they probably welcomed the added jobs; that the Coast Guard being a part of the Navy, would have created.

Q: What was the relative size of the services at that time?

Capron: Off hand, I would say, this is strictly guess work - ten to one. At that time, the Navy was very definitely not very big.

The Coast Guard Alumni Association - which basically had been an organization on paper, with one annual meeting a year, annual dues of one dollar maybe - decided to become an active organization, solicited funds in the form of an assessment from all officers in the service, and raised a quite sizable fund to be used for whatever was felt was necessary to prevent this transfer of the Coast Guard.

In addition, many officers did essentially missionary work. Practically every Congressman and Senator of a maritime state was contacted, either by ourselves or more often would be contacted by some civilian individual or organization. At that time, the rules about writing to your Congressman, other than through official channels, was very strictly enforced.

I remember particularly that another officer and myself, our engineer, visited every shipyard in the New York harbor. This was on one of the trips that the SENECA made up for overhaul. We talked to them about what the financial considerations would mean to them, if we became a part of the Navy. Bearing in mind that the great majority of drydock jobs and overhaul and such that the Coast Guard did, was done in commercial yards. Very seldom did we go into a Navy yard, except for strictly gunnery or such. We pointed out, possibly overemphazing, the fact that each commercial yard would loose an awful lot of business if the Coast Guard went with the Navy.

The upshot of the whole thing was a coalition of Congressmen and Senators from the coastal states, including the Great Lakes, visited the President and - here again it's mostly hearsay - at least convinced the President that his idea of transferring the Coast Guard was not a good idea at that time, at least. That was completely dropped and was never revived.

Capron - 117

Q: How long a period of time did this emcompass?

Capron: Possibly three or four months.

The various other changes that took place in the Coast Guard were more or less gradual.

I was transferred back to the continental U. S. as of about the 1st of January, 1934. I was transferred to, what was then, the Boston Division, and is now the first Coast Guard District; as Communications Officer.

Meanwhile, I had sent my wife home to her mother to await the arrival of another child, and had managed to come up to the states on leave when my older daugher was born.

So that, at the time I received these orders, my wife and now two children, were in Newport getting ready to come back to Puerto Rico. With these orders, I stopped their further preparations; and reported into Boston shortly after the first of January.

Q: Did you request this type of duty or was this routine?

Capron: This was a routine transfer. In those days, you didn't request any type of duty unless you had a particular hardship. As I remember it, there was no particular place on your fitness report where you could indicate the type of duty you wanted. I could be wrong on that, but that's my memory.

Capron - 118

Q: Who determined what direction each officer in the Coast Guard would take? Was their any plan where Coast Guard officers would be developed for certain duty?

Capron: There was and there wasn't. Upon the abolition of the engineer corps, for awhile it was assumed that every officer had the capability of being an engineer officer on a ship. This was true in the case of many of the older uncomplicated vessels, but not true in some of the later vessels. It certainly wasn't true in the case of higher supervisory positions in engineering. So, it was recognized that they needed more training for certain engineer officers.

Of course, this was the time when aviation was beginning to have it's early expansion. So that, headquarters would put out invitations to the service at large, for officers who wished to apply for postgraduate training in engineering and also flight training.

In that sense of the word, there was a plan. Certainly the number that they could use and so on, was carefully worked out.

In the case of engineering, the selection was based to a certain extent on what they already had in their service career. If he'd been an engineer on a vessel and had been successful, he would be more apt to be selected for postgraduate

Capron - 119

training; than if you had not.

As far as the aviators were concerned, physical fitness had about as much to do with it as anything else. That is the physical fitness of passing a flight physical as opposed to the normal physical. The training that these officers had, the aviators, were all trained at Pensacola by the Naval Flight Training School there.

Many of the engineers attended the Naval Postgraduate School over at Annapolis. Many of them went to California Tech, and I believe, subsequently, MIT.

As far as my selection as Communications Officer was concerned, there was a determination made at headquarters level that they wanted Communications Officers within a certain year group or several year groups. Within those year groups, there were some officers whose sea duty was about up, and who were due for shore duty.

At this time, I was almost completing six years sea duty. So, I was just right for that type of a transfer.

Q: Did they have any set time limit for how much time you'd spend at sea and how much time at shore?

Capron: Only on the basis of comparison of jobs. The general rules, after six years of sea duty, was shore duty for about three years. The normal tour of duty on one station was considered three years. After that three, you would go back to

Capron - 120

sea duty. Of course, as you got older and more senior, there were fewer jobs at sea than there were ashore, that is the ratio changed. So that, in the long run probably, you could expect over a thirty year career, somewhere between 50 and 65% sea duty and the balance shore duty.

To give you an idea - The Coast Guard Register at that time, broke down the amount of your duties that you had had. It was broken down into sea duty north of Cape Hatteras, sea duty south of Cape Hatteras, sea duty in Alaska, sea duty on the Pacific coast; and special duty, which included duty on harbor tugs as well as shore duty.

How they used those breakdowns, I don't know. Because, with the exception of that one tour in San Juan, all of my sea duty until World War II, was north of Cape Hatteras.

Q: Captain, at this time, could you tell me a little bit of what you know about Coast Guard aviation in its developing period? A couple of weeks ago, we did talk about the air station on Ten Pound Island.

Capron: There was a gradual recognition from the Treasury Department and Coast Guard that aviation could do an awful lot towards the enforcement of anti-smuggling - develop off-shore patrols, spotting rummies, and so forth.

One of the early stations built, a former Naval Air Station incidentally at Cape May, went into commission somewhere between 1928 and 1930. At this time, most of our aviators were former naval aviators. Our own Coast Guard aviators that had been trained during World War I, were by this time too old for really active flying. As the need was accepted, by Coast Guard and Treasury, additional stations were set up. In almost every case, these stations were at abandoned Naval Air Stations. Cape May, for instance, having been the home of the dirigible LOS ANGELES. Elizabeth City, North Carolina was re-established along about that time.

The original legislation which authorized the Coast Guard to have air stations stemed from an act of about 1916.

Aviation was more or less recognized as being important by bulletins that were put out to the service, inviting young officers to apply, and if accepted would be given flight training at Pensacola with the Navy. Quite a few of our younger officers, this was in the very late '20s and early '30s, applied and were accepted; and became aviators.

During this period, there were two of my classmates - one, W. A. Burton, who was one of the very early aviators of the second period, not in World War I; another one, classmate Carl B. Olson, who is now living in Texas, retired. Burton, incidentally, is now dead. There were several in the class ahead of me that applied about the same time - one, Clarence F. Edge, who now lives most of the year in St. Petersburg,

Florida; another one, Richard L. Burke, now living in the vicinity of New London, Connecticut. He, incidentally, was Morgenthau's pilot for a number of years. Those four were about the pioneers, of what I would call, Coast Guard officers first becoming aviators; as differentiated from those officers who had been aviators and who came into the Coast Guard to continue as aviators.

Q: Did you have any interest in aviation? Did you ever consider it?

Capron: I was very much interested at one time, at several times. I made my first application possibly around 1934, and failed the flight physical basically because I was overweight. A year or so later I applied. This time, I was told there were too many aviators about my time. They wanted a greater spread in age and rank. Several years later, when I had reached the point of being Executive Officer on a ship, I was sounded out by headquarters as to whether I was still interested in aviaton.

About this time, we had lost, mainly due to offshore landings, a number of aviators just about my time. My feeling as expressed in my letter back to headquarters refusing, was really based on two things. One- now that they'd killed off all the people about my time, they wanted to take me; and two, I'd put in relatively eight to ten years as a seagoing officer, standing all the duty and everything else. And now, I'd reached the point where I had gotten the rank and experience to be Executive Officer. I don't have to stand days' duty any more, I'm not about to become a novice in an entirely new career like aviation where I'm going to be the beginner. I never again was asked - did I want to become an aviator.

Q: You mentioned, a lot of the aviators of your age and experience had been lost. How did this happen?

Capron: Various airplane accidents. One of the hair-raising things that was done for years, that still is occasionally done - was landing a seaplane or a flying boat at sea, when some injured or sick person, passenger or otherwise, some seaman aboard ship at sea, needing hospitalization; landing at sea, taking him aboard the plane and flying him to a hospital.

Offshore landings, under any circumstances, are extremely dangerous. Gradually, about 1937 or '38 at least, the Coast Guard began to take a dim view of it. For awhile, they were forbidden.

Later on, there were cases where there might be an offshore landing. Ultimately, this is as late as 1957 or '58; we reached the point where we would refer the case to a doctor at one of the public hospitals and put it up to him point blank. "Will bringing him in probably save his life? Will he die if we don't bring him in? And will he live if we do bring him in?" Possibly it was unfair to the doctor, pointing out that we are risking the lives of a crew of four to seven people. "Are the possibility of saving his life, worth the risk of these people?" As a general rule, the very doctors who suggested originally that we take the man off, when it was put up to them - "Will he die if we don't and will he live if we do, or the probability that he'll live?" They would usually back down and say, "He'll probably live where he is, only we could cure him faster." When you got that kind of a question, your answer was, "No, we can't risk the lives of our people on that basis."

This, of course, is projecting some 20 odd years later, from the time I was speaking. However, we did lose quite a few aviators from off-shore landings - either in landing, in a high wave it nosed over; or trying to take off would run into the same thing. There were other types of deaths too, which are involved in any type of aviation - such as crash landings, one or two cases flying in the mountains, and so forth.

As I mentioned earlier, I was transferred to Boston, arriving early January, 1934. That winter proved to be one coldest winters that New England had had in many years. We actually had one week in winter, wherein the warmest it got in the daytime was 18 below and every night it went down to 28 below. That had a dual effect, as far as I was concerned.

I'd been in the tropics for two years and I felt the cold terribly. My automobile had been in the tropics for two years. It wouldn't start in the morning. I had to be towed every morning. It was miserable until I finally had the car tuned up and fixed up the way it should have been before. My blood finally thickened and I got so I didn't freeze to death.

However, this extreme cold weather, caused all of the harbors throughtout New England to freeze over in many cases solid ice of quite a few inches thick. Boston harbor froze over and every harbor north of Boston, including all of Maine harbors further over south.

One of the things that had been developing over a number of years was the change over from coal to oil for both commercial use and household heating. One of the hard facts of economics is that, you can store coal by piling it on the ground. It's very easy to bring in a lot of coal during the summer and fall storing it on the ground, and use it come winter.

From the oil standpoint, you've got to have tanks - a lot of tanks and expensive tanks to store enough oil to last the whole winter. So that, it was economically imposposible to do that.

All of these small communities throughtout New England are served by small oil and gasoline barges, which would bring the oil in throughtout the season. They were all relatively small, very much low-powered, under-powered; and capable of taking care of themselves only in good conditions. So, these communities began to be hard up for oil. Here again, roads and tank trucks being what they were; they could not be supplied by the road.

We began to get requests for ice-breaking. This was about the time that the Coast Guard's actual position in ice-breaking for commercial services began. We had one regular ice-breaker in the first district, that was the KICKAPOO, which was stationed in Rockland, Maine.

We had another vessel of relatively minor capability called the OSSIPPEE, stationed in Portland. In addition, we did have a number of regular cutters and quite a few 125-footers neither of which were designed for, or very good at breaking ice. However, they were steel vessels. Obviously, you don't put a wooden vessel into ice.

So, we were swamped with requests, demands for breaking ice into and out of these various harbors. Many of the small harbors didn't have enough water for anything other than posposibly the 125-footers.

Q: Did the Coast Guard have statuatory responsibilities for this?

Capron: At that time, the only statuatory responsibility we had was the broad one of assisting vessels in distress. It was several years later that a proclamation by the President gave us the legal responsibility for ice-breaking, as such.

So that, this winter, as Communications Officer – the Communications Officer acted very much as an assistant Operations Officer under the Chief of Staff (there was no such thing as an Operations Officer at that time); I had a very good breaking in on that kind of work.

We had various places with a lot of difficulty. The small ports, as I've already mentioned.

The approaches to Cape Cod Canal; which was a major seaway for ocean-going vessels as well as small vessels going from New York North, and up to Boston, and so forth; would be clogged with ice. Vessel after vessel would be stuck. In there, we used our larger cutters, all of which were single screw; to break ice and open up those waterways for traffic.

Q: How successful were they?

Capron: It's pretty hard to measure success in that way. From the standpoint of getting vessels through, I would say that we were pretty successful. It might take a long time. The damage that a merchant ship, freighter would receive from ice could be much greater if they were following one of our regular cutters through, than if they were following a regular ice-breaker through. The vessels would actually suffer a lot of damage - sprung rivets, sprung plates, and so forth.

Q: Were there any ships that sank because of ice at this time?

Capron: I remember none. Small vessels, yes -- fishermen that were left at anchor in the harbor might be sunk at a mooring, or something like that. Large vessels, no, I know of none.

That was a pretty rough winter and that was my initiation. I might add at this point that the Chief of Staff at that time in Boston was the same Commander Jerry Starr who had been my first skipper on the destroyer, CONYNGHAM. I found him very easy to work for, even though he still had a pretty hard-boiled reputation.

In New England, the Coast Guard had several hundred miles of telephone lines which they had inherited from the Lifesaving Service. In many parts of New England; and this also applied to Delaware, Virginia, North Carolina, the Great Lakes, Long Island; the Coast Guard had had, in order to have telephone service to the Lifeboat Stations, establish telephone lines. These originally had been built in 1917, as part of the war measure.

If there is any kind of anachronism between my saying inherited from the Lifesaving Service and the Coast Guard; the point is that the real amalgamation, as far as operating was concerned between the old Lifesaving Service and the Seagoing Service didn't really take place until the '30s. Although, officially they were all one service back in 1915.

Q: More or less worked as agencies under the same —

Capron: Under the same. They didn't really come together, until they got pretty close to the top.

With all these telephone lines, plus submarine cable, plus the radio communications that all the ships had; our communication department was pretty big - possibly 8 or 10 telephone linemen, a lot of radiomen, and so forth.

You asked earlier - We didn't have the RCC as known now, but we had a communication center which was manned by radio men, which did most of the things the RCC's do now. Except that, during the daytime, the decisions would be referred to the Chief of Staff. After working hours, would be referred by telephone to which ever officer had the duty.

Q: These telephone lines that you had - They weren't commercial lines, they belonged to the Coast Guard?

Capron: They belonged to the Coast Guard. They were not commercial lines. Everyone of them tie into a commercial exchange somewhere. But, the line itself, was entirely Coast Guard owned, Coast Guard maintained. In some case, the Telephone Company had their wires on our poles. And in some cases, we had our wires on their poles.

Q: A private person who lived anywhere, and who wanted to call the Coast Guard, could still get through on that line, in other words, through the commercial line?

Capron: Through the commercial system, yes.

For instance, these telephone lines - one went from ~~Cape Cod on~~ Wood End on Cape Cod all the way down to Chatham. In fact, it ended at the old Monomoy Point Station; which you probably are familar with. You could get into that commercially, either at Race Point ~~from~~ at the farthe*st* North ~~down~~ end or at Chatham on the other end.

So, that if you wanted to get in and talk, say, to the station at Orleans - you'd call Chatham. These, then, so-called ~~fire~~ farmer lines, magneto grounded circuit - the lookout at Chatham

Capron - 131

with a series of rings by the crank; could get hold of the Orleans station. You could then talk through. As a general rule, you would relay your message through Chatham; who in turn would then send it on up.

There were also other types of telephone lines that we had. Let's say around Machias for instance. The Telephone Company didn't go below Machias, which is about 15 miles in from the actual seacoast. We had a lifeboat station just off the coast there at Cross Island. We had a telephone line from Machias all the way down to Cutler, then a submarine cable up to Cross Island, and then another submarine cable up to an offshore lighthouse. So, that if anybody wanted to talk to the Coast Guard stations that went into the Machias exchange - they had a plug in their board to which our line was attached. The submarine cables hit practically every island off the coast of New England, with a Coast Guard cable. I think the most outstanding one was the one to Block Island.

All communications to Block Island at that time, went over our cable. We had a twenty-pair Cable that went from Green Hill, Rhode Island out to Block Island. We rented a number of circuits in that to the Telephone Company, a couple of circuits to Western Union, and then there was one circuit for the Weather Bureau. That was all Coast Guard owned and maintained. The commercial companies paid regular rentals for the circuits

Capron - 132

which they had. Actually, it was a pretty big operation.

In addition, we were charged with furnishing telephone service to every isolated lighthouse. This again, was long before anybody dreamed of the Lighthouse Service being a part of the Coast Guard. We furnished, over Coast Guard lines, telephone communications to all the off-shore islands.

Q: S. that right there you already had a direct --

Capron: We already had a direct working relationship right with the Lighthouse Service; right at ground level, basic level.

In fact, at that time, the Coast Guard had enough submarine cables to require one fairly good sized cable ship, the PEQUOT, who operated all except winter up around New England. In winter, she would operate in other parts of the country farther south usually.

Then every district had one or two cable boats, anywhere from 50 feet up to 100 feet. They could handle the shallow water cables and so forth.

Interview # 4

Captain Walter C. Capron, USCG, Ret. by Peter Spectre
Arlington, Virginia November 22, 1969

Mr. Spectre: Captain, in our last interview we were talking about your assignment in Boston as Communications Officer and we were talking about communications in general. I wonder if you'd tell me a little bit more about communications in the New England area and also about your duties.

Captain Capron: At that time, and I believe this is slightly repetitious of our last interview, the Coast Guard had many miles of land line telephones connecting the various lifeboat stations along the beach and providing service to offshore lighthouse, where no commercial telephone service was available. In most case the lighthouses would be on the same line as the Coast Guard stations, but not in every case.

We had in the neighborhood of 50 to 75 miles of submarine cable going off to these various islands offshore, in most cases connecting into a commercial exchange somewhere on the beach.

In addition, of course, all of our ships were equipped with radio - both CW, that is code, and voice radio. We had a radio traffic station located at Winthrop, Massachusetts. This radio traffic station was connected with the district communications center by teletype.

At that time, our lifeboat stations had only telephone communications. There was no way of getting in touch with them other than by telephone, and in most cases through commercial lines until we reach a point near the lifeboat station.

Q: Could the lifeboat stations communicate with distressed ships?

Capron: Only by visual signal flags.

This period found the Coast Guard financially in very very poor shape. Our appropriations had been drastically cut, both as a part of the cutback due to the depression but also the mistaken belief by Congress and the Administration that because prohibition had gone out, that liquor smuggling was automatically stopped.

So as a partial solution to our extremely limited telephone money -- when I say limited, I mean the entire district at that time had $75 a month for all telephone tolls and excess messages We just couldn't stay within in it. So we in Boston had an idea of setting up radio stations, transmitters, in many of the lifeboat stations.

When the 75 footer fleet had been laid up and many vessels disposed of, the radio equipment which was all voice had been removed and stored. We obtained permission from headquarters on our experimental basis to install at two stations, Race

4 · Capron - 135

Point on Cape Cod and Gloucester on the North Shore, radio transmitters and receivers to check the fesability of voice transmission between lifeboat stations, using completely untrained men. That is the surfmen, whose only training would be what little we could give them in voice procedure.

Q: Were the surfmen in the lifeboat stations civilians?

Capron: They were all military. Surfman was a rating which paywise, of course, amounted to a third class Petty Officer and was the lowest rating onboard lifeboat stations at that time.

Q: They didn't get any radio training when they went through basic training?

Capron: They didn't even go to basic training; the surfmen didn't. The surfmen were, at that time, more or less recruited locally. In most cases they had been local boys, fishermen and so forth, who grew up on the water but had had absolutely no basic training. Later years, that changed of course.

As I remarked before, it was around 1934 that the beginning of the real amalgamation between the Lifesaving Service and the revenue Cutter Service actually began to gel.

We set up these two transmitters with receivers at the two stations and they worked very well. Our next step was to establish other stations. We selected stations which were quite active, as far as distress work was concerned, and attempted in every case to have at least one radio equipped station on each telephone land line. So that we could get communications through into that land line and therefore practically to all the stations. We ended up by setting up probably in the neighborhood of fifteen radio equipped lifeboat stations.

At that time, when a lifeboat left the station he was out of communication until he came back. Many times they would go out on a search, particularly for a missing fisherman. The fisherman would get back a few minutes later and there was no way of calling that lifeboat back. He might search fruitlessly for half a day or a day.

Almost simultaneously with our establishing transmitters for inter-station communication, the people in the Chicago district recognizing their difficulties with lifeboats installed police radio receivers in their lifeboats. By agreement with local police, they established communication by the police radios to the lifeboats when they were away from base.

At this point some one in headquarters communications saw the light and decided to attempt to put the two ideas together. They designed and had built a number of lifeboat radio receivers. All of these, frequency-wise, being on what was then called the

4 Capron - 137

Coast Guard band which was roughly from 2660 to 2710 kilocycles. With these various receivers, we were able to install in most of our lifeboats battery operated radio receivers.

Q: Were these also transmitters as well? Were these just receivers, or could you transmit?

Capron: These were just receivers. At this period of time, there were a very very few so-called transceivers on the market. None of which really were practical to use as far as either a boat or a police car. The police did not have their own transmitters at that time; it was strictly a broadcast affair.

We installed these receivers and, of course, it took awhile for the people to get used to them. But it saved us many many hours of fruitless search and, undoubtedly, did save lives and property. It was possible after a boat left, if you received more accurate information, to divert the boat to another position.

Actually there was another indirect result which was a rather happy one from the Lifeboat Station peoples viewpoint.

Practically all of these stations on the New England coast were isolated; most of them on islands. All of those that were on islands had no electric power

As I said, before, we were pretty well strapped for money. However, our civil engineering people did have funds which they made available, to at least off-shore stations, which were using kerosene lamps and so forth. They installed generators and banks of batteries.

In most cases the generators that were installed were 110 volt Koehlers, a gasoline operated generator. In a few cases it was necessary to use 32 volts. 32 volts, incidentally, being the power supply for the radio transmitter. As a result, the placing of a radio transmitter in a lifeboat station in many cases incidentally provided electricity for lighting and refrigeration and other needs of the station.

One of our difficulties, of course, was the lack of manpower. In those stations where there was a lookout the transmitter and receiver would be placed in the lookout tower. In many of the stations, however, where the lookout tower was quite widely removed location-wise from the station the transmitter and receiver would be set up in the dining room, the mess hall. The cook was the radio man. The radio receiver would be turned on all day and once an hour they made tests. Whenever there was a call, the cook would drop his pans and run in and use the transmitter and then call the officer in charge.

From many standards it was rather primitive. Most of our surfmen were relatively poorly educated men; certainly not sophisticated in the sense of being used to using a radio. So that in the beginning we placed very little restrictions on the radio traffic, encouraging them then to use it, even if it was only shooting the breeze with a nearby station. Later on, of course, we had to clamp down.

We had built up for ourselves a pretty good coastal radio system. We had built it up to the point where our main traffic station at Winthrop could not handle all of the voice traffic, plus the ship to shore coded traffic.

So we set up at Point Allerton stations, which is located in the town of Hull at the entrance to Boston harbor, a voice traffic station. At that particular station we normally kept one or two radio men. This provided an interesting deal because we had been attempting to interest many of our Lifeboat Station people in shifting over to seagoing branch. They were separate branches then. We had gotten quite a few of them interested in radio. They had gone to radio school and become radio men.

Q: Did they go to Navy schools?

Capron: We had our own school. I'll come to that a little bit later on, in comparison between Navy and Coast Guard radio.

These boys who had gone to radio school, had been aboard ship. They would get homesick for the life aboard a Lifeboat Station. So we would rotate for a couple of months at a time a former surfman who was now a radio man. We would send him to Port Allerton. He was so pleased to get back on a Lifeboat Station that he would willingly work 12, 14, 16 hours a day, just to get back for a while. In that way we had a trained man

#4 Capron - 140

on watch at this minor traffic station at Port Allerton.

Q: How did you communicate - say a ship was in distress a hundred miles off shore? He couldn't be seen by a Lifeboat Station. How did they communicate with you, and you with them?

Capron: Every since prior to World War I, various commercial ships had been required to carry radio, wireless telegraphy. The length of time that they stood watches was, of course, more or less governed by the type of ship it was. A freighter would carry only one radio man and he would be on for periods of fifteen minutes at a time during daylight hours and so on. Most of them had automatic alarms. All traffic - I'll use wireless telegraphy for the moment, to differentiate from radio in terms of telephone - was carried out on a few frequencies. One basic frequency, which was the calling and distress frequency, was 500 kilocycles. Every Coast Guard ship and every Coast Guard radio station that was manned by radio men had a continuous watch on 500. Every ship that carried radio was required at certain times in the day to listen in on 500. So that any time that a vessel was in distress, he would send out his call. It might be the extreme, an SOS. This would go out on 500. The minute an SOS went out on 500, every station within hearing had to stop transmitting so that the channel was completely clear.

There was another signal, which was CQ, an international signal which was generally – please stand by and listen. It wasn't specifically distress. Quite often it would precede a distress.

There was another call, which was strictly a Coast Guard call, NCU. This meant any Coast Guard unit. The minute we heard an NCU, our closest station, probably a main traffic station, or it might be a ship, would immediately answer.

Basically that was how we would communicate with the larger radio equipped ships.

There was another group which caused considerable more difficulty. That was the great number of fishermen, both Canadian and American, that used to fish off of Georges Bank, LeHavre Bank, and even as far up as the Grand Banks. Some of these had the commercial ship to shore telephone. In which case, they would call us the same way that nowadays you might call if you have an automobile telephone.

To digress for a moment into an anecdote. One big surprise that I had one morning was when my phone rang and I answered. The voice came and said, "This is the Captain of the HEKLA. We're sinking." My first thought was somebody was really trying to take me over the jumps, pull my leg, or what have you. You get a regular telephone call and answer it, and someone says, "I'm sinking."

I said, "Where are you?" He gave me his position, lattitude and longitude. He said that water was coming up and so forth.

This particular case had a number of ramifications. First of all, we checked his figures and found that the depth of the water that he said he had could not have been at the place he said he was. So we called him back on the telephone and told him that. He said that he had made a mistake of about a degree, I believe, in his longitude. So that was corrected.

We had no vessel within 50 to 75 miles at least. But at that time, there was a commercial broadcasting station which specialized in broadcasting to the fishermen - market prices of halibut, mackerel, cod, or whatever it might be, and so forth. It was called a fishermen's station. It was WHDH, which has been rather in the news the last year or so for other reasons.

Q: It's not a fishermen's station any more.

Capron: No, but it was then.

We called the people at WHDH, and told them that we had this trawler sinking. And would he broadcast over his fishermen's radio, WHDH, the distress and the location of the vessel and request for any assistance from anybody nearby.

I got a phone call back from the skipper. He said, "The water's coming in at the pilot house now and I'm leaving.

A Canadian trawler, LEMBURG, had just pulled alongside. He was just over the horizon and he heard the broadcast from WHDH. He's taking myself and my crew off. Thanks a lot."

That was the end of the story as far as that part is concerned. His vessel did sink and probably that was the only thing that saved their lives. Although we might have found them in boats later on.

Q: You've been talking in terms of New England now. Were the same things going on in the rest of the country? Did they face the same problems?

Capron: No, they didn't face the same problems quite. For instance in the third district, which was then the New York division.

They had a continuous land line to their Lifeboat Stations, starting at Montauk Point on the extreme end of Long Island. It went the complete length of Long Island, a cable to cross New York harbor, and then their land line went the whole length of the New Jersey coast all the way down to Cape May.

For the communications standpoint between stations, they had no need whatsoever for radio. Although, they later on installed it for use in the lifeboats. That problem was the same everywhere.

New England had a lot more fishing vessels, small vessels. The distress activity, certainly at that time, was much higher than most of the other parts of the country.

Down off of what was then the Norfolk division, there was considerable fishing. But again, it was not the offshore type that you found around New England.

As far as the west coast was concerned, you had an entirely different kind of a picture. There were few Lifeboat Stations. All of the distress cases usually were major. It was deep water right into the coast. So that, at that time, they had not too many difficulties with the small vessels.

Q: I notice here that most of your duty was on the east coast. Was there any reason for that? Were people kept on one coast or another during that time?

Capron: Yes, to your first question; and partially for the second.

At that time, normally and I'm speaking of officers; an officer would stay on one coast for a number of years. He could then expect to be transferred to the other coast and stay there for, if not an equal length of time, a couple tours of duty.

It so happened that about the time that I could have and would have expected to go to the Pacific coast was about the time that World War II was about to break. All of my assignments from 1941 on were tied in with World War II.

So I didn't finally get to the west coast until 1955, I guess it was.

Q: There's another general question that I have. I think you've partially answered the question by talking about the number of distress cases in the New England area. I've noticed that just about the main focal point of the Coast Guard for many years, and even now, has been the first Coast Guard district in the New England area. Is there any reason for this? Other than the quantity of distress cases?

Capron: I think that is the main reason, the number of distress cases and the type of coastline, particularly the Maine coastline. But also, as you come down towards Boston and also on up to the Cape, with all the indentations. There are hundreds and hundreds of miles of coastline there, many times what a straight line would give you. At the same time, there is a lot more of commercial fishing - from the one man who is out in the Jonesport boat to the trawler with a dozen men, and so on.

I think that is basically the reason, particularly as far as the Lifeboat Stations are concerned. As far as your vessels are concerned, Boston - for instance, is relatively central for all offshore work.

I don't know whether that really answers your question or not. But I don't think that there was anything other than the requirements for distress particularly and also law enforcement that governed.

Q: Was there any lobbying by communities in Congressional districts, at this time, to get appropriations for their districts and so forth?

Capron: Probably there was to a certain extent.

Immediately following 1934, when we were faced with our big cut, the Coast Guard took a step which I do not know exactly what was behind it. They did take a step in decentralizing, by location, all of their independent vessels. By that I mean, those vessels of 125 feet on up, which could operate independently of a base. They were distributed all up and down the coast. Instead of having all of the 165 footers in New York, they were spotted. The same with the 125.

These larger cutters could, only to a certain extent, be distributed. Because their size and the number of people they carried precluded many small towns or small harbors. But, when it came to the smaller vessels, they were just distributed all around.

As an example -- we had one vessel, the FREDERICK LEE, assigned to Eastport, Maine. We still had the cutter, an ice-breaker, KICKAPOO, at Rockland, Maine. We had the OSSIPPEE, a small cutter, at Portland. We had a 125 footer, the ANTIETAM, at Gloucester. We had another 125 footer, the HARRIET LANE, stationed at Provincetown. The two 65 footers that we had in the first district, the THETIS was stationed in Boston and the ARGO was stationed in Newport. The large cutters, the Lake Class, were all stationed in Boston. Subsequently, another vessel was sent to New Bedford.

The same thing was done up and down the Atlantic coast. Whether that was done deliberately, for the possibility of local pressure I don't know.

For a little town like Eastport, for instance, the addition of a 125 footer with 12 or 13 men and their payroll and their families was a decided boost to be counted. In Provincetown with all of its tourists, who don't go there in the winter time, that was a decided help to their account.

Obviously if something happened that was going to eliminate one of these vessels or cut down this operation, (they bought most of their non-technical equipment locally, commissary supplies and so forth) the community would be up in arms.

As I say, I don't know if that was done purposely; but that was the effect it had.

Q: That's very interesting.

While you were in Boston as Communications Officer, you were also Public Relations Officer for that area. Could you tell me a little bit about that?

Capron: I learned, soon after I arrived, that I had collateral duty as Public Relations. That was the term that the Coast Guard used at that time. Later on it was changed, as every other service did, to Public Information.

I was essentially the mouthpiece for the Coast Guard in dealing with the news media of the whole area, particularly in Boston. Bear in mind that this was immediately after prohibition.

In the Boston area, at least, the Coast Guard was certainly not popular during prohibition. Because of some of the things that had happened and so forth, our publicity had been very poor. We weren't quite as bad off as Mr. Agnew is right now, but we didn't have a favorable press.

One of the jobs that I had was trying to establish good relationships with the press.

Q: How did you go about that?

Capron: At that time, all the newspapers joined together in Boston in a waterfront office which was located on the 25th floor of the Customhouse. Each newspaper had a waterfront reporter and they used to rotate on the desk at this waterfront office.

Q: Was the Coast Guard's office in the Customhouse?

Capron: We were in the Customhouse on the 14th floor.

I used to, in the morning, start reading radio traffic for any items that might be of interest that happened overnight. I'd trot up to the 25th floor and talk to the reporters there, all of whom were pretty nice people. I'd give them these little bits of dope that we had, sit down, have a mug of coffee with them, and generally they thought of myself as somebody they could talk to if they wanted to find out something, and that they could call.

That worked very well. It took a long time. Of course once we had the reporters won over, we still had the editorial desk to win over. I would say though that at the time I left, we had pretty good relations with all the press and the radio broadcasting and so forth.

Q: Did you have any restrictions on what you could release? Or was it left up to your discretion?

Capron: Actually I had very broad ground rules. Beyond that, it was left to my discretion. Sometimes there were cases that would come up when you couldn't tell everything that happened. There were also occasions wherein in talking with certain individual reporters I would give them some information explaining that it was for background only, and that they shouldn't print it. It would give some information that would help a reporter write a story. But which, if he had printed might ruin us.

Remember now, we were still fighting this rum war so far. A lot of the things that we were doing in preventive work shouldn't have been broadcast to the public or the rummies. Except for one particular newspaper chain, I never had any of those confidences violated. One of them, I learned, to never tell him anything.

Q: Which one was that?

Capron: Hearst.

Q: What rank were you then?

Capron: I was Lieutenant.

Q: What was the rank of the Commanding Officer?

#4 Capron - 151

Capron: At that time, he was a Captain.

Q: Were you considered the Commander's aide, in the sense that for Public Information a man is an aide now?

Capron: Yes. I don't think the word 'aide' is quite appropriate, inasmuch as it has now become by common usage at least to be personal aide and so forth. No, I wasn't an aide in that sense. I was his assistant for Public Relations.

He was, of course, the District Commander. He was the one that was responsible. Everything I did, I did in his name.

One of the rules I had laid down in the beginning, which helped me an awful lot I think, was that my name should never be mentioned in any news account. They could either use the word 'spokesman' or they could say the District Commander 'announced'. Never was my name to be used, unless it had to do with something that I personally had done that was newsworthy. The mere fact that I was announcing something had nothing to do with it.

They lived up to that. I think, undoubtedly, it had an effect. They were pretty sure that I wasn't looking for any personal glory.

There is one thing here; to jump over a couple of years. When I was transferred, the BOSTON TRAVELLER was kind enough to print a five or six line editorial on the work I had done while there and regretting my transfer. I still have the clipping, and you can see it would make anybody feel pretty good.

Q: It probably goes to show that you did a good job.

Capron: At least I didn't make them mad.

If you're interested further in this Public Relations angle -- Radio and it's broadcasting was moving up to big business. One of my first real contacts that I had was when we were in Springfield during the flood of 1936.

Q: Is this Springfield, Massachusetts?

Capron: Yes. The Connecticut River went on a rampage.

The people from Westinghouse stations WBZ and WBZA had gone up with portable equipment to broadcast. We had been able, without interfering with our own mission, to take them out in motor surfboats, where they could, using their portable high frequency equipment, broadcast some of their descriptions.

Along about the same time, or possibly just a little earlier, we had had the occasion of the seven CCC boys that I have mentioned in my book, wherein these boys were stranded on an ice flow in Cape Cod Bay floating around.

The HARRIET LANE was equipped experimentally with the New England Telephone Company ship to shore telephone. The HARRIET LANE happened to be the vessel closest to these boys and was assigned the job to try to save them.

4 Capron - 153

The HARRIET LANE's own job was to crash their way through part of the ice and then a dory was hauled over the ice. They used the dory more or less as a bobsled over the ice. When they came to open water, they floated across, and did not break through and so forth. The HARRIET LANE was able to rescue four of the boys. The other three had already been rescued from shore during the early part of the day.

To get back to the ship to shore telephone -- The people at WBZ in Boston were pretty sharp anyway. At that time there were the two networks of NBC, the Red Network and the Blue Network. They were part of the Blue Network.

They had contacted us. They had learned that we had this ship to shore telephone on the HARRIET LANE. So, they put in a call through the Telephone Company to the HARRIET LANE and connected it to their broadcast. They got the skipper of the HARRIET LANE to describe the last few minutes of this rescue.

Q: While it was going on?

Capron: While it was going on. We were fortunate enough to have a Chief Boatswain on there who could talk rather fluently under the circumstances. When the boys finally came over the side, he held the microphone out to them and each one of them was able to say something to his mother. It went out over the entire NBC network.

This particular thing happening when it did, these boys being *young and in the CCC* it caught the interest of everybody in the country. It was one of those things that everybody was talking about. Actually, the whole affair lasted almost two days.

That more or less instilled some bright ideas. Some time later, we had a case where the CAYUGA had a rescue job. This was to rescue a little fisherman. It looked as if it might be of interest, so I called the people over at WBZ and asked them if they would be interested in including it on the air. They thought they would be.

They got the Telephone Company, actually it was just a question of diverting one telephone line right at the building, to put in a drop at our radio station. We had the people on the CAYUGA over our Coast Guard radio describe their rescue. It came in over that and was patched in to NBC.

This was another case of fortuitive circumstance. No sooner had they taken the crew off this trawler, when they sighted another trawler within a few miles that was sinking. They went over to take off the crew of the second trawler and they got the Captain of the first one to describe it.

I never hesitated to insist that every time anything like this took place, they mention the fact that this was done over Coast Guard radio and brought that in and so forth. This was one of my own little jobs there too.

As a result, we had excellent contacts with all of the media there. As an example - WBZ gave us two hours of prime time, eight to ten, on Coast Guard Day. They even paid to bring the Coast Guard Band up from New London to play for the program. Part of the program itself consisted of a broadcast from a cutter, one from a plane in the air, and one from a Lifeboat Station, all funnelling in to the radio station. That was not a network deal; that was strictly a Westinghouse deal. (WBZ and WBZA)

Q: A little while ago we talked about the training of radio men. You mentioned that you'd have something further to say about Navy versus Coast Guard training.

Capron: In the first place, we did not at that time, with the exception of flight training, utilize any Navy schools for any type of training.

As far as radio men were concerned, the type of training that a Navy radioman needed and used was entirely different from what we used. The Navy radio, for instance, never communicated with commercial ships. They didn't even understand commercial procedure, which is entirely different from Navy procedure and Coast Guard. Our Coast Guard procedure was the same as the Navy's.

Our radio man had to be equally conversant with either one. We used different abbreviations. For instance -- On commercial radio, you'd call a ship or whatever it might be - DE and then your call letter, most of them being derivatives of French. Navy and Coast Guard procedure used V between the two calls. There was really no similarity at all, so our radio men had to know both.

In addition the Navy, at that time and still, did little intership radio communication. When they do it's voice nowdays, but at that time they didn't have much voice. There were very little communications wherein their radio men had to sit down and pound brass. All the communications from shore to ship, practically all, were done by the fox method for broadcast. The various stations, depending on the locations of the units (it might have been the old NAA station which used to be in Arlington here and later on was moved down to Annapolis, whose towers I understand are now being downed) would broadcast to the fleet. They would just start broadcasting. They would continue to broadcast message after message after message, plain language or code as the case might be. A radio man copied it. The message for the ship he'd take normally, and unless it was a particular type message where they had to have an acknowledgement, the operator never touched his key.

4 Capron - 157

We were doing two way communications all the time. The type of training and the type of duty that was involved was entirely different.

There is one that that I'd like to mention. It's certainly something that should be a matter of historical record.

In later 1934, there was a pretty high level conference held between Coast Guard and Navy concerning radio communications. At that time the head of Navy communications was accused of having very very grandiose ideas about Navy communications which would involve first, taking over all Coast Guard radio stations and subsequently, commercial radio stations. So that the Navy would operate all coastal radio stations, government or commercial.

Q: When you say commercial, do you mean stations like --

Capron: RCA, Mackay Radio, anyone of them. I say, he was accused of it. I personally believe that it was true, but I can't prove it.

Q: Who was the head of it?

Capron: His last name was Hooper. This is one of those things, incidentally, should never be in print.

4 Capron - 158

We had this conference. The decision was made, over violent opposition of most people in the Coast Guard, that on a trial basis for two years the Navy and their radio stations (this of course had the blessing of all the economists and the people who wanted to save money and everything else) would handle all our communications. This was to be done in Boston, New London, and New York. What was involved was the physical moving of most of our equipment from our radio stations into Navy radio stations, and Navy setting up their own operators to handle all of our communications to our ships and of course commercial ships. They used our radio calls, and so forth.

The experiment was not successful. In the first place, the Navy found that they could not save personnel. They couldn't double up; they had to add as many men to each individual radio station as we had had at our radio stations. They also ran into the fact that their men, as I explained, were not trained for that type of work. Even though individuals might become proficient when a transfer came the new man had to learn all over again.

Navy communications were not high priority, as we saw it. We had a requirement on a priority message, that it had to be delivered, as I remember, in twenty minutes. Routine was an hour. Navy communications were not geared to handle anything like that.

And properly so; they didn't have the distress cases. The majority of our traffic was distress traffic or law enforcement traffic.

The upshot of it was, after a year of this trial, Mr. Morganthau told the Navy that the experiment had not worked.

Q: Morganthau was Secretary of the Treasury?

Capron: At this time, yes I believe he was Secretary of the Treasury. He had been assistant Secretary and under Secretary, and then became Secretary. That's why I'm a little hazy as to which he was.

Q: But he was in the Treasury Department?

Capron: He was in the Treasury Department and he was directly responsible for the Coast Guard. He told the Navy that the experiment hadn't worked and to return everything pronto.

Of course, those of us who were in Coast Guard communications were tickled to death. We did everything as fast as we possibly could. During the transition period, it involved not only a lot of work but a lot of planning. Because we were going to be using much the same equipment, during the period that it was being dismantled at a Navy station, moved ten miles to a

Coast Guard station and set up again. We had to be able to cover these frequencies, particularly the distress frequencies.

We did it, up in Boston, by backing up our emergency radio truck and using our emergency radio truck transmitter keyed from inside the building.

It was a period that Coast Guard operations did, without question, suffer considerably because you couldn't get messages through. And let's face it; any Commander has got to have control of his own communications. Furthermore no Navy radio man was going to, if it came to a show down, give preference to Coast Guard traffic over Navy traffic. It just isn't the nature of the beast.

Anyway that ended, and as far as I know that particular subject has never come back. I think it's a pretty good example of what official relationships existed at that time. I say 'official'. The Navy communicator of the first Naval District was a pretty good close personal friend. When it came officially, I wasn't about to help him.

Q: Captain, can you tell me about some of the operations that you were engaged in at this time?

Capron: There are one or two that really stand out in my memory. One of them I was personally involved considerably.

That was the flood in 1936 with the Connecticut River, which ultimately overlowed it's banks from about the northern boundary of Massachusetts, well down into Connecticut, well south of Hartford. There had been a heavy thaw and considerable fear on the part of the state police particularly, who were responsible for the state, that the river would overflow and one or two dams on the upper part of the river would break.

Q: This was in the spring?

Capron: Late winter, early spring. I'd have to actually dig out some old papers to pin it down as to the exact month, but I think March.

We in the Coast Guard realized that this was the sort of thing that we should probably be involved in. As Communications Officer, I was particularly interested in the communication angle. I learned from the state police that practically all telephone service from that area into Boston was gone. Much of the communications were done by police radio, using them as radio transmitter stations rather than merely broadcasting to cruisers.

We volunteered our communication trucks, and this offer was accepted. The request was made that we go up to Hadley in the beginning.

I might say at this particular time that a law which authorized us to go into any flooded area required that we must be supported by some recognized agency, often the Red Cross. And that all of our expenses, other than salaries, must be borne by the requesting agency.

Q: Could it be a government agency?

Capron: Not necessarily. The Red Cross was the usual agency. In the Mississippi valley area it was always the Red Cross.

In this case, it was the Massachusetts State Police, We had to have their official request. Even though in this particular case, we invited it.

We went on up with communications equipment. About half way up I was met by a state trooper who advised me that I should communicate with my headquarters in Boston. I learned that there were a number of motor surfboats being sent up on trucks for use in evacuating people and so forth, and that I was to assume command of all the Coast Guard forces (at that time, consisting of me and two radio men augmented by boats) in the Massachusetts area part of the Connecticut River.

Q: They were sending crews with the boats as well?

Capron: Of course, the boats weren't there yet. Oh yes, when the boats came up they had very adequate crew.

I had started using my own car and the two communication cars. I brought along clothing enough for about two days, believing that I was merely going to station these trucks and then go on back.

4 Capron - 163

With these boats coming up, first of all we had to arrange a rendevouz, which we did west of Worcester. We met. One of the boats came from Point Allerton, with an officer in charge that I knew quite well. Another one came from Nahant, with an officer in charge that I came to know quite well. Then several small pulling boats, which were more or less tagging along with the power boats.

From the conditions, as I understood them at that time, I sent one of the boats over to a town called East Hatfield on the western bank of the Connecticut River. It was probably one of the last things to go over the bridge. The other boat I sent into Hadley on the eastern bank of the Connecticut River.

We arrived and found there was plenty of work to do. In East Hatfield there were still a lot of evacuation of people from second floors and so on. Over in Hadley, where we were, most of the evacuation had been done the night previously. One of the best organizations in this evacuation had been a Sea Scout Troop, which had gone up from the neighborhood of Salem. With their small pulling boat, they had evacuated a lot of people. With a snide remark - they weren't faced with the government red tape that we were.

I set up my little command post, if you call it that, in the Town Hall at Hadley. The state police lived up to their promise of support. I'd parked my car well back from the flooded waters. We were given transportation by police cruisers when we needed it. We slept on the floor of the Town Hall, but the police took us in to Amherst to the Lord Jeffery Inn. It was a very fine restaurant where we had our meals.

Q: It still is a good restaurant.

Capron: From the sublime to the ridiculous, from sleeping on the rough wooden floor and then going in for breakfast to one of the nicest restaurants in the area, was kind of an anachronism.

We stayed in that area for quite a while. Meanwhile, troubles down in Springfield and West Springfield were multiplying. We had a request from the Red Cross down there. Things around East Hatfield had quieted down, so I sent that boat down by truck to West Springfield and they moved over later into Springfield. We stayed where we were for several days more.

For instance - By this time, the bridges were all out. We provided transportation for Red Cross representatives, who were now surveying the damage and what was needed. We also had numerous incidences of rescue - such as cows that were swimming around and about to drown.

The one I remember most vividly was getting a fat porker into the boat to keep him from drowning. Incidentally, pigs have extreme difficulty swimming. Their cloven hoofs cut their own throats.

We later on moved down to Springfield and we had all of our people in Springfield. We remained there several days and finally were able to pull out and go back to Boston.

Meanwhile the third district, New York, had their people up in Hartford. As you know from reading about floods, the crest goes on down. They caught it after it went past us.

From the personal standpoint, it was very interesting. Probably from the overall standpoint, it was pretty small potatoes. But the following year when the Mississippi, Missouri, and Ohio went on a rampage, my experience, meager as it was, helped a lot.

As I mentioned before, the Communications Officer was kind of an assistant Operations Officer. The district office was very very lean on staff. It had a staff of about five officers, as opposed to I don't know how many nowdays. So, I won the job of organizing the expeditions from our district to the flooded areas.

Q: Was the Coast Guard very strong in what's now the Second District?

Capron: No, we were not. We had practically nothing. Everything that we have in the Second District, to all intents and purposes, is a heritage of the Lighthouse Service. They were very strong in that area; they had to be. We had nothing; in fact, we didn't have a Second District. It was part of the old Chicago District.

So we had to, in a hurry, collect boats and crews. As I remember, in the first train that we sent out we had in the neighborhood of somewhere between 30 and 50 26-foot motor surfboats.

The order, to collect them and bring them in, came in early Sunday morning. We ordered surfboats in from all the Lifeboat Stations in generally the Massachusetts-New Hampshire part of the Coast Guard. We brought them all into Boston.

We worked an arrangement with the Boston Navy Yard where they called in all their riggers and carpenters and so on. We had to wake up all the railroad officials to get gondola cars to carry these boats. A railroad official, on Sundays, is not like a Coast Guard officer who stands duty. They're hard to come by.

We were finally able to get enough gondola cars backed into the Navy Yard. We brought these boats in. They started arriving three o'clock in the afternoon, or what have you. They'd arrive and the crane would pick them up and set them down in a gondola car. Immediately two or three civilian carpenters in the Navy Yard would be under them and they were building a cradle to hold them. As I remember, two 26-footers would go on one gondola. That went on practically all night.

I won that job. Meanwhile, one of the Warrant Pay Clerks was working on the other end of it arranging the trains. In the first place, we would not send all these boats out without all their own crews right on the same train.

ICC rules don't permit, except under exceptions, freight cars and passenger cars on the same train. Furthermore, we were sending these people out there and it was going to take them a couple of days to get there. We had to have pullmans and a place for them to sleep.

As an added thing, ICC when they finally granted permission to let this combination train go through, decreed that we had to drain the gasoline out of everyone of the boats. So, we had to go around and drain gasoline out of everyone of those boats. A day and a half later when they went through Buffalo, they brought a tank wagon alongside the train and filled everyone of the tanks with gas.

We were able to get that train off. Finances were a problem. The Red Cross was perfectly willing to put up the cash based on what estimates were that it would cost. They wanted the Officer in Charge of that train to personally sign for all the money.

Q: Was that you?

Capron: No that was not me. I didn't go to that flood, thank God. That particular one was commanded by an officer who is since dead, who was a product of the Lifesaving Service. One of the very finest of the lot that I ever saw by the name of Erwin B. Steele. Incidentally, his son later on entered the Coast Guard Academy. He went through the various ranks and ultimately became a flag officer. He was Commander of the Second Coast Guard District and died of a heart attack about three years ago.

Q: Is that Chester Steele?

Capron: It was his father who was in charge of this first train.

Arrangements were extremely difficult anyway. Enough so that I rode the train out as far as Ayre, Massachusetts. I got off at Ayre and came back on a local back to Boston. We all gave a sign of relief and thought it was all over.

Within a few hours, we got orders to send more boats out. This time it involved mostly lifeboats - the 36 footers. It was necessary in this case to collect boats. We collected them at Portland, Maine, Newport, Rhode Island, Rockland, Maine, and Boston. So they were collected in those places and moved various places and put aboard trains. In the case of Rockland, maybe only half a dozen which came down to Portland and then picked up the Portland group. The Newport group proceeded independently for awhile. They all came together somewhere around Northfield, Massachusetts on the Boston AND Albany Railroad. One train was made up and they all went up to the flooded area. There were some 50 boats in that group with crew.

Within another few hours, we were told to send some 36 foot picket boats out. They went through much the same thing. By this time, we'd learned an awful lot of the ropes and so on. It wasn't too much of a headache.

They were actually out there about five or six weeks all told, most of them. We had difficulty because of them being out there. Under the old pay rules an individual had to sign for his own pay and receive it in cash. These boys were all out in Mississippi, but their families were all back east and they were going broke.

The Coast Guard League of Women was an organization of various Coast Guard wives, which is really the forerunner of the present Coast Guard Welfare. They used to do the small welfare business and so forth in the various places. They finally ended up by loaning as much as they could afford to a lot of these families, who were really almost destitute because there was no legal way to pay them.

Q: Who was minding the store meanwhile back in these Lifeboat Stations? Did they have enough boats?

Capron: Yes. Every Lifeboat Station had a motor lifeboat and at least one motor surfboat, in many cases two, and a picket boat. Of those motor surfboats, all our cutters had at least one. We took them off the cutters too. So that we had to be careful, obviously, that we didn't strip anyone's station of everything they had. The people that left, generally it was a three man crew for a boat - a coxswain, an engineer, and a bowman.

Of course there isn't any question, in one sense of the word, it was a calculated risk that a station would be able to perform while they were gone. Probably in a long length of time, they couldn't. They couldn't give adequate liberty to the people that were left and things like that.

That was a big effort, as far as the Coast Guard was concerned. I think probably it was the last one wherein we had to send in a lot of equipment in this case from as far away as the east coast, and I know some came from the west coast.

In later years, in the first place the floods were a different type of floods out there, the Coast Guard was able to procure through the Army Engineers for instance the types of equipment which was much more suitable for flood work than our regular equipment. At the same time it could be stored, using an outboard motor in one of these flatboats. You store the

#4 Capron - 171

flatboat at a convenient place, then all you bring in is your outboard motor.

Q: Captain, in 1937 you got a new assignment. Will you tell me about that?

Capron: I was detached from the district office in late winter of '37 and assigned as Executive Officer to one of the 165 foot patrol boats, the THETIS, based in Boston.

As I mentioned before, the end of prohitibion had not ended smuggling. The Coast Guard was still working very very hard to prevent smuggling of liquor. We did have a certain amount of advantage now, inasmuch as foreign countries had been relatively unwilling to assist prohibition. But it became a strict point of customs, they were willing to help us because they knew we could help them.

As an example, American cigarettes were being smuggled into Canada by thousands of cases. We in the United States were able to tip off Canadian authorities. Whenever one of these small vessels loaded with cigarettes would clear Boston or some American port, the Canadians were waiting with open arms to grab them. 'You scratch my back; I scratch yours'. They were quite willing to help us on the liquor.

I hadn't been aboard the THETIS more than three or four days when we were sent out as part of a group. We were a group of four 165 footers, who were picketing a rummie pretty well off the New England coast. This was one of the last that was left, rather persistent. The Coast Guard was really trying to break it up. There was the general feeling that if they busted this one, it would probably stop.

So there were two 165 footers continually picketing this rummie. The other two had gone to Halifax for fuel and supplies, and then come back.

We kept this rummie under surveillance for a very long time. My memory fails me as to how long it might have been. Ultimately he was forced to proceed to Bermuda for fuel and supplies, and forfeit the bond which he had been required to post under British law.

The balance of the time on the THETIS was, what we felt then, routine. Frequently taking sick or injured men off of trawlers, who were out on the banks.

Most of the fishing done by trawlers is done on a share basis. Every member of the crew on board gets a share. If a man is injured so he can't work, if he's aboard, he still draws his share. The fishing people, including the master and the crew, were very anxious to get rid or unload any non-worker that they might have. So they immediately yelled for us to take him off and take him to a hospital. Sometimes it was necessary, but quite often he would have been just as well off staying where he was. We had many many times where we took these people off. It almost always turned out to be at night.

A 165 footer not being very stable, it was a question of going near the trawler, stopping the engines, maintaining a speed of five or six knots, the boat swung out on the sea painter and then pulled over to the trawler, and getting a man aboard. Occasionally he'd be in a straight jacket, having gone off his rocker. Then our boat dropped down to leeward of the trawler and we'd come back and pick him up.

It was really quite risky, as far as the people in the boat were concerned. We had that many times.

About the only other noteworthy thing that occured while I was on the THETIS, we participated in the patrol in 1937 of the America's Cup Races off Newport when ENDEAVOR raced RAINBOW.

For many many years Sir Thomas Lipton had been the only one had ever had enough money and enough courage to challenge the New York Yacht Club group for the America's Cup. This year a new man appeared on the scene and challenged. I've forgotten his name.

That was an interesting period of patrol. This time I was close enough to the racers to be able to actually see some of the race.

Q: Did you want this assignment?

Capron: I was pleased to be assigned as an Executive Officer. I didn't particularly want it, no.

I liked being in Boston, but a 165 footer was probably the most uncomfortable thing the Coast Guard owned. When you went out, you just took a beating. We didn't have much water, no capability of distilling or evaporating water. So that the minute you left the dock you went on water hours and they were very limited.

Q: The 165 footers were designed specifically for the Coast Guard, weren't they?

Capron: They were designed specifically for the Coast Guard for operation against rum runners, and they did replace the destroyers.

Q: How come they were so uncomfortable? Was it just because of the requirement of speed?

Capron: The requirement of speed with that size hull meant that you had a relatively narrow vessel. The engine room space was almost half of the under deck space. The number of men required to operate the vessel was not in direct ratio to the size of the vessel. We still had to have 36 or 37 men, plus four officers to operate. We could have operated a vessel twice the size of that with the same number of people. As a result, the quarters were very restricted. Basically to get the speed they wanted with the size hull and the amount of power they put in, it was a narrow vessel, you just took a beating.

Q: What happened to the destroyers?

Capron: The destroyers were turned back to the Navy gradually starting about in 1932 or so, when the first 165 footers came out. They were gradually returned to the Navy, probably the last ones going back somewhere around the first of January 1934.

Q: Did the Navy keep them in operation?

Capron: No, they laid them up. To the best of my knowledge, they were never operated again.

Q: They didn't reactivate them for the second World War?

Capron: You must remember that the flush-deckers, a later ship, were pretty old hat by World War II. They gave 50 of them to the British on the Lend-Lease.

The United States started building new destroyers in the thirties. Not many of them, but they started building them then. So that by the time World War II came along, not only were our destroyers long since forgotten, but a good part of the flush-deckers were gone. As I say, the 50 we gave Great Britain before we got into the war were the flush-deck type.

Q: What about the Coast Guard building program? Were any other ships being built besides the —

Capron: During the late twenties and early thirties, the so-called Lake Class was built. Those were the vessels which in 1940 were given to the British on Lend-Lease.

In the middle thirties, Congress authorized under a PWA Program seven new vessels. These were the Secretary Class. Those vessels were 327 feet long, relatively fast, quite comfortable, and something very very new as far as we were concerned. They were again the result, let us say, of Morganthau and his interest.

At that time, there was a lot of smuggling of dope taking place on both coasts. Morganthau felt that we needed some long-legged fairly fast vessels capable of staying at sea a long time, to combat this dope smuggling - opium mostly. So as a result of his interest, those ships were designed and built.

I know nothing personally about any new ships we have right now. As far as I'm concerned, those 327s were the best things the Coast Guard ever had. They're still running and they're still pretty good ships.

Q: What about ice-breakers, were they building any then?

Capron: Yes, again in the middle thirties and again under a PWA Program the Coast Guard was authorized five vessels to be built as small cutters with ice-breaking capability. They were pretty good little vessels, had a fair ice-breaking capability, but at the same time had the disadvantages that any compromise vessel has. They were ~~excellent~~ fair ice-breakers and they were good sea-going ships. You can't have both in a vessel that size. I belive the number was five that were built during that period. As a matter of interest, they were: the ALGONQUIN, the COMMANCHE, the MOHAWK, the ESCANABA, and two more. That's a total of six.

Q: The ESCANABA was the one that was lost in the second World War.

Capron: Yes.

Interview # 5

Captain Walter C. Capron, USCG, Ret.   by Peter Spectre
Arlington, Virginia   November 30, 1969

Mr. Spectre: Captain, your next assignment was with the U. S. Coast Guard cutter COMANCHE. Could you tell me something about that?

Captain Capron: My duty aboard the THETIS had been rather short, six months or so. In the fall of 1937, I received orders to the COMANCHE based at Staten Island, New York.

The COMANCHE was one of those newly built vessels, which I mentioned last week, that were really a cross between a regular cutter and an icebreaker. Their bows were somewhat cutaway to permit them to ride upon the ice. They had a very very heavy belt of steel around the vessel at the water line and relatively short bilge-keels so that in a seaway they had a tendency to roll considerably. Like any compromise, they were not ideal for either type of work. However, used properly they did an excellent job of icebreaking in the rivers and lakes of the United States.

Q: They weren't intended for the Arctic or Antarctic?

Capron: No, they were very definitely not intended for any Arctic or Antarctic work. They were specifically designed to operate for icebreaking purposes in the rivers and harbors of continental United States.

They were 165 feet long, in this case, between perpendiculars rather than overall. Thus differentiating them from the patrol boats, which were 165 feet long.

Q: Were they entirely different design?

Capron: Entirely different design; there was no similarity other than the fact that the word '165 feet' applied to both of them. They were relatively wide for their length. They had not much speed, in the neighborhood of 12 to 14 knots at the most. They were steam turbine, geared drive, single screw. Whereas they had considerable horsepower for towing purposes and at slow speed, they were designed such as they could not make any great speed under any conditions.

Six of these vessels were built. Ultimately they were stationed: two on the Great Lakes, three on the Atlantic coast, and one, for some unknown reason, on the west coast.

Q: Why do you say that?

Capron: There is no ice on the west coast of the United States. So that icebreaking capabilities were completely wasted. That was the ONANDAGA stationed, as I remember it, in Astoria, Oregon.

I reported aboard the COMANCHE in New York in early November. Soon after we began our winter schedule, which would lead up to our icebreaking job in the Hudson River.

For many years the Hudson River had frozen over and was permitted to remain frozen over during the whole winter. But during the early and mid thirties, demand for wheat in European countries and of course our own depression stimulated the use of the Hudson River for hauling grain. That may seem somewhat of an anachronism.

You must bear in mind that Albany, which was the head of navigation on the Hudson River, was also the eastern terminal of the barge canal which was the following canal of the old Erie Canal (Clinton's Big Ditch). There were large grain elevators located in Albany. So that even though the canal froze in the winter time, the storage capacity of these grain elevators was such that there was sufficient grain to supply as many ships as might desire to go up the river during the winter time.

About this time was when Franklin D. Roosevelt issued the executive order which gave the Coast Guard the responsibility for keeping open the various rivers and harbors of the United States.

Q: Did any other agency have that responsibility before the Coast Guard?

Capron: No other agency had that responsibility. The Coast Guard had, to a limited extent, been performing that for a number of years. But as I pointed out a week or so ago, the advent of oil as the main fuel, for not only domestic heating but commercial power replacing coal, had really spurred on or initiated the requirement to have ice free or open rivers and harbors, particularly in New England and the northeast part of the United States.

The six vessels of the COMANCHE class had really been built, although they were out of PWA funds, for the purpose of being a general duty cutter and an icebreaker. They were completed generally during the years between 1934 and 1937.

The first thing having to do with icebreaking that we did was to go up the river prior to any freezing with a commercial pilot aboard, who showed us the various marks and changes in the channel from the previous year.

It must be borne in mind that most of the marks, man made marks, for navigation on the Hudson River are buoys. Once the river freezes over, the buoys would be either dragged out of position or submerged. As a result, the then Lighthouse Service normally removed all buoys during the late fall and only replaced them in the spring after the ice had gone out.

It was therefore necessary for us to use various marks ashore and the same marks that were used by the commercial pilots. These marks were quite interesting, reminiscent somewhat possibly of Mark Twain and his Mississippi River stories.

Actually from the Battery to Albany, a distance of about 125 nautical miles, there were only two man-made ranges or marks, for navigation purposes on the shore. The marks, as used by the pilots and also by us, consisted of various types of formations you might say along the shore.

For instance -- One beacon was on the point in the Hudson River just below West Point. You steered a course toward this beacon, keeping the clock tower of Lady Cliff Girls' College directly over this beacon. That provided an effective range for that particular course.

Various course changes were made when a beam of certain points along the shore, such as a beam of a dock or a tank or even a house. I remember one particular range that we used in the vicinity of Tivoli, where we used the left hand edge of a house which always had the shades drawn, under the distant steeple of a church as our range. Facetiously we used to wonder what would happen if they ever pulled the shades up.

The various courses in the whole Hudson River from New York to Albany probably numbered at least 100. The longest stretch on any given course being possibly five miles. We had charts with rough sketches showing what each mark was supposed to look like, and the course for that stretch. We had upstream charts and downstream charts.

Q: Did any of the charting agencies provide you with piloting charts?

Capron: The only charts we had were the standard Coast and Geodetic Survey charts, which showed the regular aids to navigation, which were sufficient for use in the summer time when buoys and so forth were all on station.

We had to supply, by adding these various diagrams to those charts, our own charts. The marks, as I say, that we used were exactly the same marks that the pilots used.

There's another reason for that too. The controlling depth of water to Albany, at that time, was 27 feet. The COMANCHE drew about 13 feet. Obviously we could go in much more shallow water than a fully loaded steamer. But in the ice, the steamer was strictly limited to the channel that we had broken.

If we inadvertently strayed off the proper line into shallow water, the vessel that was following us would either have to stop or if unable to stop would go aground. So that for navigational purposes, our thinking was entirely in terms of 27 feet and never in terms of our own draft.

5 Capron - 164

Q: What did you do after your initial exploration of the river?

Capron: After the initial trip, we continued on more or less routine patrols out of New York harbor with one of the cutters in what is now the third district until the river had frozen over.

We received word from the pilots that passage was becoming difficult. Most of these vessels could handle one or two inches of ice without any difficulty.

One of the big troubles was, however, the fact that the Hudson River has a number of tides in the stretch from New York to Albany. I believe it's three different tides and therefore, tidal currents. Between the wind and tidal currents big sheets would move up and down the river (particularly in the broader reaches, such as near Poughkeepsie or near Haverstraw) with the force of the wind or the current would, upon reaching the narrow part of the river, more or less pile on top of itself. So that you had what we called windrows of ice. So that at these various places you might have patches of ice all the way across the narrow part of the river, of several feet thickness, with open water just beyond.

So it was necessary for us quite often to go up, this is in the beginning of the season, and station ourselves at a particular point and remain in that area to assist vessels going through that particular area.

For example -- Fairly often, we would remain at either West Point or Newburg, and only get underway when vessels were coming through. This would only last maybe a week in the fall and in the spring. It was indicative of the fact that the whole river was not always difficult for commercial shipping.

During my first winter, I might add that I was Executive Officer of the ship, which was pretty cold; there was one period of about a month that there was no attempt to get vessels any farther north than Poughkeepsie. There was a certain amount of barge traffic from New York up to Poughkeepsie and to Kingston, a town some fifteen miles north of Poughkeepsie. The larger vessels made no attempt to go all the way to Albany.

Q: You only broke ice when there was somebody that wanted to go through?

Capron: That is correct.

Q: You didn't constantly break ice?

Capron: We didn't constantly break ice. As a matter of fact, it was somewhat of a dangerous manouevre to do that.

#5 Capron - 186

When you went through ice, this applies strictly to river ice, (it does not apply to what you would find in the lakes or arctic ice) if you went through too fast your wash would break away the ice from the shores of the river. You would have a mass of floating ice, going up or down stream as the case might be, until it reached a narrow bend and then pile up and give you another windrow that was pretty hard to get through. So we always used a minimum speed necessary to maintain that channel, to avoid tearing the ice away from the sides of the river.

We did, however, go through ever so often. Even though we might not have any vessels, we would attempt about once a week to go through by ourselves if we had no vessels, merely to keep it from freezing too hard.

Now again in that first year that I was on the vessel, excepting that one month approximately, deliberately the river was permitted to freeze over north of Poughkeepsie.

The following year the Commanding Officer, who was Lieutenant Commander A. G. Hall, was detached about early November. Another officer, of similar rank, was ordered to be his relief. It so happened that this other officer was involved in certain international conferences having to do with telecommunications, and he never did arrive on the ship. So that I inherited comman and acted as both Executive Officer and Commanding Officer from early November 1938 until about the first of August 1939.

Q: What rank were you then?

Capron: I was Lieutenant. The proper rank for the vessel was a Lieutenant Commander.

So I was personally faced with not only the position of having to perform two jobs, but also when the icebreaking season began, to teach the river to the other officers aboard the ship. There had been a complete change over of officers, so that none of those who had been aboard the previous winter were still aboard, leaving me as the only officer with experience of the river.

I might say that I welcomed this. It was the first chance I had in any kind of a command. To repeat myself, I really welcomed it. It was an opportunity which most officer of my particular rank and seniority didn't have. However, it did mean that when we were up the river that I would spend ten or twelve hours each day on the bridge. At least, until late in the year when the other officers had become familiar enough to be left alone.

Q: Did you break ice at night?

Capron: Only under very exceptional circumstances. We would break ice at night up as far as Germantown. We didn't like to. Above Poughkeepsie we objected at every opportunity. However the Hudson River pilots would run their ships, freighters, as far as Germantown at night.

One of the things that we were very careful of was never to interfere with the operations of these merchant ships, by refusing to do anything that was within our power. If we couldn't break ice, we couldn't break ice. If we could, we did. Essentially we did not operate at night.

Q: When you were taking merchant ships up the Hudson, did you organize convoys with more than one ship at a time?

Capron: Practically speaking, we had convoys. If one ship was going up, we would, one way or another, convince them to wait until there were several other ships. As a general rule, we didn't have any particular difficulty that way. Most of the ships going up were foreign ships - Swedish, Norwegian, Danish, and so on. All of them had to take aboard American pilots. These pilots depended on us to take them through. That was one reason why they always gave us a pilot when we asked for one, with no charge. Without us, they wouldn't have been operating. So that, these pilots, who were of course very well experienced mariners, would never if they could possibly help it, try to take a single ship up. They much preferred to have a convoy of three or four ships. It was perfectly possible and occasionally we did it; if one ship insisted on going up, we'd let them go. When he got stuck, we'd let him stay there for a day maybe until we got up there with several other ships.

In the river, a vessel stuck in the ice was not in any danger. He merely was stuck there, and that was it, period.

Q: Did the COMANCHE ever get stuck?

Capron: Oh yes, many times we got stuck. We were always able to get ourselves free. We had to use lots of tricks and extrordinary seamanship lots of times. About the heaviest ice that we could break and this was not continuing at a slow speed right through the ice (this was by backing off, slamming into it and backing off) was around twelve inches. Anything more than that we could break, yes, but it was an awful slow process.

You'd back off and you'd slam into that ice, and maybe you'd make 50 feet, and then back off again. Of course that didn't do the ship any good and it didn't do the people on board any good. When you get at a speed of 8 or 9 knots when a ship hits a solid chunk of ice, it's just like having a collision at that speed. Everybody was hanging on all the time.

That second year the district decided that they would try to keep the river open to Albany for the entire winter. That meant spending a lot of time up there. It was during that period, particularly, when we did a lot of cruising up the river even through we might not have a vessel with us. Because the upper reaches of the Hudson are narrow, in most cases the channel was 300 feet wide, at a few it was 400. That was not necessarily from bank to bank, but that was the channel.

We normally had temperatures at least as low as zero. So that the river would make half an inch of ice over night. Now if the channel had been kept open, the freezing was much slower because of the current. However the chopped up chunks that resulted from your passage, propeller and bow and so froth, would freeze together very easily. Those had to be kept kind of stirred-up.

Q: You were the only icebreaker operating on the Hudson?

Capron: No, that isn't quite correct. We had the primary responsibility for the district for the Hudson River. However the MOHAWK, a sister ship, which was stationed at Cape May would be sent up every several weeks to give us relief. To give us a chance to come back down to New York and give our crew some liberty and a certain amount of rest. So that we probably would not be up more than two weeks at a time, and then come home for a few days and then go back up again.

Practically speaking, we reached the point where we almost asked that the MOHAWK not be sent up. They had nowhere near the experience that we did. They liked to tear through a floe of ice at full speed, thereby setting adrift these big pieces of ice, which would ultimately jam the channel. Then by the time we got up there, would be the time when it got tough and we'd have to start all over again.

I'm quite sure that any former member of the MOHAWK would resent very much my saying this, but that was our reaction.

We fueled at either Poughkeepsie or Albany; we took aboard stores up there. So coming back to New York was strictly an R&R deal, if you want to call it that.

Q: After August of 1939, you left the COMANCHE?

Capron: I left the COMANCHE, yes. I would like to not necessarily cover too much in-between, but I must point out that this icebreaking was roughly three months in the year. During the rest of the time, our operations were the same as any cutter operating out of New York.

I don't know that we had any specific instances that are particularly worthy of note. As I mentioned earlier, during one period of time there I was both Exec and Commanding Officer for about eight months. There again, I welcomed it but it did mean an awful lot of work.

Then of course interspersed with all this, annually we had battle practice. Which in most cases, the two years I was aboard that vessel, was conducted down off the Virginia Capes off Norfolk. Which involved a lot of preparation getting ready and a week or so of rather intensive training down there. That, of course, was what every Coast Guard vessel was involved in.

We did provide one thing that was probably good. That is, of the three similar vessels on the east coast - the ALGONQUIN, the COMANCHE, and the MOHAWK - it was the one time in the year that we were all in the same place at the same time. It gave us, the Commanding Officers, Executive Officers, engineers and so forth, an opportunity to compare notes with the other people. To find out what they were doing and what their solutions to certain difficulties were that we were running into. It was good getting us together that way.

Q: Where was the ALGONQUIN based?

Capron: At this time, she was stationed at Portland, Maine. Her first station had been Woods Hole, Massachusetts. After about a year there, she was transferred to Portland. She had plenty of icebreaking up in that area, but again a slightly different type that what we had. In that hers was in harbors and bays, and not much in rivers themselves. There again, there was a decided difference.

When you were breaking in a harbor or a bay, there is a place for that ice to go. When you're breaking in a river, the only place that ice can go is down. I think probably fresh water ice or brackish water ice in a river is about the most difficult you can run into. This is for that type of ship. While the wind ships, of course, can sail up the Hudson River and not even slow down.

Q: This is immediately prior to the second World War. Was the Coast Guard getting prepared in any way? Did the Coast Guard see the writing on the wall?

Capron: At this particular time, the answer to that question is almost a "No" but not entirely.

Mr. Morganthau, who was Secretary of the Treasury, in my opinion was one of the best Secretaries we ever had as far as the Coast Guard is concerned. Although I personally disliked him very much, having served as his aide a couple of times. From the Coast Guard standpoint, he was one of the best Secretaries we ever had.

He decided rather early to do something, soon after the first hostile steps were taken. My memory fails me just a little bit as to when Hitler actually took his first war-like steps.

In the spring of 1939, the Coast Guard took up a type of neutrality patrol. I'll call it neutrality patrol, for lack of a better word. What was involved was that in major ports, such as New York, a Coast Guard vessel was stationed at the entrance, possibly anchoring, possibly underway, to identify every ship that went out. Hopefully to identify it by name, by home port, and of course nationality, and by destination. That of course could only be done by signals, flashing light. The cooperation we got from some was very good and from others not so good. We did that for a long period of time.

The COMANCHE used to take it's station for seven days off the entrance to Ambrose Channel, and there identify and daily transmit into the district office the ships that had gone out.

Mr. Morganthau's theory was this: That if the Germans were going to make a move (this must have been before they actually did) it would be preceeded by an exodus of German flag ships from ports of the United States and other ports, to get them off the high seas before any war started.

Whether that's a good theory or not, heaven only knows. But that was the theory, and that was why the Coast Guard at Mr. Morganthau's orders was identifying all of these ships as they went out.

Q: Did that happen when war actually broke out. Did German ships leave the harbors?

Capron: I was in an entirely different kind of business by that time. Although I suspect that it did, I really couldn't say.

That, of course, is closely tied in with what later on happened with what few German ships and Italian ships that were in our harbors after war had broken out. That is some time later on when so many of them were sabotaged.

At this particular time, we had that job. It was a highly unpleasant job, I might say, because a good part of the time you would be caught 'twixt wind and water.'

With a southeasterly wind blowing and the current coming out of New York harbor, you would lie right beam on to all the swells coming in from the ocean. We used the expression, 'roll your guts out'. There was no place to go.

In fact one night we were anchored under those conditions with the PONTCHARTRAIN, one of the Lake Class ships, anchored on the other side of Ambrose Channel. He was the patrol commander and also a larger vessel than us.

The winds began to spring up and the tides to change, and we began to take quite a beating. I stood it as long as I thought we could. I sent a message over to the PONTCHARTRAIN, asking him for permission to get under way. He came back with a negative. As I pointed out, he was a much larger vessel and he also happened to be on the other side of the channel under slightly different conditions.

We finally took one extremely heavy lurch. One officer in the wardroom, it happened to be Steele (that you asked about the other day), went over backwards in his chair and almost knocked himself out. I decided, orders or no, we should get underway. So I went on the bridge and we made all the preparations. I sent a signal over to the PONTCHARTRAIN and told them that weather conditions were such that we had to get underway. So we started to heave around; this was at night and raining pretty hard, possibly ten or eleven o'clock at night.

This is a story that some day I'm going to send in to "Humor in Uniform."

On the forecastle we had a Chief Boatswain's mate who with his flashlight was watching the chain. Of course as you know, as the anchor windlass brought the chain in he would report - 30 fathoms at the water's edge, 30 fathoms on deck, 15 fathoms at the water's edge, and so on and so forth. Finally, 'short stay', at which time I said, "Break it out." From him, all of a sudden, was, "Up and down, anchors away."

So we started slowly to try to bring our head around and suddently, as the anchor chain came up, I heard this expression from the forecastle. He said, "Jesus Christ, we've lost our anchor."

And we had. We never found it, although there was a lot of dragging done in that area trying to locate it; it was never found. One of the shots near the crown of the anchor had parted and it was all gone.

That basically, I would say, was the type of activity that was wartime associated that we had while I was on the

Q: Was there any military preparation before the war? For instance - ASW or convoy work, or anything like.

Capron: Yes, the Coast Guard did a lot preparation. In the first place all the way through, we had maintained, hopefully at least, our combat readiness with the type of equipment that we had. Which was relatively light.

For instance - The COMANCHE had two three inch 50 broadside guns and the usual number of smaller weapons, one-pounders and machineguns.

The 165 foot patrol boats, as distinguished from the COMANCHE class, had a three inch 23 gun mounted forward.

We had our annual battle practice, target practice, and so forth. I would say, within the limitations of the types of weapons we had, we were fairly well prepared.

The Coast Guard under Admiral Waesche, at this point, showed a lot more vision than the Navy.

Here again, don't misconstrue what I'm saying as being antipathy or anything else. But it was an actual fact.

Admiral Waesche, whether he got it from Morganthau or not I don't know, recognized the fact that we were going to be in a war and going to be in one pretty soon. So he obtained from Congress-appropriations to outfit practically all of our ships with sonar equipment. This was fairly early in the game.

I, at this time, was on the CALYPSO. We went south to Jacksonville in late October of 1940 to have the initial work done leading to the installation of sonar equipment and degaussing equipment.

At the time we went south, most of the 165 footers on the east coast were sent to Jacksonville, and all of the 125 footers. The initial work, which involved piercing the hull, building in new magazines, ammunition boxes on deck, a Y gun for depth charges aft on the fantail, and all of that type of equipment to make us hopefully at least anti-submarine vessels.

We all remained in Jacksonville at this shipyard with the preliminary work being done for a couple of months. We then returned, inasmuch as the equipment itself had not been delivered. The equipment we were using was the so-called QC, which was for the day, very modern, inasmuch as it utilized not only the pure hydrophone for listening, but you could use the pinging to measure the echo for distance ranging.

We returned during the winter, and subsequently in March of '41 we went back south again and had all the remaining equipment installed.

So that I would say, from what I personally knew about the 165 and 125 foot patrol boats, that the entire Coast Guard and all the vessels that could be used for anti-submarine warfare had been so fitted before July 1st, 1941.

We then returned home and went on about our business.

As an aside to that, and I'm jumping ahead a year. At the time when I was in what was then called the Transports Atlantic Fleet, which ultimately became Amphibious Force Atlantic Fleet, we had the first division of the Army aboard, after war was declared, going from Norfolk to New York. Of our screen of destroyers, there were only one or two who had sonar equipment.

Whether Admiral Waesche, or his advisors, had this vision I don't know. It was enough so that he was able to persuade Congress to get the money to get all of this installed long before Pearl Harbor.

Q: Did you know Admiral Waesche yourself?

Capron: In the way that a Lieutenant could know the Commandant, yes. I had met him several times. At one time, this was in 1942, I was called in and received more or less a personal pat on the back for something that I had done. This was long before the days of medals and commendation ribbons and so forth.

Q: What kind of man was he, from what you know of him?

Capron: In my opinion, he was one of the outstanding Commandants the Coast Guard has ever had. That's about it. He had vision. He had a good personality. He was able to talk to the Congressmen and Senators on the Hill. He was also able to talk to the administration and his own boss, Morganthau. He also listened to his staff. So that if he was convinced of the correctness of some move, he was perfectly willing to carry the ball on it. As a general rule, he won.

I'm getting way ahead of our story, as you no doubt know, because I'm covering almost a ten year period of his career now. He was appointed three times as Commandant. I'd have to sit down and do a little counting to come up with the exact number of years.

Q: You went from the COMANCHE to the CALYPSO in Baltimore.

Capron: That's correct.

Q: Can you tell me something about that? I also understand you were Captain of the Port of Baltimore, and various other locations.

Capron: I think probably the best way for me to approach this is to try to cover it, more or less, chronologically.

Again, I went to the CALYPSO in Baltimore about the first of August, 1939. Most of us felt that if there was a war in Europe, it wouldn't affect any of us at all. This was about the time when Congress almost defeated the draft and so forth. As I say, most of us felt that anthing about the war would have nothing to do with us.

The CALYPSO, at that time during the summer months, was involved to a great extent in the patrol of regattas, races, and so forth. At that time the Chesapeake Bay area was almost the center, as far as the east coast was concerned, of power boat racing. It averaged about two regattas a week.

The CALYPSO's number one job was patroling these various regattas. In patroling them, there were certain items of routine which we had inherited from the old APACHE. The APACHE had been the Baltimore station ship for years and years and years. When she became unservicable because of age in about 1938, the CALPYSO was brought around from the west coast and assigned in her place. So, we inherited the patroling of these races.

From our present day standards, it was a kind of silly action. We always acted as committee boat in all these regattas. We would anchor so that a certain point on our deck would be exactly on the starting and finish line. That meant from the manouevring standpoint of dropping your anchor and backing out your chain for maybe 30 or 45 fathoms, putting a stern anchor over, heaving around, and then positioning yourself in this river or bay or harbor that you might be in so that you were right on the line. Then the committee would use the vessel as their committee boat and so forth.

The actual patrolling would be done by our own boats. We had, for that purpose, two quite speedy small speed boats - Hacker-Craft with a capability of somewhere between 30 and 35 miles an hour. In addition, we had the standard 20 foot motor launch that all 165 footers carried, and another motor launch that we carried under exceptional circumstances. We would use these small boats or ours for patrolling these various regattas.

The basic part of the patrol was the actual saving of life. That is, these speed boats and outboard motor boats going around a half mile course and so on were continually upsetting and so on. That's where the speed boat came in; you could dash in and fish a man out of the water and get out again before the racers came by.

This was quite exciting and quite interesting. But, it was tough on the nerves. Because you would be spending roughly five days a week as a center of these howling screaming dervishes called outboard motors, going around and around and around. At the end of the day, you were just about ready to blow your top. We had that roughly five days a week. With enough time to go back to Baltimore for supplies and fuel and then go on another regatta.

That occupied us up to the final regatta which was the President's Cup Regatta here in Washington. We came up here and I was patrol commander for that. That was in 1939. At this time, they were held almost the last of September.

Then after that, we assumed the regular distress work which was for the Chesapeake Bay. There was the DIONE, which was a similar vessel to the CALYPSO, a 165 foot patrol boat, stationed at Norfolk. The CALPYSO was stationed in Baltimore.

Basically for distress work, I had the responsibility down as far as Sandy Point Light, actually Solomons Island. The DIONE had the responsibility from Norfolk to there. We were always on two hour standby.

However you also had a patrol seven out and seven in. These patrols were conducted in the Bay. Actually the skipper of the DIONE and I had a private agreement that any time there was a distress in the other guy's area and you were out on patrol, if you could possibly make it you did. To keep him from having to get underway and go out. We operated during the later part of that fall.

Q: What happened to the search and rescue cases in the summertime when you were patrolling regattas?

Capron: In the first place, the type of search and rescue cases you had in the summer were entirely different from the winter ones. Many times, we sent a small boat out. However, the DIONE had the responsibility for our area in the summertime.

Occasionally, the PAMLICO would come up from Pamlico Sound and either handle a regatta or search and rescue. Basically, the summer cases were such that a 125 footer would be able to handle it; or the DIONE would come up from Norfolk. If we had a real honest to god case, we would just slip on out and go. That didn't happen very often, in the summertime, during the regatta season.

During that winter we had our regular patrols and so forth. I might also add, we had a 26 foot motor launch that belonged to us, on the dock. We docked at Fort McHenry. There was a government dock there, just outside of the Fort McHenry reservation. We had davits on the dock; we had a 26 foot motor launch. For local cases, we'd put our motor sailer over with a crew and they'd go and handle it. This would be around in the harbor. In addition, there was a 125 footer at that time in Baltimore. There was also a 75 footer, which was doing intelligence work.

However, neither one of them had much to do with the Bay proper.

Q: What kind of intelligence work was this?

Capron: Actually they were working for the Customs. They'd take the customs people around and go onboard on various hot tips the customs people had and everything else. There was a tug there that did the regular boarding. But this 75 footer would take the special Customs agent around and so forth.

Q: What about your duties as Captain of the Port?

Capron: Again I've spent an awful lot of time on this other.

As time went along, theings began to get worse. During that spring of 1940, what was called neutrality patrol was established. The Navy operated their destroyers in this 300 mile line offshore and the Coast Guard was given the neutrality patrol for the harbor entrances.

It ended up that the Coast Guard handled the entrance to Cheasapeake Bay, Hampton Roads, and so forth. This ships assigned to that were the CALYPSO, the DIONE, and a 125 footer, the McLANE which was based at Morehead City.

We operated there, on this particular patrol, seven days at a time. We were permitted to anchor considerably. What we had to do was to collect from every outgoing ship and incoming ship, but outgoing particularly, much the same information that we'd had to up in New York, plus the cargo.

The only way that this could be done as we finally figured it, out was to have the pilots do it. If we had tried, with our limited personnel and limited experience, to put an officer aboard one of those outgoing ships to obtain all this information - first of all, we would have delayed the ship considerably. Secondly, we just didn't have the kind of capability of putting boats over and going alongside. This was practically in the ocean at the entrance to Chesapeake Bay.

So a deal was worked out between the two groups of pilots that operate out of Chesapeake Bay. One was the Norfolk Pilots and the other the Baltimore Pilots.

We would put one of our enlisted men on each one of the pilot boats every morning about nine o'clock. The pilots bringing these ships out would collect this data as they came out. When the pilot ship would take him off and he went aboard his pilot boat, our man on board there would get that information and correlate it and put it on a tabulated form or what have you. Then every day at nine o'clock, we would swap men on that pilot boat.

This was really hairy business. We actually only missed about once or twice in a year, when the weather was so bad we just couldn't do it. That meant putting a boat over, sending your own man over to the pilot boat, bringing the other man back. And doing that with two pilot boats, Baltimore and Norfolk.

Then we had to correlate all that information. Normally, rather than sending it by radio, we would take into Little Creek where a messenger would meet us and take it on in.

That went on for quite a while. Then while these patrols were still going on, things began to get hotter and hotter as you know.

In the very latter part of June, the President invoked by executive order the Espionage Act of 1917. This Espionage Act of 1917, first of all established Captains of the Ports who would be Coast Guard officers. It placed under the authority of the Captain of the Port, to the degree necessary, all movements of vessels within the harbor within the port, and any necessary security requirements for the protection particularly for the vessels and the ports themselves. This was in the latter part of June, 1940.

I was skipper at this time of the CALYPSO. We were just sailing our patrol; we'd backed out of the slip. The radio man came running up; we were still at "all hands". He said, "There's a message for you, Captain." The message was relatively simple.

It said, "Lieutenant W. C. Capron, you are temporarily detached command CALYPSO. Proceed to the Customhouse. Request office space from the Collector of Customs and assume the duty of the Captain of the Port."

I had no more idea what the duties of the Captain of the Port were than the man in the moon.

By this time, we were out in the stream ready to go on a seven day patrol. I did some hurried packing. The Executive Officer relieved me. I climbed into a boat and they pulled me ashore.

I might say going back to our talk about the speed boat, those speed boats were purely for regatta purposes.

When we were on regular patrol, we carried good old-fashioned surf boats (pulling boats). They took me ashore and I ended up on the dock.

At this time you could make a telephone call for a nickel. With a nickel I called my wife and said, "Here I am, come and get me." Which she did. Much to her surprise, I was not sailing on a seven day patrol or anything else.

The next day I got up and went in. The big thing for us in the Coast Guard is that the people in Customs had never heard about us. The Collector of Customs was a big time politician and he didn't know what it was all about or anything else. Finally one of his subordinates took mercy on me and assigned me a desk in a big office with a lot of other people.

Suddenly the night of the 3rd, right before the 4th of July, this whole thing hit the newspapers. Why it took that long, I don't know. We had been to a part at the Officers Club over at Curtis Bay and from there went to a rathskeller over there in east Baltimore. While we were there, a newsboy came through with this newspaper. This was probably around eleven o'clock at night. It was the first edition of the morning Hearst newspapers with a big headline - CZAR of THE PORT. Being curious, I bought a copy and discovered it was me that they were talking about.

The following day, the 4th of July, I was hoping to stay in bed getting over this fairly late night party.

The newspapers started calling me up about seven a.m. They wanted a comment; they wanted pictures; they wanted everything. I finally agreed that they could come out.

There were three papers involved; one was the Baltimore SUN. I've forgotten what the other two newpapers there were. There was a photographer there too. I hadn't shaved; I'd just gotten up that morning and put on kind of a rumpled white uniform. This was long before we ever had khaki. My uniform was white. The photographer insisted that he take my picture, and that the fact that I needed a shave wouldn't even show up. As you no doubt can guess; it showed up plenty.

I had a news conference. Frankly I couldn't tell them any more than they knew, having been on the job only for a couple of days and having there been no Captain of the Port since World War I. Anyhow that is how I became the first Captain of the Port of Baltimore.

Q: What did your duties ultimately involve?

Capron: First of all, there were no established anchorages in the port of Baltimore for different type vessels. A vessel would come in and anchor any place it pleased. Which is fine from the standpoint of the freedom of the seas, but when it comes to proper utilization of a restricted area it isn't very good. Because they'd be anchored all over the place and it would be clogged up, and you'd have half a dozen more ships that wanted to get in. There was no explosive anchorage. At this time, they were loading explosives that were going to Great Britain.

There was absolutely no regulations of traffic in the harbor. Incidentally, it wasn't needed at that time. But there was also no security on the docks.

At this particular time, there were some very active organizations in the United States, both pro-British and pro-German. The German Bund, of course, was the most famous one. They were continually trying to gain advantages and so on.

At this time, our government leanings were very definitely toward the British — that is the allied side.

One of the very first things we had to do was to try to figure out a voluntary security system at the various docks. It had to be voluntary, because we did not have the legal authority to lay down rules and say this is what you're going to do.

Q: Did you get a staff for this?

Capron: After about a week, yes. My staff consisted of a 2nd class yeoman. How he ever made second class, I don't know. As long as I was Captain of the Port for this period, my staff consisted of this particular yeoman.

One of the very first things I did was draw up these various anchorage charts, and have them photostated and distributed. We had a temporary anchorage for vessels just coming in, and wanting to anchor overnight before they went to a dock. We had another anchorage for vessels and barges that were going to stay there for awhile. There was still a third anchorage that we called a dead anchorage, where we put some Italians and Danes who had been demobolized. We put them in the dead anchorage and required them to anchor bow and stern, because they were dead ships. In addition, there had been an immigration anchorage which was not policed very well. We had to establish an explosive loading anchorage.

The very first thing I ran in to - the Army Ordnance Department which had an Ordnance Depot in Curtis Creek, right across from our Coast Guard yard, was charged with handling and loading various munitions which were going to Great Britain. Baltimore City had numberous regulations governing the handling of explosives. So that, basically, the only anchorage there was with enough water and outside of Baltimore City limits where munitions could be loaded was the quarantine anchorage. Historically, the quarantine anchorage is controlled by the Public Health Service.

At that time, there was a decided feud between the Commanding Officer of the Ordnance Depot of the Army and the number one doctor at the quarantine station as to the loading of munitions in the quarantine anchorage.

I think I came into the picture at just about the psychological moment because it was practically a knock down fight between the two. They had almost reached the point, as far as taking positions was concerned, of no return.

Of course, Public Health and the Coast Guard have always been very close. For many years, we were both under the Treasury Department. All of our doctors were always Public Health Service doctors. This particular doctor, head of the quarantine station, had been on duty with the Coast Guard a number of times.

I was able to talk to him and to the Army Colonel and ultimately work out a deal, whereby I would be the one who would say 'yes or no' on use of the quarantine anchorage for munitions loading. My one tugboat would patrol or make sure that everything was all right down there.

Once we accepted the fact that the quarantine doctor had the authority over that place, he was perfectly willing to delegate it to me. So we worked out this mutual deal wherein the Army came to me, then I'd call up the doctor and say, "We're going to use this corner this time," and he'd say, "Fine." We managed to handle the munitions loading in Baltimore harbor. That was the very first thing I ran into.

From then on as Captain of the Port, there were numerous things. Basically my force consisted of this 125 foot patrol boat that was stationed there, the harbor tug we had, and the 75 footer that I mentioned that worked with the Customs agents.

As far as I was concerned, I was just feeling my way along. There were no rules and regulations governing what the Captain of the Port could do, what he should do, or anything else. Basically all we had was the Espionage Act of 1917 which, as any law properly is, just broadly spelled out things without any detail at all.

After I'd been there several months there was another officer a Commander, (I was still a Lieutenant at this time) who was ordered there on permanent duty to become Captain of the Port.

After he reported in, I returned to my regular job as Commanding Officer of the CALYPSO, probably somewhere around October. From then on, we worked on these various neutrality patrols that I mentioned, numerous distress cases, and so forth.

Within a month or so, I was shipped down to Jacksonville for the rearmament as we called it. We put in a rough winter on neutrality patrol; again went down and completed our rearming. I got back to Baltimore somewhere around early March of 1941.

Meanwhile, wartime conditions of course had deteriorated as far as the allies were concerned and as far as the United States was concerned. Basically my interest was the interest of the Commanding Officer of this particular ship.

One Saturday night we were at a dance over at the Maryland Yacht Club. One of the very nice things about the CALYPSO, ex oficio you might say, was that all of the officers were members of the various yacht clubs by special invitation with all the priviledges of the members of the yacht clubs but not including paying dues. So we were at a dance over at the Maryland Yacht Club.

At about ten-thirty or eleven o'clock, someone came up and said I was wanted on the telephone. I answered the telephone, fully expecting it to be my officer of the deck who knew where I was. Bear in mind, our ship in Baltimore was always on two hour standby. We only had about one period during the year when we were off of that, and that was a month for overhaul.

I had this call; it turned out to be the Chief of Staff for the district down in Norfolk. He was a rather explosive individual, who continually jumped to conclusions and so on.

He immediately started out by saying, "Where have you been?" I replied, "I've been right here." He said, "I called your ship. I first called at nine o'clock, and they didn't know where you were. I finally traced you down." The ship being on standby, the Captain is always available.

I asked him, "Who did you ask on the ship?" He said, "I asked the quartermaster." I said, "Commander Lucas, I don't tell the quartermaster where I'm going. It's not the quartermaster's business. When I'm going anywhere, I tell the officer of the deck. If you had asked him, he could have told you. Isn't that the way you finally found out?" He said, "Yes."

Commander Lucas then went on to explain - first of all that Commander Able, who was Captain of the Port of Baltimore, was in the hospital and was seriously ill. And that his assistant, a Chief Warrant Officer, did not have available to him any of the codes and ciphers. (I might add that the staff had been built up during the several months that I was away to a respectable amount.) There were several messages to the Captain of the Port that had not been acknowledged and could not be, inasmuch as he was in a coma in the hospital. The safe could not be opened immediately by anybody else. So that he, the Chief of Staff, would have to paraphrase and give me over the telephone the contents of these various messages.

This first one was to place a watch as soon as practicable on any Italian vessels which might be in the harbor, to be prepared to go aboard and seize them at almost a moment's notice, being particularly careful to prevent any possible sabotage. And as a final caution, give absolutely no publicity. One or two other messages went in to a few more details.

Then a plain language one from the district given over the telephone was, "Assume Captain of the Port of Baltimore."

It was twelve o'clock at night. The possible time given for the seizure the next day was nine a.m.

I had available my own crew of the CALYPSO of 35 or 36 men immobolized because our main engines were torn down, a tug with a crew of approximately 9 or 10 men, a 125 footer with about 18 men, a 75 footer with 7 or 8 men. And a job of taking over two Italian freighters, each with a crew of 35 or 36 men aboard, out in the harbor.

Q: What was the purpose of this?

5 Capron - 217

Capron: That subsequently developed. There was, what turned out to be, a plan *developed* by the Italian Naval Attache here in Washington to sabotage all of these Italian ships which had been to all intents and purposes interned in United States ports. They didn't dare go to sea because the British would sink them. They were not legally interned, but to all intents and purposes they were.

There were, throughtout the United States, probably a dozen Italian ships and maybe three or four German ships, all of them coming under the same catagory.

That was another point of the Espionage Act, forbiding the damaging of a vessel. There are some technicalities to that, which I won't go into.

I was also told that I could call on the Training Station, which was then located at the Coast Guard yard, for any manpower I might need. So I called up Captain Reinburg and received a promise of a platoon of troops with one or two Petty Officers and a couple of Warrant Officers to help me the following morning.

I personally stayed up all night. My wife had been at the dance with me, of course. I didn't feel like letting her go home alone and park the car in the commercial garage that we had to use and walk the half a block or so from there to the house around midnight. We did have a live-in maid at that time for baby sitting, so we could leave the children. So, I brought her aboard ship and ~~her~~ had her turn in in my bunk. Of course, I violated every regulation the Coast Guard ever had about women aboard ship over night.

I was up practically all night making the arrangements and so forth.

The following morning at about seven o'clock, the detail reported from the Coast Guard yard and my own people were ready. I had the CALUMET, the tug, which was to be our transportation out to the ships which were at anchor. I assigned various jobs to people.

I particularly worried about the sabotage angle. The main thought on sabotage was the opening of sea valves and so forth and sinking her. I had two engineers available, both Chief Warrant Machinists. To each of them I assigned a job on a particular ship of immediately going down and finding the sea valves, with a guard, and assuring that they weren't opened up.

I broke up the rest of the party and so on. About that time, I received orders from Washington that we were to go out and actually seize the vessels.

About that time an enterprising young man from the Baltimore SUN, who I had known for some time, (he was the waterfront reporter) showed on the scene and asked what we were doing.

5   Capron - 219

This being Sunday morning, I allowed as how we were holding landing force drill. Without question he laughed in my face, allowing that it wasn't usual at that time on Sunday morning to hold landing force drill on the dock. He went on to say that they had a tip that we were going to seize the Italian ships.

Bear in mind we were told first of all, no publicity. And second the Italians were to have absolutely no warning, whatsoever, until we actually walked aboard.

Here I was with this reporter. I was in the proverbial dilemma as to what to do. I finally decided that if he was with me on a tug, he could not spread the word. As long as I had control of that tug, he was with me. I also knew if I didn't take him with me, it would be on the radio probably within 15 or 20 minutes. So I approached him with the proposition, I said, "All right, I'd like you to come along." "Yes, we're going out and seize the Italian ships. I don't know why, but we are. I'll let you come along provided: one, you stay on the CALUMET. And everything you watch will be from the bridge of the CALUMET".

I was interested in the angle of 'if we had a fight', of having a civilian along to get plugged.

I said,"The other one is that you lay off the use of my name in this."

5 Capron - 220

I still didn't know what was going to happen to me for directly violating an order. He agreed to that and we went out.

We went aboard just about nine o'clock. Immediately our people spread out, some went to the engine room, some went to the bridge, and so forth.

I sought out the masters whom I knew and had already met in my previous tour as Captain of the Port. We had been on a rather friendly basis, even had dinner one time with them onboard ship. I was able to explain why we were there and so on.

Actually it wasn't until 24 hours later, that I learned that the ships had already been badly sabotaged. One of them had fired a boiler dry and ~~loaded~~ melted the boiler completely down. A number of valves had been smashed by sledge hammers, and the anchor engine on one of them was wrecked. One stupid group had even hacksawed through the propeller shaft, which was probably the easiest repaired thing that could have happened. At that time, I did not know that this had gone on.

One of the instructions that I had was that I was to take these people ashore immediately and get them off the ships. To take them ashore immediately was not too bad a job. We rounded them up, had each man get all of his personal gear together, (clothing, shaving gear, and all that sort of thing) and we were able to get them off fairly early in the forenoon. I took them ashore at the Coast Guard yard.

While all of this was going on, this is where logistics come in, nobody including myself had even thought of or wondered where these particular people were going to be stowed. They couldn't be turned loose. Immigration laws of the United States wouldn't permit it.

Here we had some 70 odd foreign seamen with no place to eat and no place to sleep, and yet I had the personal responsibility for them.

Here is where my earlier friendship with the doctor in charge of the quarantine station came in. He had a couple of empty barracks at the quarantine station which could be used. He couldn't feed these people, but he could sleep them in these barracks. Captain Reinburg, whereas he couldn't sleep them, agreed that for a day or so he could feed them. So, we found a place for them anyway.

They took care of them until about a day and a half later the United States marshall took them off of my hands and put them in local jails and so forth.

Interview # 6

Captain Walter C. Capron, USCG, Ret. by Peter Spectre
Arlington, Virginia December 6, 1969

Mr. Spectre: Captain, could you tell me a little bit more about your tour in Baltimore?

Captain Capron: We were mentioning last week, we had received orders and executed them to seize the Italian ships which were in the harbor. We had our difficulties, as I said, in finding a place for the crews.

Late Sunday afternoon having finally just about completed the job, put guards on these ships and the crews disposed of in the quarantine station, I received a radio message directing me to telephone a certain number in Washington, D. C. immediately.

Upon making this phone call I found that the number was that of the Commandant, Admiral Waesche. After I had identified myself, I was given instructions by him to take into custody all of the Danish ships which were in the Port of Baltimore.

At that time, we had eight Danish ships. Some of which were moored out in the stream, not too far from the Italian ships, and one or two at the dock.

6 Capron - 223

The words, and I can almost remember them specifically, that Admiral Waesche used were, "We had planned on waiting, but we are beginning to be afraid that there may be some sabotage committed on these vessels. So we have decided to take them into custody immediately."

That was my directive. I immediately tried to get hold of all the people I had had for the other job with the Italians.

As far as the Coast Guard Yard and the Training Station were concerned, Captain Reinburg was willing to give me a brand new crew of people, but not the same people. He insisted that they had worked long enough.

I still had to use, however, my own people from the CALYPSO and the tug and the 75 footer which were now under my temporary command.

We had to make our arrangements pretty fast and went aboard simultaneously, as much as we could, the various Danish vessels in the harbor. They were moored in two clusters in Curtis Bay, so that it was possible to go aboard them all at once. Then send another crew to board the two vessels which were at a dock in another part of the harbor.

By this time it was fairly late in the evening, around nine-thirty and dark. We had no idea what we were going to run in to. My instructions had been that we were to take everybody off, except the Captain and the Chief Engineer and the Chief Steward.

6 Capron - 224

The first vessel I went aboard the Captain, whom I had known for a year or so, practically met me at the gangway with the remark, "Where have you been?" Expressing a little surprise at his question, he mentioned the fact that one of the news commentators of the day had announced at nine o'clock over the radio that the Coast Guard was taking all Danish ships into custody. So that our element of surprise, for any of those who had radios and understood English (which applied to most of them) was completely lost.

On another one of the vessels, which was in the same group, I went to the cabin and knocked. As I say, we were a little bit worried about what kind of reception we would get. I had commissioned a sailor, who was armed with a Thompson submachine gun, to stay right with me. I personally had a .45 pistol under my raincoat, completely out of sight. But I had told this boy to stay right with me, and not to lose sight of me.

When I knocked on the cabin door of this particular vessel, the Captain came to the door and invited me in. Upon going in, I found that his wife and little boy were there also. The sailor who had taken my orders literally, and properly so, followed me right in. Apparently this sailor with a tommy gun really frightened the Captain's wife. Her exclamations and so were just enough to really scare the little boy, who was five or six years old. I spent some 10 or 15 minutes trying to quiet them and point out that there was absolutely nothing that was going to happen to anybody.

We had to begin the job of taking off these Danish sailors. All the ships were manned and they had all been paid quite recently, within the last week. This being Sunday, they had just laid in all their personal stores. I guess probably every seaman on board had a least one quart of liquor, if not more.

My orders were that they could take ashore only their personal belongings. I took it on myself to let them know they could not take ashore any liquor. In the first place, I didn't know where I was going to put them. I knew I couldn't put them where the Italians were. Becuase if I had, there would have been a young war right there. The Danes had absolutely no use for the Italians, and there would probably have been a number of murders.

They had a number of hours to get ready to leave. They couldn't take their liquor with them, so they started to drink it. Bear in mind, most of my guards were these 'boots' from the Training Station, nice kids. Before I knew it, quite a few of my guards were helping the Danish sailors get rid of their liquor by drinking it themselves.

It was close on to midnight, if not later, that we started to bring the first group of Danes ashore. For that night, I had arranged with Captain Reinberg that they could sleep in one or two of the buildings at the yard. (Actually, sleep on the deck, is what it was, until morning.) And that he would feed them in the morning. And then we would find out where we were going to put them.

Q: Where did you finally wind up putting them?

Capron: We finally prevailed upon as I remember it, one of the city institutions for putting them up.

There was a decided difference in the way we had that treatment. In this way - the Danes were under no compulsion from us to stay with us. We merely took them off the ships. If the individual wanted to go anywhere, he could. Whereas the Italians were actually in custody as individuals, and couldn't go anywhere they wanted to. The distinction there being, of course, that Italy was at war officially and Denmark was not.

Q: What did they finally do with the ships?

Capron: Ultimately the Danish ships were chartered by the U. S. Maritime Commission and their own crews returned to the vessels. They sailed under the United States flag, as I remember. There was, at that time, a Danish government in exile. This being after the Germans had invaded Denmark. This Danish government in exile gave their blessing to our utilizing those ships under charter.

6 Capron - 227

Q: What about the Italian ships?

Capron: The Italian ships in the first place were badly sabotaged, as I mentioned before. They had to be repaired in our shipyards. They were then placed under, I believe, the Panamanian Flag and were sailed as U. S. owned vessels for the balance of the war. I think both of them ultimately were sunk. The Italain vessels were not particularly modern vessels, not fast, and in the war zone they would have been sitting ducks, even in a convoy.

The Danish ships however were all modern, fast ships, mostly diesel. I might add, we had our trouble with those. Where with the Italian ships we had completely killed everything aboard, even the refrigerators; on the Danish ships we had kept them alive. I put my own people down there with the Chief Engineer, to keep the generators running and to keep all the machinery running. That in itself presented some problems, because all the instructions were in Danish. None of the engineers that I put down there could read Danish or understand it. However, it did work and we had no particular difficulties there.

In fact it wasn't more than a day or so that, after this Danish government in exile had screened the crews, the great majority of the crews were permitted to go back on board.

I had one little incident that is of interest, I think. There were two Italians who had returned to their vessel late at night, having been on a 48 hour liberty or whatever. This was long after we had taken the vessel over. So we had to take them off. We brought them in the CALUMET alongside the Danish vessel that we were then working on.

I mentioned to the master of one of them, who was a very good friend, (Bear in mind on my previous tour several months before as acting Captain of the Port, it had been my responsibility to assign anchorages to all of these practically interned vessels. So I knew the Captains, the first mates, and the engineers quite well.) that I had a couple of Italians aboard.

He said, "For God's sake, don't let them be seen. If any of our people that you are taking off see them, I'm afraid there's going to be a murder." So we put those two Italians in the brig of the CALUMET and kept them completely isolated while we took the Danish off.

Of these eight ships and all of the problems that were involved in getting these people off and so forth, it was late in the afternoon of Monday when I finally got everybody ashore and had gotten them taken care of - with a place to sleep, a place to eat, and all that.

I had not been to bed since I got up around seven o'clock Saturady morning; I was dead on my feet.

An interesting aside - Just at the head of the dock where we had come in was the dental office of the Coast Guard yard, which was physically a part of the quarters that were assigned to the Public Health dentist. Being the nearest place, I went up and asked to use the telephone to call my wife and have her come down and get me. I was still wearing my patent leather dancing shoes, incidentally. After having called her, I was pretty much pooped.

The dentist whose name was Canby, a rather young chap (I was young too, although I didn't think so.) said, "Is there anything I can do for you?" I said, "Yes if I can have a drink it might help me a little bit to relax." Frankly I had the jitters. He poured out a good generous slug of bourbon and fixed me a highball. I had that and maybe another one. They had the absolutely desired effect. By the time my wife came, I let her drive me home.

As an interesting follow up on that - Dr. Canby continued his career in the Public Health Service. Within the last two months, he was named as the Chief Dental Officer of the Coast Guard. I believe he assumed that as of the first of December.

I met him for the first time in some 20 odd years several weeks ago. He very vividly remember the incident. Of course, I remember it because if I hadn't had those two slugs, I might never have gotten home.

Q: This is pretty close to the end of your tour in Baltimore.

Capron: This was very close to the end. Then I was taken off the ship, on a temporary basis, and assigned to this acting Captain of the Port to meet this emergency. I remained in that job for roughly two months.

In the meantime President Roosevelt had the Presidential yacht POTOMAC, which had originally been the Coast Guard patrol boat ELECTRA and taken over by the Navy and converted to be his yacht. He had a 125 footer as an escort vessel, the CUYAHOGA, which was nowhere near fast enough. So the decision was made at this time to take the CALYPSO, my ship, as the escort vessel for the POTOMAC. This took place while I was at the Captain of the Port's office.

The CUYAHOGA was returned to the Coast Guard and took the CALYPSO's place in Baltimore. The CUYAHOGA didn't call for anywhere near the same rank that the CALYPSO did. So I was practically without a ship. I remained as acting Captain of the Port.

When Commander Able, who had been in the hospital, returned I was made his assistant. This didn't work.

Probably this is the only individual in my whole series of interviews that I'm ever going to have anything to say against.

Commander Able, upon his return, became the Captain of the Port. I had been acting Captain of the Port for two different periods. The first period was setting up the job, and the second was seizing these vessels and so on. I had made numerous friends among the shipping people.

We had instituted a voluntary system of identification for all longshoremen working on the docks in Baltimore. It was underwritten by the steamship agencies. It was fully supported by the union and it was the first thing of it's kind in the United States. Later there was statutory authority to require it. This was strictly a voluntary proposition as far as the unions and the steamship agencies were concerned. It really was quite a deal, because we were able to screen every person who went aboard ships. At that time, before we went into the war, on most ships carrying cargo to Britain there were a lot of Nazi agents, Bund members, and so on who were very anxious to cause trouble.

So that when Commander Able came back, whenever there would be a luncheon to which the Captain of the Port was invited, they always asked Commander Able to bring me along. Able resented this very very much. He was a much older man and he really resented it.

For me it was very definitely a very unhappy position. The final payoff of it was, for me, one day I dropped in to see a very good personal friend who was the head of the Furness-Withy Agency in Baltimore, one of the biggest British steamship agencies in the country.

6 Capron - 232

As I went in to see Captain Cloud, (his title Captain actually stemmed from his being a Captain in the field artillery, USA, World War I) his remark as I entered was, "I thought you were going to be out of town today." I said, "No, I had no idea of being out of town." He said, "We invited Commander Able to be our guest at the Association of Commerce luncheon and to bring you. Commander Able said you were going to be out of town."

About this time, Able himself walked in. Cloud challenged him with, "I thought you said Capron was going to be out of town." Able said, "Well, I thought he was." Cloud said, "You better come along." I said, "If Commander Able wants me out of town, I think I will be out of town."

That, as far as I was concerned, was the last straw. So that evening, I telephoned the officer in Washington in personnel who had charge of officer assignments. I told him that if he wanted to keep me from getting a general court martial, he'd better transfer me and do it quick. I just couldn't take it any longer, and I was going to lose my temper, and either say or do something that shouldn't happen.

The next day at about eleven o'clock, over the teletype, came this set of orders for me, Lieutenant W. C. Capron.

"Proceed immediately to Hampton Roads. Report to Commander, Transports Atlantic Fleet for duty as Coast Guard Liaison Officer And that was it.

Q: Before we get into your new assignment, we passed over inadvertently the integration of the Lighthouse Service into the Coast Guard.

Capron: That is correct. I somehow or other, completely missed mentioning that last week. Probably because the impact of that didn't really reach me for some time.

On July 1st of 1939, the Lighthouse Service officially became a part of the Coast Guard. My first contact with it was when two lighthouse employees, who were over at the Lighthouse Depot across Baltimore harbor from the CALYPSO, came over and requested that I swear them in. They were being commissioned in the Coast Guard. As Commanding Officer of a vessel, I had the authority to swear them in as commissioned officers in the Coast Guard.

Subsequently on several distress cases we had in the Chesapeake Bay, one of which was a very large steamer which went aground, we had the assistance of lighthouse buoy tenders. Whereas formerly, under those circumstances, they would have gone merrily on their way with no responsibility whatsoever to help. Now being a part of the Coast Guard, they did have that responsibility. I might say that many many times the excellent seamanship of their crews and the ability of the vessel helped us on big distress jobs.

Q: Were the people in the Lighthouse Service civilians?

Capron: Everybody in the Lighthouse Service had been civilians. Upon the amalgamation, this came as a result of a year long study that was made, all of the seagoing people and many of the shore based personnel were offered military positions, which salary-wise were commensurate with what they were receiving as civilians. The law which followed up the executive order authorized crediting the Lighthouse civilian service toward military retirement.

The one thing that they had to do was to meet the physical requirements of the particular position in the Coast Guard that they were going to take. If they did not wish to assume military status, they were permitted to continue in their civilian status. Even as late as 1946, we had one or two master of light ships who were civilians with all the rest of the crew being military.

Q: How did you and the people around you in the Coast Guard feel about these new officers? They were in a sense competing with you for promotion.

Capron: My own feeling, and I think my feeling was probably general, was this - they were in a way, yes, competing with us for promotion. But at the same time, their numbers increased the total number of officers in the Coast Guard, which of itself increased proportionately the number of people in each individual rank. So that basically the actual competition was slight. There must have been some people that didn't like it, but I don't know of any.

I'd like to just bounce back for a moment to our discussion of the Lifesaving Service, joining with the Revenue Cutter Service and becoming the Coast Guard. As I pointed out, the Lifesaving Service never did really become a part of the Coast Guard until 1934. It would not be assimulated.

I think I also mentioned the fact that there was quite a period of time wherein the feeling between so-called regular officers and temporary officers was rather strong. Oddly enough, it was not between individuals but between classes of individuals. And as I think I mentioned, the womenfolk were stronger on it than the men.

But all of us I'm sure in 1939 remembered the bitterness of those early days with these temporary officers, and the fact that the Lifesaving Service had not been assimilated for so many years. Remembering that, I think we leaned over backwards to make sure that this amalgamation with the Lighthouse Service would be successful. And I think it was.

Q: Did any of the Lighthouse Service people, the ones that were commissioned, serve during the war in the same way that the Coast Guard officers did?

6 Capron - 236

Capron: Absolutely. For instance - The assistant Commissioner of Lighthouses at the time of the amalgamation was a gentleman by the name of Charles A. Park. He became a four-striped Captain on the amalgamation. During the World War II expansion, he became a Rear Admiral and was Chief Operations Officer for the entire Coast Guard. In fact, I worked for him at one time. He was one of the most able people I ever met.

Another one of those, higher ups, was named Dillon. During World War II, he became a Commodore.

All of these people were integrated, but were extra numbers. That will answer your earlier question too. They were extra numbers, so that they would have a running mate in the regular Coast Guard (or what had been the regular Coast Guard) and would be promoted with their running mate. So there was no real competion there.

In my opinion, they were never discriminated against, certainly not because of their background.

We had an interesting coincidence. The gentleman who had been Superintendent of Lighthouses in Puerto Rico, at the time I was down there on the SENECA, named Manyon became a four-striped Captain in the Coast Guard. He was head of the Aides to Navigation Division of what was then the Norfolk division and is now the Fifth District, up until the time he retired quite a few years later.

Q: Could we move on now about your assignment. What exactly were the duties of your new assignment?

Capron: In order to lead up to what my duties were, there's a little more background that I think ought to be brought out.

As part of the Lend-Lease deal with Britain, the United States gave to Great Britain our ten Lake Class cutters. These were the original Lake Class which were built between 1928 and 1933. They were electric drive ships and pretty fine ships.

At about that same time, the United States was expanding it's capabilities on amphibious warfare. In the Caribbean, specifically around the island of Vieques and right around Guantanamo, there were joint manoeuvres going on with the Navy and as troops, Marines and soldiers. The Marines were the first Marine Division and the soldiers were the first Army Division.

At that time the Army had it's own transports, all civilian manned. They were engaged in these manoeuvres with the Navy transports, which were all militarily manned. The Navy transports carrying Marines; the Army transports carrying soldiers. Part of this involved going to sea in manoeuvres and so forth.

The very first thing that happened was that the civilian crews refused to sail their ships without any lights, with the ships dark. So they had these manoeuvres with everybody running dark, except these four or five big Army transports which were lit up like a proverbial church.

They also had landings. Landing craft, as a general rule, were put over not only from davits, but more often put over using cargo booms.

Quite often these maneuvers would last beyond quitting time, say five o'clock or whatever it was, in the afternoon. The civilian crews point blank refused to man the hoists, the winches, and so on, and to hoist the boats and bring the troops back on board unless they were guaranteed double overtime.

Furthermore the meals were irregular, because the troops had been ashore all day. When they came back, often the cooks refused to prepare the meal.

Actually the battleship TEXAS, which was part of this particular group, in one case sent all of their cooks over to one of these transports to cook meals for the soldiers. They also sent winchmen over to operate the winches.

In every case where this happened, the civilian crew man who's job it was to do it stood right alongside of a sailor who was doing the job, and later on put in for double time overtime.

This all took place in January and February of 1941. They came back to continental U. S. completely disgusted. The Army then asked the Navy, "Will you take over these particular transports?" They happened to be the HUNTER LIGGETT, the LEONARD WOOD, and the JOSEPH T. DICKMAN.

The Navy's response was that they could not; they didn't have the experienced people to man them. The Navy was already some 15 to 20 other transports. These were all later on called APAs, but at that time there was no distinction.

The Coast Guard, having just turned over ten of their cutters to the British Lend-Lease, had several thousand trained men available with no place to put them. So the Navy asked the Coast Guard (this is long before the Coast Guard became a part of the Navy), "Will you man these Army transports?"

Q: This is where you came in?

Capron: This is where I came in. Because at that time all these ships were in the shipyard being modified and so forth and crews being put aboard, all Coast Guard crews. They had to have a Liaison Officer on the staff of Commander, Transports Atlantic Fleet.

It so happened that the requirement for it came up probably within, maybe at the same time, the time that I called and said, "Get me out of here."

In addition, there was one other ship at that time which was the original MANHATTAN. This was the big steamer MANHATTAN, which was re-named the WAKEFIELD. She had not been under the Army, or anything else. But she was also Coast Guard manned at this time.

Having a whole division of ships, all Coast Guard manned, it was felt that on the squadron staff there had to be a Liaison Officer and in addition an assistant Operations Officer for the squadron. And that happened to be me.

After chasing them around and finally catching up with them in Charleston, South Carolina, I went aboard the BARNETT which was then the flag ship. I reported aboard as Coast Guard Liaison and assistant Operations Officer.

Q: You served on many of these transports. Was this in organizing these crews onboard these transports?

Capron: In only one case. The various transports that I served on was because the flag ship would change. During the period from about June 15th, 1941 until about the 1st of June '42, I was on the staff of Commander Transports Atlantic Fleet. His title was changed half a dozen times during that. He became Service Squadron 3, he became Training Squadron 3, and so on. It was still the same group. We would shift flag.

In some cases, the BARNETT which was supposedly our permanent flag, if she went in the shipyard, we didn't go with her.

We shifted to another ship, which was the MACAULEY, a sister ship to the BARNETT. Later on, when both the BARNETT and the MACAULEY and a number of transports were sent out to the Pacific to ultimately be in the Solomons Islands invasion, we shifted over to the LEONARD WOOD as flag ship. The LEONARD WOOD, as I just mentioned, was a Coast Guard manned transport.

As a matter of interest, some months later Admiral O'Neill was Commanding Officer of the LEONARD WOOD. He was Commanding Officer in the North African invasion, at Sicily, and later on one or two in the Pacific.

That is how I came to be on that job. It was at this time, going back to my various comments about Navy versus Coast Guard and so on, that a mutual respect began to grow up between Naval Officers and Coast Guard Officers. We were working right together now. I was unusual, in that I was the only Coast Guard officer in the whole ship.

Q: In other words, the ships were manned by Coast Guard enlisted men.

Capron: I personally as Coast Guard Liaison Officer on the staff was the only Coast Guard officer on these various ships that were our flag ships, until finally we went aboard the LEONARD WOOD.

#6 Capron - 242

So that I kind of stood out. I did something well, I was Coast Guard. If I did something poorly, I was Coast Guard. That was it.

At that time this mutual respect began to grow. They saw that the Coast Guard people could run these transports just as well as the Navy could run the transports. Deep down, maybe we thought we could do it better. At least, all hands were doing the same job, and doing it equally well.

As another item - The Commodore on whose staff I was, Captain Emmett, had originally had the idea that operating landing craft (the small 30 and 36 footers) was the type of work that Coast Guardsmen, particularly Lifeboat Station people, should be particularly adept at.

So that in possibly January of '41, prior to this debacle that I mentioned with the Army and the Marines and so forth, the Coast Guard had sent several hundred surfmen right from Lifeboat Stations to the Navy. They manned all of the Navy's landing craft.

So that every one of the Navy transports had somewhere around 30 to 50 Coast Guardsmen aboard. That was another reason for having a Liaison Officer. These were all enlisted, with no officer on board with them. They very definitely needed somebody that they could go to for the number of minor difficulties that came up, usually having to do with pay.

Q: They were still under Coast Guard control?

Capron: They were paid by the Navy Paymaster, but they were paid under Coast Guard law.

As an example - We had authority to pay expert riflemen $3 a month, for being an expert rifleman. Once a year he had to qualify, or lose it. The Navy had no such authority. So the Paymaster on a Navy ship refused to pay the boys their $3 for being experts. And they came to me.

In those days, every officer had to have his own copy of 'Regulations', his own copy of 'Pay and Supply Instructions', his own copy of 'Ordnance Instructions', and his own copy of 'Communications', and all of them. You had to have your own, and you had to keep them up to date.

So, I was able to pull out my 'Pay and Supply Instructions' and go to the particular Paymaster and show him the regulations and the citation of the law which authorized these people to get that money. They would have ultimately gotten it, yes, but it might have been six months or a year later.

That's merely an example of the type of thing that came up.

Q: It was during this time, that you were there, that the war actually began. At what point did the Coast Guard come under the Navy?

Capron: That was kind of a gradual proposition. Those of us who were on board these transports were under the Navy, very definitely. Although it was still the same type thing, in that we were under Coast Guard courts and boards rather than the articles for the government of the Navy. For the personnel instructions and everything else, the Coast Guard applied.

Our going under the Navy was administratively done by the Commandant of the Coast Guard and the Chief of Naval Operations. It was not a presidential proclamation. So, actually we started in June.

Late that summer the 327 footers, the Secretary Class of vessels which were on the east coast, of which at that time there were six, were all ordered to duty with the Navy. They were operating as part of the neutrality patrol, offshore patrol, and so forth under the Navy. These vessels continued to operate that way. That was late summer of '41.

As things got progressively worse some time during that fall, I believe it was around October, the President by proclamation placed the Coast Guard in the Navy Department.

Q: You mentioned that the Secretary Class cutters became part of the Navy. Also that the Lake Class went to Britain under Lend-Lease. What was left to do search and rescue work and the other functions of the Coast Guard?

Capron: We had the 165 footers which could do pretty well for a small vessel. We had the 125 footers. We still had the MOJAVE class, of which there were four, having been built in 1921 or '22. We also had a number of other older cutters which were able to operate. In fact, one or two that had been laid up were placed in commission.

At this time, there was nowhere near the same amount of search and rescue work from the peace time standards. The real danger of the submarine hadn't shown up on this side of the ocean, but there wasn't anywhere near the type that we had had. Of course, at this time everything that went across the ocean was in British convoy duty. So that in that way we were able to keep up with the existing search and rescue load.

As I said, it was some time around October when the Presidential proclamation placed the Coast Guard in the Navy.

I, in fact, was so much divorced from what the Coast Guard itself was doing in my particular job that I didn't even know when it happened.

Q: Captain, could you tell me a little bit about some of the amphibious training that took place before the outbreak of the war?

Capron: We had a big manoeuvre off what is now Camp Lejeune, North Carolina, which at the time we started had just been taken over by the Marine Corps. New River was the name of the particular small community. The manoeuvre was basically the landing of two divisions. One was the first Army division, and the other was the first Marine division landing on the beach with landing craft. Then moving on inward for what would be an advance into enemy territory.

We had the problem of supporting these troops from the ship for the ten days they were there. It was quite illuminating because I personally was main beachmaster for the first Marine Division. Another Coast Guard officer, Dwight Dexter, was main beachmaster for the first Army division. (Dwight Dexter, incidentally, later on was main beachmaster at Guadalcanal.) Over us was a Navy Commander by the name of Jamison, who exercised overall control.

It was interesting to see the differences in the way the Marines and the Army operated. The Marines were fed from the ships with a hot meal being brought ashore in thermos jugs or anyway possible. Whereas the Army sent their people ashore with field kitchens. Except for raw supplies, food and so forth, which was prepared in their field kitchens; they operated almost independently of the ships. Fresh water had to be taken care of, it was brought in.

At the end of the exercise, we executed a so-called strategic withdrawal and reloaded the ships. We brought the troops back and so forth.

One of the interesting things of this is that contrary to most practice operations, we were handling live ammunitions. All of the ammunition that came ashore, the boxes and so forth for the Army and the Marines, was live ammunition.

We were given to understand privately that this was a prelude to an invasion of the Azores, and this was the reason why were using ammunition and that everything was the real thing. Historically I can't prove whether it was or not, but that was the understanding that several of us who were in the upper echelon were given to understand.

Q: I have heard that they at one time had thought about invading the Azores. So that could possibly be true.

Capron: We actually had, in the safe, the top secret order. All it needed was an execute, which never came. Later on there was the same thing in effect for Martinique, which again was never executed.

After we finished that operation, it highlighted a number of bad deficiencies that we had. Fortunately most of those deficiencies had to do with training, some had to do with equipment, and some had to do with doctrine.

One of the most difficult things was the dividing line between the Navy and the troops. Where does the Navy's authority stop, and where does the Army's or Marine Corps' begin? That was really a problem, because some six or eight months later I was on a committee that finally came up with the recommendation that high water line was the dividing line.

Looking at it from the number of years, it sounds kind of silly. But it wasn't silly because you had to have somebody responsible. Should it be the Naval Officer who's had the responsibility all the way up to here, or should it be the Army Officer who's going to have the responsibility going in? Basically, was it then mostly a military maneuver? Military meaning troops, or naval meaning boats and ships and so on. That wasn't decided right then, but the problem was highlighted.

After that, we went on about our business. Pearl Harbor came along.

As a simple aside to that - on Pearl Harbor day, the Commodore and myself and two other members of his staff were playing golf in Norfolk. (There was a Marine on the staff also.) The Marine's wife ran out and said, "The Japs are bombing Pearl Harbor." We questioned her. Yes, they are,

I heard it on the radio." About this time, over on the next fairway, we heard other people discussing it. They had heard it.

The Commodore turned to us, with what I consider a rather classic statement, "Boys, we might as well finish this round because it's the last one we're going to play for a long long time." So we did.

When I went home, I found that a number of my Coast Guard friends, who were on the other transport, had congregated at my home. They and my wife were all huddled around the radio hearing all the reports of Pearl Harbor. By this time, they were working on Clark Field in the Philippines and all the rest of it.

Meanwhile there had been a final operations scheduled for these two divisions, which were the only divisions we had trained in amphibious warfare (the first Marine division and the first Army division).

My statement isn't quite correct. The second Marine division on the west coast had had some training too.

This exercise had been scheduled for January and was to be held down off New River. The people who were responsible for this scheduling and so forth, a Naval Officer was basically in command, most of the decision that were made were based on the recommendations of the Marines and the Army high command. They more or less agreed that they would go ahead and have this manoeuvre down off New River.

New River is a stretch of beach north of Cape Fear, along the North Carolina coast, wide open to the sea, and with reasonably deep water in fairly close to the beach.

My immediate boss, Commander Jamison, Navy, and I were the operations officers. I was assisant to him. We felt, both of us having read a little bit of history, it was rather stupid to hold a manoeuvre on an exposed beach, that like. Which no matter how much you tried to keep secret, was pretty much of an open secret.

Using all the transports that the United States had which were trained in amphibious warfare, and using the two divisions which were really trained in amphibious warfare to put them out as sitting ducks when we knew that in World War I the Germans had the capability of sending a submarine all the way across here to the United States. They certainly would have it in World War II.

We argued very hotly and finally convinced our immediate boss, the Commodore, Captain Emmett. At a conference held aboard the flag ship of what was then called the Service Force of the Atlantic Fleet, of which Admiral Randall Jacobs was then Commander in Chief, the Commodore presented all these arguments that Red and I had given him as to why that manoeuvre should not be held in that particular place. He had limited success in convincing the people, particularly the soldiers.

Ultimately during that conference Jamison and I were sent for, to come over to the flag ship and present our arguments. I was Lieutenant Commander and Red had just made Commander. Most of these people were at least two-stars, and one of them was four-stars. We felt rather diffident going in there with our little argument that what they were planning to do was stupid. However, we did go in. We partially convinced them, at least to the point where we were told, "All right, you find a place for us to have the manoeuvres. We've got to have them."

This is where my little tour on the CALYPSO came in, because I had become quite familiar with Lynhaven Roads and with that area in the southern part of the Chesapeake Bay inside of the Capes. Red and I scouted out that area, and a day or so later we presented the proposition that that would be a good area. It was limited, yes, but a good area to have these exercises. It was accepted.

Subsequently we embarked the first Army division in New York and brought them down. In this particular case, it was slightly different from the earlier manoeuvre in that the first Marine division was to be the defenders and the first Army division were the assult troops.

We brought them down from New York and brought them in. They went through a period of a three of four day manoeuvre in January. Most of the time the air temperature was 26 and the water temperature was 36. Those of us on the beach had to be in the water as much as we were out of the water. Frankly it was pretty miserable. However, we had the exercise.

During that exercise, German submarines showed up off the coast. The first torpedoings of tankers were out off of Hatteras, actually off the Lighship at Diamond Shoals. This was within 50 miles of where we would have been, if we had had our landings down New River.

Q: Your stock in trade must have really gone up.

Capron: I think it did. Red and I personally figured that the submarines were on the way over, and it was only the change in location which prevented those transports from getting it. That's conjecture.

After the exercise was over, we took the troops back to New York. On the way up, we saw two or three violently burning tankers that had been torpedoed and passed them. Then we stayed at New York for a short period of time.

At that time we received orders to take troops, in this case the 34th division, over to Ireland. This was a relatively routine kind of a deal. Our landing craft were all taken off; we didn't need them for that purpose. Our boat crews were all temporarily transferred off. We took aboard the 34th division and took them over to Belfast, without any particular incident other than the type of scare that we all had in the early days of the war when those U-boats were so prevalent.

Q: Were you convoyed?

Capron: We had escort, yes. We went as one large convoy, half of them were bound for Iceland and the other half bound for Ireland.

At a point south of Iceland, a British escort met us. Prior to that, we had an American escort. This consisted of the battleship TEXAS, the cruiser QUINCY, and probably a dozen destroyers. They broke off at what was called MOMP, (mid-ocean meeting point), and headed for Iceland. Then a British escort, with five destroyers, met the rest of us and took us the rest of the way. We weren't too happy with this British escort, mainly because there weren't many of them. Practically speaking, I suppose, because of experience, we were probably just as well protected, if not better, by the five British escorts as we had been by the dozen escorts of the U. S. fleet. That's a comparison that you couldn't prove one way or another.

6 Capron - 254

We took these troops into Belfast. We stayed in Belfast for awhile. We went on up into the Clyde to the town of Gourock and stayed there awhile.

Our group, it consisted of about five or six transports at this time, loaded more or less of a heterogeneous group consisting of a lot of Americans who had been stranded in England at the outbreak of the war, an awful lot of wounded (back and head wounds particularly) that were being brought back to Canada. None of our troops had ever been engaged. In fact, the 34th division was the first group that had gone overseas. Also a lot of non-coms of the Canadian army that were going back as cadre for a new Canadian division.

Late in February we sailed from the Clyde, going out to the Irish Sea in a very dense fog with a British escort and a British destroyer leading it.

I had come off watch at four o'clock, I had only turned in for a short period of time, when all of a sudden all of the lights came on. All of the lights were controlled by a master switch. Everything was out at night, except for the battle lights. All the lights came on, and over the P.A. system came the words, "Collision. This is not a drill." Within seconds, there was a clang and the whole ship really shook.

I got dressed, which didn't take much time to do, except for shoes. I went up on the bridge. Upon getting up there, I looked and there was a small freighter which had been cruising down. the Irish Sea.

Q: It wasn't a part of your convoy?

Capron: Not part of our convoy. It had gone across our Bow and everybody was running dark. At this time, radar was practically unheard of. There were a few ships which had it, but very very few. We had almost cut him in two.

By the time I got up there, there was a boat in the water that had gone over and taken off the crew of this vessel while it was lying there. The question came, here was this vessel still afloat. We couldn't go off and leave it. It certainly was a menace to navigation. Nobody knew how long it was going to float, or anything else.

We were in waters that, quite often, were submarine waters. It was still dark with heavy fog. The Commodore told Red Jamison, the operations officer, to get in a boat and go over and see if you can find out how long that vessel is going to float. Because if it was going to float very long, we'd have to send somewhere for a tug or something and go on about our business. We couldn't hang around, with these so-called floating apartment houses, the transports.

6 Capron - 256

Q: Did the whole convoy stop?

Capron: They had to. They were all milling around; we had a couple of minor collisions too.

Anyway Red started to get ready. The Commodore said, "Take Owens, the engineer with you and see what you can find out." Red then spoke up and said, "Commodore, if it's just the same, I'd like to take Walter with me. He's in the Coast Guard and he knows about these things." Frankly, I knew no more about it than he did, but that's the reputation.

The old man said, "That's an idea Red. You don't need to go, let Walter go. He can do the whole thing." So in this bitter cold foggy day, I went down in the cargo net over the bow into a boat. It happened to be manned by Coast Guardsmen, part of these boat crews.

I went over, taking the Captain of this little freighter with me. I insisted that he go with me. We got over there and went aboard. I took a look at the thing. The tarpaulins that were over the holds were all puffed way up, which showed that water was coming in underneath and the air was tring to escape. I went down in the engine room, it had a combined engineroom and fire room, and water was coming up all the time. It wasn't more than six inches from the fire boxes. When they abandoned ship, they left the generators going and everything.

So I got out of there in a hurry with the Captain and called the boat over. They had a little trouble getting the boat over; the engine conked out and they got it going again. I was just about to go over the side and swim, but they got there. So we climbed in.

I went back to the ship. When I got nearby, I yelled up to the Commodore, "She won't last more than 15 minutes."

He said, "Okay, now go over to the FULLER. The FULLER has had a collision with another ship, and he won't answer my radio. Go over there and find out how much damage he's had." So I went over.

There was a little difficulty with the people on the FULLER who weren't too sure whether I was a German U-boat or not. They didn't want me to come too close. I finally got the information from them that they had been hit aft about frame number three. I couldn't get that through my head, but I went with the word.

On the way back, I looked and the small freighter had sunk. It just was gone, my fifteen minutes was pretty close.

I went back and got aboard. I later on learned the thing on this frame number three being aft, the FULLER had originally been one of the old Baltimore mail steamship line which the British built, the British numbered frames from aft forward. We number them from forward aft. That explained the discrepancy.

6 Capron - 258

From then on the return trip was completely uneventful. After we got back they started making up the Task Force that ultimately went to Guadalcanal, although we had no idea where they were going. That included our flag ship, the BARNETT.

The flag was ultimately transferred to the LEONARD WOOD. The LEONARD WOOD was modified to have flag quarters. We were transferred to the LEONARD WOOD some time around April of that year, 1942.

That, for the time being at least, wound up any particular things that I had to do with what was now the Amphibious Force Atlantic Fleet, which had started out as being Transports, Atlantic Fleet.

Q: You did go on to a new assignment at this time? Can you tell me about that?

Capron: Very shortly after this, while we were engaged in training other troops, (By this time, nobody every talked about going outside for training.) we were training up at Cove Point in Chesapeake Bay just above Solomons.

I received orders to proceed to Washington for a conference. I came up. This particular conference was a rather high level conference. I wasn't the only one from our group; there were several down here. I had apparently attained a reputation as knowing something about landing craft particularly. So I was ordered up to this conference. This was a pretty high level conference, just below the Joint Chiefs of Staff as far as level was concerned.

At that time they were considering the feasibility of an operation which would land troops across the British Channel in France, Flanders, Belgium, Holland, and so forth. The idea was to take them by landing crafts from the British Isles, across the English Channel, and land them.

We had already had reports on what happened at Narvik, when the British had a landing at Narvik, when the people had been exposed to the cold and in the boats for a long time. There were numerous estimates of the efficiency of the troops somewhere around ten percent, after all that exposure.

Furthermore the plan, as proposed at that time, was that they would try to land three divisions abreast. At one time I had figured out, but I've forgotten exactly, how many boats would be involved in such a thing. You'd have had a line miles long. They would have over a hundred miles to traverse.

Furthermore it would take you two days to load the boats, with that number of troops. You just couldn't load them that fast. You don't have that many docks, piers, beaches, and so on. So you would have troops that would have to wait from 24 to 48 hours, before they could even start. It would have been a hundred mile trip.

This whole thing was discussed. I was asked, from the standpoint of small boats, what I thought of it. I was rather blunt that I didn't think it had a chance of success. I gave various reasons that I had, all based on my own experiences in small landing craft. This was long before we had LCIs and LSTs.

The conference broke up. The upshot of it was that the Navy refused point blank to have anything to do with it. The then Chief of Army Engineers spoke up and said, "We can furnish the boats and the boat crews and so on to do this job." So it was decided that the operations would take place some time in the spring of 1943. And that the Army Engineers would train the boat crews and everything else, and they'd all be soldiers. I think this was called 'Bolero', the operation.

I went back and about several weeks later I had orders again to report to Washington and report to the Chief of Army Engineers, to whom I did. They told me that they were going to set up their training facilities in the vicinity of Camp Edwards, Massachusetts on Cape Cod. They would like to have me go with them when they selected the specific places and make recommendations for what would be needed in the way of docks, repair facilities, oil storage, gasoline storage, and so on.

6 Capron - 261

We left Washington by plane and flew to Providence. At Providence we were met, and then went on down to Camp Edwards. I spent a couple of days down there with them. We, as a result selected Waquoit as the initial place, Washburn Island was the actual specific location, and the places where we would have docks, where we would put the enormous tanks we would need for both gasoline and diesels, and various other things.

Q: Captain, before we go on with that, you mentioned before that you didn't like the idea of the operation. How did you feel about being engaged in training people for this operation?

Capron: The way I felt then was basically this: After I'd finished up at Camp Edwards for these couple of days, I came back through Washington. I met the officer who was to be the Chief of Staff of this, what came to be know as the Army Engineer Amphibian Command. He asked me, "How would you like to come up and be in charge of all our boat training?" I said, "You know my feeling. I've told you, I told them in the conference, that the whole idea of the plan is screwy. It can't work. Furthermore, I said that I felt that the Army had no damm business running boats. So how come you're asking me to come up and run your training?" He said, "It's very simple.

You were honest enough to tell us what you thought, under those conditions and under conditions where you might have been *slapped* down. We figured that if you'd come up and work for us here when we start doing something wrong you'll tell us the same thing." I said, "If I'm ordered to go up there, I go. If I'm not ordered, I don't. It's that simple."

I went back to Norfolk. Within two or three weeks I received orders to proceed via Washington to Camp Edwards, Massachusetts and there report to the Commanding General, Engineer Amphibian Command as a member of his staff.

Upon arrival, which I had already known of course, my job was to be in charge of the entire boat training program.

At this time we had two or three bodies of water. We had some empty barracks right in Camp Edwards, which is six or seven miles at least from the water, and a nucleus of maybe a dozen officers. This was very early June. Our deadline for turning out the first thousand boat crews was the 1st of August. We didn't have any boats.

Q: That was 1941?

Capron: That was '42.

Then began a very hectic time. I had nothing to do with the procurement of boats, or anything like that. But they started coming in; they came in on flat cars. They came into the town of Buzzards Bay, which is quite a few miles away. The boats, incidentally, weigh about five tons. We had the problem of getting these boats off the flat cars, into the water, getting them serviced, and bringing them around by water to Waquoit Bay.

By this time, there were more people coming in. I had a couple of very fine boatmen who were Army officers, commissioned specifically for the purpose, who knew what the score was. We managed to hire a crane that could pick the boats off the flat cars and set them in water. During a period of two or three weeks, we received well over a hundred boats. A little later on we began getting tank lighters, that came down from Boston.

We got out first detachment of troops, which had originally been the 36th Army Combat Engineers. They would automatically change into a boat regiment. For most of these people, the biggest body of water they had ever seen had been the bathtub.

I should add that I was given 120 Coast Guardsmen, all landing boat trained, as part of my force. They did the actual physical instructing.

We had the job of turning out these boat crews, and they were supposed to be turned out at the rate of 1,000 a month, which we started to do.

6 Capron - 264

Ultimately some time in August, we turned out this first bunch and the second batch were already in. When I say trained, I mean they could operate a boat, and not necessarily put it aground. The engineer knew enough about the thing so he could push the starter button, and so forth. They were not trained boat crews by a long shot, but they had reached the point where by their own practice they could become proficient.

We got a second bunch. They came in strictly as individuals and not as a regiment as the others had. So we had the problem of not only training them in boats, but also in making them a unit.

The powers to be in Washington made a decision, after the Dieppe raid, which took place early in August. This was really, in my opinion, a feeling out of this massive invasion that they were talking about. As you probably know, the Dieppe raid turned out to be a complete fiasco.

As a result of that and other things, the plan for the mass invasion across the English Channel was indefinitely postponed. It was decided that the Army Engineers would continue training boat crews.

About this time the final division of responsibility, as far as boat crews were concerned, was arrived at. The Navy would handle all ship to shore, whereas the Army would handle shore to shore, looking forward to island hopping in the Pacific, for instance. That was the artificial dividing line between the responsibility.

Along in September, I suddenly received orders. I had been ashore; I had been promised a years shore up there in Edwards. I had taken a house in Falmouth Heights and had a year's lease. In September, having been in that house 2½ months, I received orders back to Norfolk. I was to go back and to report, not this time to Commander Transports, but Commander Amphibious Force Atlantic Fleet.

Q: They were going to continue on at Camp Edwards though?

Capron: They were to continue with Camp Edwards, Another Coast Guard officer was sent up to relieve me, or to follow me.

Q: Why did they transfer you?

Capron: It had been at that time when they threw out the idea of the cross Channel landing and as a substitute was to be the North African 'Torch', the North African invasion.

I got back to find that my job was to train the joint beach and shore party, Navy and Army. Navy being beach party; Army being shore party. I was to train them for another invasion. None of us knew where the invasion was to be. All we knew was that we were given a deadline of when we had to have these people trained.

6   Capron - 266

I got in around the 5th to the 10th of September '42, and reported in at Norfolk, and found that this was the job.

At this time the amphibious force consisted entirely of transports; they had nothing ashore at all. Up until this time, they had needed nothing other than the Commander's staff.

Admiral H. K. Hewett, who incidentally lives over in Annapolis, one of my old friends, (I say friend, asmuch of a friend as a three-star Admiral can be with a three striper on his staff) was located in the Hotel Nansemond. They had taken over the whole Nansemond Hotel at Ocean Beach.

I reported in at NOB and was told that my job was to train beach parties first. Then ultimately to take the Army Engineers that came in and train them together. How many they weren't too sure, at that time. And where it was going to be, none of us knew.

Q: Where the landing was going to be?

Capron: Where the landing was going to be, we didn't have the remotest idea.

I was told that you will be based down at Little Creek. I had been in there a number of times on the CALYPSO. Actually it's a very narrow waterway entrance, with stone breakwaters extending out into the Bay. It's the place where all the car floats bringing the freight cars from Cape Charles over to Norfolk came in. Also the ferry which met the Pennsylvania Railroad passenger trains over on Cape Charles and brought them over to Norfolk. Inside it was a fairly wide waterway, even though the entrance was very narrow.

I went down there and looked around. There were two or three new sheds that had just been built, and a company of Army Signal Corps. That's all that was down there.

Q: No barracks?

Capron: Hell no. There was a contractor there who had big piles of lumber, but no barracks, no nothing, except these sheds which they used to shelter the field kitchens.

I went back up and spoke to my immediate boss there and told him what I had seen and about everything else down there. He said, "Your men have started to come in already. Over here in the gymnasium we've already got between five and six hundred of them." These had ratings, some were Chiefs. But the basic ratings we had were signalmen, boatswain mates, machinists mates, enginemen.

Q: Did you get people sent there who had experience already?

Capron: No, these people were just plucked from the whole fleet all over, and all Navy. There were also pharmacists mates and all the people that go to make up a beach party. A beach part for one ship at that time was 56 men, plus three officers - a beach master, an assistant beach master, and a boat officer - and a doctor.

These people had come in and here I was. They had given me a desk in the upstairs second floor of what had been a World War I barracks. It was just a desk, that's all it was. I did have a telephone.

The boss told me, "We've got to get those people out. They're yelling about us having those people in the gymnasium, and we've got to get them out of there." "Where will we put them?" He said, "Somewhere in this area, the Norfolk area, there are 500 pyramidal tents. What we've got to do is get those tents and set them up, and then move these people down there. They would feed in these Army field kitchens which were under these open sheds."

I said, "Well, how about it, do I get any assistance or antyhing?" He said, "The first officer that comes in and reports in, you get." The first officer came in, reported in, and came up. He was a man several years older than I, he was a Lieutenant, his name was Cook. He was very military and so forth. I said, "Mr. Cook, just what is your experience?" How long have you been commissioned?" He said, "I've been commissioned three days." I said, "What is your experience, your background?" He said, "I was in the artillery during World War I." "What have you done since then?" He said, "I worked for Curtis Publishing Company." "What do you know about the Navy?" He said, "I don't know much." I said, "All right Mr. Cook, here's our problem. You're the only assistant I've got, and I've got to stay here because somebody has to received the rest of the orders. Somewhere around in this area there are 500 pyramidal tents. We've got to get those tents and get them down to Little Creek. We've been assigned an area that we can have the tents put up. We've got to get them up and get these men into those tents." Incidentally, a pyramidal tent normally takes six men.

By this time, we had 650 men over there, 27 doctors, and I don't know how many Ensigns and J.G.s had been reporting. All of those were graduates from Harvard. I didn't get Kennedy because he'd already gone to a P.T. boat. I got the classes behind him.

So I told Cook to go up, find those, and we'd have to get them set up. So he went and found them. Two or three hours later, he called me up, very exultant. He'd located the tents; they were at the Army base; he knew exactly where they were. I said, "That's fine. How about getting them down to Little Creek?" He said, "I don't know how we'll get them down there." I said, "That's your problem." He said,

"All right," and hung up. Then in one way or another with trucks, he got them all hauled down to Little Creek, and a distance of eight or nine miles.

Again he called me up, he said, "I've got them down here." I said, "Are they set up yet?" "No." I said, "If you need any manpower, let me know. We've got all these men over here sitting around doing nothing. They can set them up as soon as you are ready for them. Let me know. We've got to get those tents up." Meanwhile, with the tents we also got enough ~~sufficient~~ canvass cots.

I guess Cook by this time had given up on me. He called up the next day and asked for a working force of 50 men. So I sent them down, and I went down later. He told me he was all set, so I went down.

I don't know how the devil they ever did it, but he got a couple of the top sergeants of that Army Signal company to come over and teach them how to set up the tents. And how to set up a company street. He chiseled a bulldozer and a road grader from the contractor, and they made a company street.

Then when he got these men down, they set up all of these tents. Dammed if he didn't chisel from the contractor pipe and a crew and they set up running water. They had water running down a ditch with pipes with faucets about every 50 feet; they had set up running water. This had been a bean patch; we actually were digging beans out for a long long time.

6 Capron - 271

The whole job took about four or five days. Then we moved those people down there, and started getting them trained and getting ready for the North African invasion.

Q: Looks as if you latched onto a good man then.

Capron: Oh he was.

Interview # 7

Captain Walter C. Capron, USCG, Ret. by Peter Spectre
Arlington, Virginia December 20, 1969

Mr. Spectre: Captain, could you tell me some more about your experiences with the Amphibious Training Schools?

Captain Capron: I think the last time we talked we had reached the point where we had set up our school in tents at Little Creek, Virginia. The men, of course, had already been ordered in.

We had the problem of organizing various beach parties. Up until that time the beach party, as such, had been strictly part of the ship's company that was put ashore to handle the boats and to assist the troops in crossing the beach. But at this time there started a realtively new idea, which would be that the beach parties would be trained as such ashore and then placed on a transport for a given campaign or landing. This was the beginning of that idea.

All of the existing transports at this time had their own beach parties, which were well trained. They had been operating for a period of one to two years, including the Coast Guard manned transports as well as the Navy manned transports.

7 Capron - 273

For the North African invasion, which was what we were getting ready for even though none of us knew it, there were a number of new ships being put in commission. They were being converted at that time from their original purpose, ~~being~~ cargo ~~purpose~~, to being combat transports. Many of them were ships that were being built for the Moore-McCormack Steamship Company, and several others. But most of them were C-2 or C-3 type of ships.

So that the group that we were training down at Little Creek were to be the beach parties for these new ships, which were just even then being completed.

Q: So you not only didn't have the ships, but you didn't know where you were going?

Capron: We didn't have the ships and we didn't know where we were going. All we knew was that we were training these people for an operation.

There was no real doctrine for beach parties at that time. What doctrine there was was a result of earlier practice operations, mostly with Marines. There still had never been decided what was the dividing line, particularly between the Navy Beach party and the Army shore party, between their responsibility. Furthermore what was basically the Navy's responsibility and the Army's responsibility? The Marines

7 Capron - 274

were all going to the Pacific, and their responsibility had been laid down. The Army was doing it all (amphibious landings) in the Atlantic. This having been a Joint Chiefs decision of some time back.

So that we were really starting from scratch. We started training these beach parties at Little Creek. One of the things that I had noticed in past operations was that as a general rule the sailor, as differentiated from the soldier, physically pooped out rather soon. He was used to decks and to being aboard ship. He was not used to plowing up and down through the sand for hours on end, and it just wasn't what he was used to.

So one of the things that I initiated was a very very strict physical training course. Included in it was a series of obstacle courses. At this time this was relatively new. Don't think it was my idea, it wasn't. But it was a relatively new thought. Actually the people who had originiated it were the Seabees.

I was very fortunate in having a Chief Petty Officer Specialist made available to me, who had been in charge of the physical training of the New York City police force. With him, it was a natural.

We devoted at least an hour a day to straight physical buildup for these sailors who were use to walking on wooden and steel decks, who were now going to have to plow through ankle deep sand.

The course, as devised by this Chief Petty Officer, consisted of quite an obstacle course including scaling a wall, climbing ropes, and doing all the other things that as of now we all expect to have to do to get in physical shape. We had a pretty good course.

I think I mentioned in my last interview that I had been given a bunch of officers right from the Harvard Indoctrination School, some were Lieutenant, junior grade, and some were Ensigns. I think I mentioned the fact that when I questioned them I learned that the man over 30 was a J.G. and the man under 30 was an Ensign. And they all had exactly the same experience.

I was also given some 27, I believe the number was, doctors. Most of whom had had very little indoctrination. In fact, most of them didn't know how to wear their uniform yet.

Q: Why did you have doctors?

Capron: One part of the beach party's responsibility is the evacuation of wounded on the beaches out to the ships. In an amphibious operation, you do not have any hospital ships along.

\# 7 Capron - 276

So that the wounded are evacuated to the empty transports from the beach. It was the beach party's responsibility to receive them from the combat troops who were supposed to be gone inland, and to take care of them in a hospital tent or what have you until they could be evacuated by boat, on stretchers as a general rule, out to the ships.

As time went on the operation became specialized enough so that a head wound would go to one ship, abdominal wound would go to another one, and so forth. The doctors that would be aboard would be more or less specialists.

We had the responsibility of training these people. I had all these doctors, and like any group of men there were some good and some bad. I say good and bad, I'm not speaking from the moral standpoint, I'm speaking from the ability to be absorbed and take the rightful place in that kind of an operation. Every one of them had gone into the Navy voluntarily. Most of them had dreams of these big white hospital ships where they would be 'angels of mercy' and so forth. To be suddenly confronted with duty with one of these beach parties, whose sole reason for existance was to support an armed landing by the Army, a lot of them just couldn't see it. They were very unhappy, some of them. We managed to get rid of the ones that were mostly unhappy. The balance we were able to pretty well indoctrinate.

Included in the 56 men beach party was about eight hospital corpsmen, who had the responsibility of staffing and operating the evacuation center which directly evacuated the wounded to the boats and thence to the ships.

The other members of the beach party were mostly technicians, carpenters mates, electrician mates, machinists mates, a couple of signal men, and various ratings that you would imagine would be needed along the beach.

Q: Where did the soldiers come in, in the training?

Capron: The soldiers were the so-called shore party. The actual handling of supplies, for instance, was not the responsibility of the Navy beach party. It was the responsibility of the Army shore party.

Q: The Navy's party was called the beach party and the Army's was called the shore party?

Capron: Right. Their responsibility was unloading the boats of supplies that came in. The shore parties were always made up of Army Engineers, originally they were all Combat Engineers. They did a lot of the unloading.

In these early days, all unloading practically was done by hand. Later on various other things developed, pallets and occasionally fork lifts. Although in most beaches you couldn't use one. But they did use the pallets, which would be towed by a bulldozer back into the boondocks where you would set up your dumps.

Q: Did you train them with the actual equipment that they'd use?

Capron: They were ultimately trained with the actual equipment that they would use, yes. These people that we had here were all going to the new ships. We had a list of the ships. So we just arbitrarily, when we made up a beach party of 56 men plus three officers, gave them the name of one of the ships they were going to.

Ultimately they changed the names of the ships. Originally it was the MOORMACSUN and the MOORMACthis and so forth, but they ultimately had good old Navy names.

But we named them right in the beginning. So this was actually for morale as well as anything else. Because these people were very unhappy. The only reason they were in the Navy was because they liked ships. All of a sudden we were making them all the same as engineers on the beach.

I might say that during the whole time I was there with that one our biggest problem was morale among the Navy sailors. They same thing applied to the Coast Guard sailors too. Because they thought they hadn't joined the Navy to fight a war on a sandy beach.

We trained these people for some four or five weeks. They were trained completely separately as Navy beach parties. All of this started somewhere around the 1st of September.

After about four or five weeks, my memory fails me as to how long, an Army Combat Engineer Regiment was ordered in. The first one that came in was the 36th Combat Engineers.

We then took these combat engineers and our beach parties and we started putting them together. We ran into considerable difficulties for a long, long time. The biggest difficulty was always the command difficulty -- who was in command here, and who was in command here. It was very much of a problem and some of it was finally decided at a pretty high level in Washington. We put them together and trained them as a group.

Just about the time that we got that much finished, I received word that we had another group coming in. It was just the same number of men and the same number of beach parties to set up. We had to start all over again.

Q: What happened to the ones you were working with? Did they stay?

Capron: They moved down into Camp Bradford, which had been a Navy Seabee organization down there. It was gradually being phased out as Seabees. It was going to become the future home of the Amphibious Force.

#7 Capron - 280

Q: But they were still under your command?

Capron: They were still under our command. Remember now, at this time these were all individual beach parties. Each one being it's own unit, but not independent by a long shot, but no grouping either. Each one was going to a ship and when they went to that ship they would become a part of that ship's company.

We still hadn't quite visualized the ultimate which was that you trained beach parties, handled them as separate units, put them on a transport for a given operation, and take them off again when the operation was over. That was the ultimate, but we hadn't visualized it as yet.

Q: You were putting them on the ship to stay?

Capron: We were putting them on the ships to stay, yes.

We trained this second bunch and got them all finished. I might say that it was quite a problem.

As far as I personally was concerned, I was in this peculiar position. They had set up the Amphibious Training Command down there at Little Creek. It so happened that there were only two Coast Guard officers in the whole lot. It was myself who was in charge of the joint beach and shore parties school. There was another Coast Guard officer who was second in charge

7 Capron - 281

of the signal school, which was another joint affair with Army signal corps and Navy signalmen and so on. We were the only Coast Guard people in the whole place.

We went ahead with our training. I personally ran into an awful lot of difficulty. First of all all of our men had to be armed, in order to defend themselves in case the beach itself was overrun. I just couldn't visualize sending a man with a rifle and bayonet, who had never used the damm thing. He'd never pulled a trigger. Our Petty Officers had had a certain amount of training in the use of the rifle, but the seamen we had, none of them had. Ammunition became scarce at that time. We had a devil of a time getting ammunition, so that we could finally give these boys one day on the rifle range with the weapons that they were going to carry into combat. That's not the way to fight a war.

But unfortunately, that's the way we started out in World War II. I'm afraid if we get into another one, all the lessons will have been forgotten and we'll do it all over again.

About that time we learned that part of our people were going to join ships that were already in England.

You probably wouldn't know, but the invasion of North Africa was actually carried out by two task forces. One sailed from the British Isles, which landed in Algiers and the north coast of Africa. The other one was the task force which sailed from the United States, which landed on the northwest coast of

Africa, specifically at Port Lyautey, Casablanca, and Safi - which was the southernmost point.

We, the group coming from the United States, (I'm getting a little ahead of my story.) were to have the Second Armored Division plus a regiment of the 9th Infantry Division. The bulk of ours was going into Casablanca, with a small amount of it going up to Port Lyautey.

To get back to this Chief Specialist I had. I had always lived up to a particular proposition that I would never tell people to do anything that I wouldn't do myself, within a human capability of course. As we went through those toughening exercises, some of those doctors did gripe and gripe and gripe. They had no use for physical exercise.

I had never been through a real shooting operation. But I had been through many practice operations, and I knew very well that your legs were the thing that gave out. They gave out awfully fast. If you trudge up and down a sandy beach for 12, 24, or 36 hours, you get awful tired.

I went through all the exercises, including going over the hurdles and climbing the walls and everything. Finally the Chief Specialist, who was my good man Friday as far as conditioning was concerned, called me aside one day and said, "Look you're too old to do that." It so happened that I was late in my thirties. He said, "It's alright for these kids." Most of them were kids; very few of them were over 30.

After quite an argument, I finally agreed that I wouldn't do some of the tougher ones. Or wouldn't try to do some of the tougher ones. Scaling a ten foot wall was never one of my outstanding abilities.

Q: When did the shore parties actually begin to embark?

Capron: We began to embark somehwere around the 25th of October, 1942. Meanwhile the ones that were going to the ships that were being assembled in Great Britain, were shipped overseas. I was going to be Operations Officer on one of the transports divisions, and would be main beachmaster at Safi, the southernmost landing.

We embarked and sailed up the Chesapeake and had a number of manoeuvres off of Solomons Island there at Cove Point.

Q: What transport were you on?

Capron: I was on the HARRIS, which was I believe the flag ship of Division 7, as Operations Officers. After I got aboard, we began working on our plans. During this period, there was a conference over on the flag ship QUINCY. That's when we learned where the landings were going to be. Prior to this, we had no idea. When they issued woolen clothing

7 Capron - 284

to the troops, we were positive that it would be up around Norway or somewhere like that. It shows how innocent or ignorant of North Africa that we were, not to know as hot as it is in the daytime in Africa, at nighttime it's bitterly cold.

The Commodore there, the Commander of the Division on whose staff I was, had originally been skipper of the BARNETT while I had been on the staff aboard the BARNETT. So I knew him quite well. We worked there and wrote up all of our op orders and the operation plans and so forth for the operation at Safi.

One little item that's kind of interesting - I was present at a briefing that the Army was giving. We had the troops aboard all this time. They were still practicing, lowering the boats, going over the side, and all that. I was present at a good size staff meeting of the Commanding General of the Second Armored, whose name was Major General Ernest Harmon. After we got through one briefing one day, somebody made the remark, "You Navy people just don't understand some of these things." That was enough to make me blow my top.

I said, "I'm not in the Navy. I'm only assigned to the Navy for the war. I'm the Coast Guard." Then General Harmon spoke up, he said, "I know it. I know all about you. I know all about the Coast Guard. I know all about the Coast Guard

Academy. I was Commandant of Cadets at Norwich University when Commander Hinckley was Superintendent of the Coast Guard Academy. Between us, we arranged the first football game between the Coast Guard Academy and Norwich University."

You can readily see that shut me up and shut me up awful fast. I didn't need to tell him what the Coast Guard was.

After we had been up there several days, a message came through from Cominch which directed me to proceed by the first available transportation to Norfolk and report to what would be the remnant of the Amphibious Force after the forward element had sailed.

Q: Why was this? Why did they send you back?

Capron: At the time I didn't have the slightest idea. I had already attended that briefing over on the flag ship, that I told you about, wherein we had been told that nobody was able to go ashore again if he was present at that briefing. Because that was when we found out where the landings were going to be.

Here were direct orders to me by name. They transferred me over night to one of the cruisers. I spent the night in the day cabin. The next morning, bright and early, they put me aboard the Navy destroyer EDISON which took me back down to Norfolk. Me with all my gear, which included a tommy gun and all the equipment you personally carried on the beach, because I had been going to be main beachmaster for Safi.

I still didn't know what it was all about until I got back. I then learned that what had happened was this: Ernie King had learned that all the staff of instructors and what have you that had been assembled to train these people for the North African invasion were all going on the invasion. There was nobody left behind other than a very few senior people, none of whom had been active in any training. That's when he blew his top and issued orders that a certain number were to be left behind. I think there were five of us who were taken off the ships, myself and two Navy and two Army. We were taken off. I learned this after I got back to Norfolk.

I got a command car which took me to my home, which was a beach cottage down on Willoughby Spit, the only thing we'd been able to find. I surprised my family very much by showing up, with them thinking I was somewhere at sea. They had no idea where this landing was going to be. I was from then on until the time it took place, which was early morning of Novebmer 8th, almost afraid to go to sleep for fear I'd talk in my sleep.

Then I learned that those of us who were brought back were to set up a permanent curriculum for training of all the various elements that go into an amphibious operation.

Q: How did you feel about that?

Capron: I was very much put out, to put it mildly. Because after all, I had gone through all the tough part of this getting ready and so forth. Whereas I don't think I was any more bloodthirsty than anybody else, I still felt pretty badly at being pulled out without the chance of even seeing the results of the work I'd done.

We spent the time, while all the ships were gone, setting up training aides and so forth. I was given the job of writing what became the Fleet Training Phamplet for beach and shore parties. We did all the things that were involved in getting the amphibious force set up on a solid basis for continuing operations.

Q: A short time after that you were transferred?

Capron: Six months after that.

In the meantime, after all of our beach parties came back, one of the staff, a Navy Captain, had what I believe was the first idea of setting up beach parties as a permanent organization rather than having them a division on any ship.

We got back most of the beach parties that we had trained earlier. We established an organization, of necessity more or less patterned after the Army organization rather than Navy, which were called beach battalions.

One beach battalion would support a division of troops in a landing operations and would constitute almost a part of, during the landing operation itself, the Army Engineer Regiment, which was a shore party. However at the end of the operation, the shore party would keep on going with the Army and the Navy beach battalion would be withdrawn and come back. That was when they first had the idea that once you get these people trained you can't dissipate them on the ships.

That was one of the difficulties that they had in North Africa. We had some pretty well trained beach parties. When they went aboard these ships, some of the Commanding Officers of the ships decided that - here's a good boatswains mate. So he swiped the boatswains mate from the beach party that had been trained for the beach party, and put one of his own people, who might or might not be any good, in the beach party.

So at this time, this naval beach battalion idea was to be a complete unit with it's own records and operating as a unit. So we got them pulling all together. I was named Commander of the First Naval Beach Battalion. Here again, I was more or less in the position of being the only Coast Guard officer in the whole place.

We started training this group ultimately for the landings in Sicily. Meanwhile I managed to pull together something of an instruction staff that I felt could very easily take over from me and me get out. It turned out, it wasn't to be.

Until the time the First Naval Beach Battalion embarked to go over to Oran, or one of the North African cities, to complete training there in order to get ready for Sicily, ~~then~~ orders came through that we were to train some more naval beach battalions.

Actually we formed one with no training whatsoever and shipped them to Great Britain where they would undergo their training there.

The next one, the third, we took down south. By this time Fort Pierce, Florida was our southern training base. We took them down there and put them through training, ultimately with the Army Engineer Regiment.

By this time, I had reached the point where I felt that I was stuck practically for good with that training angle of the amphibious forces. I just didn't like the idea. So I finally went up to the Naval Chief of Staff in the Amphibious Force.

I might say that the Amphibious Force Atlantic Fleet was so organized that it had a complete duplicate setup of Navy and Army.

The Commander had been Admiral Hewitt, later on it was Alan G. Kirk who some years later was our Ambassador to ~~Norway~~ Russia. Below him there was a complete duplication of personnel and they worked together at the same desk. They had double desks and sat opposite each other. We had a Navy Chief of Staff, who was Commodore Johnson. We had an Army Chief of Staff, a Brigadier General whose name escapes me. We had an Army G-1 and a Navy N-1, who sat right across from each other. This had been Admiral Hewitt's idea. He was a keen student of history and realized that every time there had been a failure in amphibious warfare it had always been because the sailors and the soldiers didn't understand each other. He was going to make sure that it didn't happen here.

I had an Army Major who was my counterpart. The unfortunate part about it for a long while was the fact that the Navy didn't go in much for spot promotion while the Army did. This Major had to be junior to me. I was Lieutenant Commander. Until I was promoted to Commander, that poor bugger couldn't go up. Ultimately, when I was promoted to Commander, the very next day he went up to Lieutenant Colonel.

All the way through you had your running mate. In my case, I was representing the Navy as the head man of this particular school. At another school, the head man would be an Army man. It was not an all Navy deal by a long shot.

After we had written up all this doctrine to train these people, I finally went up to Commodore Johnson. I told him, "I think I ought to get out of here. As far as my career is concerned, there isn't anything here for me. You've got plenty of people that can take my place. We've already done the hard work, the exploring and breaking the ice. I want to get out and get back with the Coast Guard."

He was quite sympathetic. He said, "You write your letter and I'll put a favorable endorsement on it."

So I wrote my letter to the Commandant of the Coast Guard via the Navy chain of Command. The Commodore put his endorsement on, in which he felt that out of fairness to my career that I should be given a different assignment. That went through.

Within three or four days at the most, meanwhile I had gone back to Fort Pierce with this training group, I received dispatch orders to proceed to Boston and report to the Commanding Officer of the SPENCER for duty as an observer, and to proceed via Washington, D. C.

Q: What's an observer?

Capron: At the time, I didn't know. This was explained to me as I went through Washington, I was to go aboard the ship and make a trip as an obersver with the full understanding that at the completion of the round trip, I would either take command of the SPENCER or command of another 327. This observer was to give me a chance to see and learn everything that I possibly could.

Q: Sort of training there.

Capron: In training, yes. It is true, at that time, they did have schools for escort officers. But they were essentially for younger officers. They didn't have them for officers senior enough to be in command of a large vessel.

Having shaken the dust of Norfolk, and particularly the Amphibious Force, I proceeded up to Boston and there reported aboard the SPENCER.

Q: What kind of duty was the SPENCER involved in?

Capron: She, at that time, was escort of convoy. She had been, up until that time, operating on the North Atlantic routes from Argentia to the British Isles, specifically Londonderry. Most of the time, she had been flag ship with a Navy four-stiper aboard as Commodore of the escort group.

At this time, they were just setting up the trans-Atlantic convoys which were to go from New York or Norfolk to, in the beginning, Casablanca. Later on they went all the way into the Med, but at that time it was Casablanca.

I'll amend that. The merchant ships themselves went on into the Mediterranean, and in some cases went in as far as Malta.

The U. S. escort groups were to escort these convoys, these were good size convoys of 100 to 120 ships, –

Q: How many escort ships were there?

Capron: Usually in the neighborhood of nine to twelve. In this particular escort group, that the SPENCER was to be with, there was two divisions of 1600 ton Navy destroyers, squadron Desron 19, plus the SPENCER, the CAMPBELL, and the DUANE. So in that particular group, when everybody was present, we had 15 ships, the 12 Navy destroyers and the 3 Coast Guard cutters.

We proceeded from Boston to New York and there joined up with the other group. Somebody there had fouled up because we still had the North Atlantic camouflage. North Atlantic camouflage was that razzle dazzle blue and white with jagged stripes. Whereas the mid-Atlantic were the various shades of gray. There wasn't time to repaint it, so we made our first trip with that particular camouflage. In mid-Atlantic, that meant that we just stood out like a sore thumb.

Q: This was while you were an observer?

Capron: Yes. We made our first trip across and I went as observer. The Commanding Officer was then Commander Harold S. Berdine, who had been on her for some time.

Q: Was he helpful in showing you the ropes?

Capron: There are several odd coincidences right at this point. I had known Berdine for years. We had been together in Boston for awhile. He had been command of a ship at Newport, which had been my home town. So I knew Berdine quite well, and we'd been quite friendly.

The SPENCER, on the trip they had just completed, had had a rather famous fight with a submarine. They sunk the submarine, and took all her crew prisoners. It was rather spectacular because there was a lot of shell fire. What happened was that the SPENCER followed this submarine, who was submerged, right down through the convoy. That was early morning, just before dawn. ~~They could have gone and broke before the real fighting started.~~ They had quite a scrap.

All this time, of course, I'd been with the Amphibious Force. So when I reported aboard, I found that two other officers from headquarters that were coming aboard as observers also

They were only going to be aboard for the trip from Boston to New York.

Berdine was a little bit bitter about these people. I got him aside privately and told him that I was going to make the whole trip with him, and that I had been told that at the end of that trip that I would either relieve him or one of the other Commanding Officers. Berdine was a little bit on the peeved side.

He said, "That's the trouble. As soon as a ship makes a name for itself, everybody wants to get on it." I said, "What do you mean?" He said, "Haven't you heard anything about our sinking a submarine this last trip?" I said, "No, I haven't heard anything about it."

That took the curse off right there, as soon as he realized that I wasn't scrambling to take his ship away because she had a reputation. Our old friendship was re-established. I lived up in the cabin in the spare stateroom the whole time.

Q: What were the two officers from headquarters doing there?

Capron: One of them was down there to see if he could figure out some answers for some gunnery problem. Frankly I don't even remember what the other one was down there for. It was just an overnight trip, as far as they were concerned. Where for me, it was the three months or so for the crossing and return.

Once Berdine realized that I wasn't a publicity seeker, because the ship had just made a big name for itself, and it was that I had been with the amphibious force andhad never heard anything about it; as soon as he realized that I wasn't out to steal his ship out from under him, because he'd made a name for himself, from then on relations returned to their *normal status* that we had had for all these years.

Q: Did you stand watch?

Capron: No, I didn't stand any watches at all. Nobody knew, and nobody was supposed to know, why I was there. I was there just as an observer. Berdine was the only one who knew why I was there.

As a matter of fact, some times I asked questions of the Exec and he got rather short with me several times. He was busy and as far as he was concerned I was just a super cargo and I was getting in his way asking him all these questions.

To jump a little bit, this trip was relatively uneventful. When we got back, we ran into a heavy fog off New York and we had to anchor outside of New York harbor. While we were there, a radar radio message came in directing that I relieve Berdine and he proceed to a new job. It so happened that the Exec brought the decoded copy of the message up. He looked just a little bit dejected, because I think he remembered some of the times he'd been quite short with me and was afraid that I would remember it too.

To make a long story short on that one -- He was an outstanding officer and we became very very good friends and still are. I had the opportunity, some eight months later, to recommend him as the Commander of the BIBB, a sister ship.

Q: What was his name?

Capron: Zittel.

Q: Can you tell me in general the type of duty you did? What your escort work involved, how the convoys were organized, disbanded, and so forth?

Capron: In the beginning, we were a part of a task force which consisted of this destroyer squadron plus the three Coast Guard cutters.

Q: Was it always the same squadron?

7 Capron - 298

Capron: It was always the same squadron for some months. We operated with them. Their Commander of the squadron was also the escort Commander. Right here is where my earlier time with the amphibious force in transports came in very handy, because I found that I didn't have to learn much more about ship manoeuvring. I had already learned it the hard way in the transports. There was a very slight difference in the way the ships in the columns were numbered, between destroyers and *large* ships, but that was easily taken care of.

I found that I could hold my end up, I believe, equally well with the other Commanding Officers. We operated with them until early November of 1943.

We normally would sail from New York. Part of the convoy, a good part of it, would originate in New York and part of it would originate in Hampton Roads Norfolk. We would join outside.

Q: You didn't have anything to do with the actual putting together of the convoy?

Capron: Yes and no. We had nothing to do with the assignment of the ships in the convoy, that is as to which column they'd be in or which number or all that. That was all done Commander of the 10th Fleet, who was Ernie King with another hat.

We did have the responsibility of more or less assembling them outside. Each convoy had a convoy Commodore, who was usually a retired naval officer who'd been recalled to active duty, who acted as convoy Commodore. He would ride one of the merchant ships, which was always in the center. He would have a small staff of signal men and so forth, so that he could communicate with us and also communicate with all of the ships.

In a trade convoy, which is what all of these were, there was a peculiar relationship between the escort Commander and the convoy Commodore. In that, the escort Commander was not directly, as far as military command was concerned, over the convoy Commodore. Very seldom, if ever, would the escort Commander issue an order to the convoy Commodore. By the same token, the convoy Commodore would never issue one to the escort Commander either. If you wanted him to do something, you'd more or less ask him to do it.

I can see now that there were elements which could lead to violent disagreements. I don't know of any that ever took place.

The convoy Commodore would handle all the communications to the various merchant ships. You had a pretty broad front there. Usually you had roughly 15 columns of ships, with a thousand yards between columns. There be 4, 5, or 6 ships in each column, 500 yards apart. You covered an awful lot of territory, a lot of ocean.

#7 Capron - 300

Q: You probably couldn't see either end of the convoy.

Capron: You couldn't see, no. From one end, you couldn't see the other. The various responsibilities that the escort Commander had and the convoy Commodore had were pretty well spelled out. Very seldom did I ever hear of any real difficulties along those lines. When it came to the final show down, the escort Commander could just tell the convoy Commodore what to do and that was it. Usually it was unnecessary ~~and rather polite~~

We operated up until November with this group.

Q: How many convoys did you bring back and forth?

Capron: During that period I would say about three round trips.

Q: How long of a lay over would you have between trips?

Capron: Over on this end, we had a ten day availability in the yard. Then we had about three or four days up at Casco Bay, which was a ~~trading~~ training area. We'd go up there and tame practice with American submarines. We'd ~~hang~~ ping on them and learn dummy attacks and we'd usually get some shooting in.

After that, we'd join up with wherever your convoy was starting from, which usually at that time was New York. Later on, it was usually Norfolk. Of course, ships would come in from the other seaports to join you.

Then we would usually on the other end, originally we went to Casablanca, turn the convoy over at the Straits of Gibraltar to a British escort. Then we would go to Casablanca, with a five or six day lay over on that end. Your lay over depended entirely on how long it had taken you to go across.

The first trip across I made, which was when I was an observer, took 23 days. There were a number of wolf packs around and they kept diverting the convoy this way and that way.

Later on, I think probably 18 days was more like the average length of time.

Inasmuch as the convoy sailings were rigidly scheduled, it you had a fast crossing, your lay over was much longer than if it was a slow one.

Q: Did you have any exciting moments? You must have had some.

Capron: Yes, we had a number. We never actually had a wolf pack attack during my time. I think probably some of the biggest excitement would be if you happened to get caught in a fog with a hundred ships and you were all milling around there wondering how many collisions you were going to have.

Q: Were the ships equipped with radar?

#7 Capron - 302

Capron: We were, but not the merchant ships. These were all originally mostly Liberty type ships, and later on the Victory ships. Very few of them had radar, but we all had radar.

We had a number of attacks or contacts when we thought we were being attacked. Unless you actually saw a submarine or brought him up, you had no specific proof that what you were working over was a submarine instead of a whale. I don't think we often made that mistake, but we undoubtedly did sometimes.

After we'd been with this group up until November, all of the Coast Guards 327 footers that were on the east coast of which there were five at that time, (The ALEXANDER HAMILTON having been sunk in the very early days of the war.) we were all orderd down to the Carribean to report to the Carribean Sea Frontier for escort duty. We didn't know for how long.

Four of us went to the Carribean Sea Frontier and one, the INGHAM, went over to Panama and operated over in Panama as a target ship for submarine training. Those of us who reported to the Carribean Sea Frontier were all assigned as Escorts, Commanders to escort groups which were escorting from Cuba down to Trinidad. These were essentially South American convoys which would originate in New York, sail down the coast, between Cuba and Haiti (Hispaniola) and then down on to terminate at Port au Spain, Trinidad. At which point, they would be regrouped into convoys which even went further down to South America, or in a few cases across the Atlantic to Africa.

Q: Submarines were operating strong in that area?

Capron: Oh yes. The Carribean was the happy hunting ground for the submarines.

We relieved Navy destroyers, who were escort Commanders. All the rest of the escorts were Navy PC boats. Of the four cutters, SPENCER, CAMPBELL, BIBB, and DUANE, we were all escort Commanders with about six PCs attached to our escort group. Convoys were operating roughly every five days. We based on the northern end at Guantanamo, Cuba. The southern end was the Naval Base which was just outside of Port au Spain, Trinidad. We had that period there, where we all operated down there in relatively good weather conditions. There was never any fog, hardly ever poor visibility, unless a heavy rain storm, and warm. In fact, in Trinidad it was damm hot.

We learned later that it was a deliberate action on the part of COMINCH to bring those ships, which had been operating in the North atlantic originally from Argentia to either Iceland or Londonderry. They started operating in the summer of 1941. Then shifted to the mid-Atlantic from New York to the Mediterranean. They had been operating that way for well over two years. So this was a wonderful opportunity to send us into the warm climate and get away from the awful North Atlantic. The winter time in the North Atlantic is no place for anybody.

#7. Capron - 304

Q: It was really a semi-vacation.

Capron: It was. From the standpoint of climate and weather it was, yes very much so.

In fact one of the difficulties that I had, the other Commanding Officers said the same thing, was trying to keep our people to keep their shirts on. Because an explosion blast where ever it hits bare skin, it will just fry you. Even a light shirt will protect your body, in the event of a blast. I think it was impossible to make them keep their shirts on during noon hour with this warm weather. It was the first sun they'd seen all these years. So I more or less compromised that each man had to have his shirt with him, rolled up under his head or something like that.

We stayed down there until about the early part of February, after which the other destroyers with the people we relieved came back. There were two American destroyers and two Dutch destroyers, who had been caught out when the Japs first jumped out in the Pacific. They had been caught out there and had come east to the United States. They had no place to go; they couldn't go to Europe. They came back and relieved us, and we went back up to New York.

At this time powers that be in Washington made each one of the 327 footers, with the exception of the DUANE, a flag ship for one of the escort groups crossing the Atlantic. As individuals, not commanders, we carried a Commodore aboard. We had the quarters, not in the cabin, with two staterooms. Actually we were ideal to be flag ships.

We came back up and operated from then on. I had a Navy three-striper, originally a three striper and later on made four-striper, aboard my ship as the flag ship. This time we had a division of four-piper destroyers and a division of the new DEs, plus ourselves and a couple of extra DEs that weren't a part of the division. We operated most of the time from Norfolk. Although when it came time for your overhaul at the end of a trip, you never knew where you were going to go. You might go to New York, you might go to Boston, or you might go to Norfolk. They tried to send us most of the time to Boston when they could, mainly because a lot of the crew's families still lived there. That had been our original home port. As time went on, we went into Norfolk more and more and up north not so often.

Q: Was your wife still in the Norfolk area?

Capron: I'd moved because of the fact that our home port had been changed to New York. I moved my family to New York. The result was that I didn't get into New York very often.

7 Capron - 306

The Exec's family lived in Boston and my family lived in New York. If we happened to go into Boston, he wouldn't take any leave at all. If we went into New York, I wouldn't take any leave at all. When we went to Norfolk, we'd split a couple of days apiece

What my wife would do, at the time I was aboard, get a baby sitter for the kids and she'd come up for a few days.

Of course, the battle of the Atlantic was more or less won but it wasn't over by that time. The general feeling that you always had was that this might be your last trip.

Frankly if the Germans had ever gotten smart in the beginning, as they did later on, instead of torpedoing merchant ships, they had gone after escorts when we didn't have many, they'd have won that war.

Q: I always wondered about that. I knew that at the beginning of the war practically every country on the allied side very short on escort ships, and they were more or less untouched.

Capron: We were very short on escort ships. It wasn't until about late spring of 1943, that we began to have enough. Before that, they didn't have them. The national priority on ship-building, in the early days of the war, were not escort vessels. They were amphibious vessels. It wasn't until later that they started building these escort vessels.

Before my time, I used to hear the other people talk about it, they would have a 70 ship convoy going across the North Atlantic with maybe five escorts. They couldn't spare an escort, even if they saw a submarine off on the horizon. They couldn't spare an escort to send him out, because they just didn't have enough.

Q: It's pretty interesting because I would think in a situation like that with five destroyers around a convoy, why the submarines wouldn't get the five destroyers first and then have a free hand.

Capron: I don't know whey they didn't. Let's face it, the escort vessel itself is a relatively shallow draft vessel and is much less susceptible to torpedoing than a 25 foot draft cargo vessel.

Later on when they had the influence-type torpedoes, sonic, they began to go for escorts. If they had done that in the early days of the war, at the time when the British particularly were using one of our old four-pipers (that had gone to Great Britain on Lend-Lease) as a flag ship escort command and the rest of the escort being corvettes, the submarines would have surfaced and shot it out with any one of the vessels, with the exception of the four-piped destroyer. They wouldn't have had to torpedo.

#7 Capron - 308

I've heard a number of explanations. None of them seem to make sense as to why it was pretty late in the war before they started going for escorts.

Q: We've been talking about your experiences with the convoys. We've left out quite a bit about what was happening to the Coast Guard in general during the war. For instance - What happened to Coast Guard aviation? Did the aviators stay a part of the service or go into Navy aviation?

Capron: In the first place, the entire Coast Guard went under the Navy. I use that 'under' rather than 'into', because it remained in a sense a separate corps. (In later 1941, probably October,) The Coast Guard aviation in the early days were used for scouting work for submarines particularly. They received a certain amount of modification to make it possible for them to bomb, with depth charges, submarines.

After several months to a year, Navy aviation had been built up with personnel and planes and so forth. The requirement of Coast Guard planes to do work which was actually involved in contact with the enemy, such as covering convoys, and the need for Coast planes to do that sort of work greatly diminished.

Yet there was a great need for rescue work, both the from the scouting standpoint and even the potential of an occasional landing in the water to pick up somebody. That, of course, didn't happen very often.

There was one squadron of Coast Guard planes that were stationed in Greenland. Most of their work was what was then called air sea rescue, which now is search and rescue.

With the exception of some incidents during the early days of the war, most of the Coast Guard aviation efforts were still along the peace time line of attempting to save lives, with wartime activity giving them plenty of opportunity.

There were at least one or two cases where a Coast Guard plane, in the early days of the war, actually sunk a German submarine by bombs. Our planes were not really configured for that type of work.

When they more or less fell into the traditional rescue angle, it made a lot more sense than it did to have our people be a small part of a fighting force.

Understand, Coast Guard aviators have always been trained at the various naval stations. Our Coast Guard aviators are Navy trained. The basic training is exactly the same. It's only when they get into more advanced training that there's a certain amount of difference. The advance type training that our people would be getting into would be, in the early days, flying boats. With Navy people it was torpedo planes and things like that.

Q: This sort of leads into another question. Who was performing the traditional 'search and rescue' functions of the Coast Guard while the major cutters were involved in escort duty?

7 Capron - 310

Capron: In the first place, bear this in mind. By 1943, everything was in convoys. At least as far as around the United States was concerned. In trans-Atlantic, everything was in convoys with the exception of a few neutralist ships, particularly Spain. With those exceptions, everybody was in convoy. In that sense of the word, our fellows were still doing it because they happened to be right there with the vessels.

In the very early days when the submarines first hit this part of the world, about the middle of January '42, at that time there really wasn't anybody doing that. That's when so many ships, particularly tankers, were torpedoed and sunk and lost with practically all hands.

There's this other angle which you really have to bear in mind. That is that the Coast Guard was given numberous duties, more extensive duties. Some of which were more or less traditional, and others were brand new.

I personally was involved almost entirely with either amphibious forces or later on escort of convoys, on our ships.

There was an enormous beach patrol established, on practically the whole coast line of the whole United States. Which was all operated by the Coast Guard.

Q: Who was manning the beach patrol? Were they regular Coast Guradsmen?

Capron: When you talk about regular Coast Guradsmen, you've got to qualify the expression. The Coast Guard at the time that we first thought we were getting into the war, back from Pearl Harbor about six months or so, prior to the amalgamation with the Lighthouse Service was only 10,000 people. We had a number of expansions, 1,000 men at a time. My guess is that, at Pearl Harbor, the Coast Guard may have had as many as 20,000. At the maximum during World War II, we had 176,000 people.

The question of, "Are they regulars or aren't they regulars?" is pretty difficult to answer. It so happened that everybody that came into the Coast Guard after about February of 1942 came in as a reserve, with one group exception.

The laws governing the Coast Guard Reserve only permits citizens of the United States. The laws which govern the Coast Gurad Regulars, at that time at least, did not require citizenship. So when we had people - draftees - who came in and were not citizens, they came in the Regular Coast Guard whereas your citizen came in the Coast Guard Reserve.

There was occasionally a little bit of feeling between the so-called regulars and the so-called reserves, It didn't exist very often and it didn't exist in many places.

I do know one ship where through the stupidity of the Commanding Officer there was a decided difference of feeling between the so-called regular and the so-called reserve. That was the only place I knew it to happen.

Q: The question has always bothered me about the wartime expansion of the Coast Guard. That is: You might be able to answer it since you were in personnel after the war. Why did the Coast Guard expand if they needed 100,000 more men, why didn't they just put 100,000 more men into the Navy since the Coast Guard was operating as part of the Navy?

Capron: Remember what I said first about the Coast Guard being 'under' the Navy. We were a separate corps under the Navy. We operated under Coast Guard regulations, not Navy regulations. We did operate under Navy courts and boards, rather than Coast Guard courts and boards. But as far as regulations were concerned, we operated under Coast Guard regulations.

When they first started out, the Coast Guard as such was given certain jobs to do. In the first place, we manned those transports in the beginning; the Navy couldn't man them. The only reason we could was that we had just ten *given Great Britain* of the Lake Class cutters under Lend-Lease and we had those crews available. That's the only reason we could do it. And we had trained men for the job.

There were certain things that we did that the law specified the Coast Guard do. Such as the Espionage Act of 1917, under which most of the things we did then and the things we did during Korea were based.

The Magnuson Act was strictly an amendment to the original Espionage Act of 1917, and the Coast Guard had that authority. The Navy, as such, did not have that authority. We had it, no matter whether we were operating under the Navy Department or under the Treasury Department. It was still our authority.

So in the beginning then, we had taken certain Navy jobs which were really essentially Navy jobs. We manned transports. That was a Navy job that was not Coast Guard at all. We did it because we had the capability at that time..

Then we manned escort vessels. Again we had the capability. In the beginning, they were our own ships. Later on, they were DEs that the Coast Guard manned. I don't know how many DEs there were during World War II, up in the fifties. We also manned all the frigates that were built.

Those were strictly Navy jobs that we did because we had the capability, that the Navy could have done just as well as we could.

Then we had certain Coast Guard jobs, which basically we probably could do better than the Navy could. Originally we had the beach patrol of the whole coast of the United States. We already had our surf stations, lifeboat stations. In many cases all we did was expand that. We already had the people there with a certain amount of know how. They knew the territory. At that time, in those early days there, was a lot of infiltration by German agents into the United States. Later on, as the war moved farther away from our coast, the requirement for the beach patrol went down.

In addition we had many other duties in the harbors and so forth. Again statutory laws specified that the Coast Guard should do it.

In early 1942, the old Merchant Marine Inspection Service (Bureau of Marine Inspection) was placed in the Coast Guard. That gave us through the old BMIN, as it was called, responsibility for inspection and certification of all American ships. Those people came over bodily into the Coast Guard. Their actual transfer was not made permanent until about 1946 or '47.

The question of pilotage was extremely difficult. They established a temporary reserve, so-called, which had several facets. One particularly included the pilots. All of the pilots of the United States became members of the temporary reserve. They were never paid by Uncle Sam. They still were paid by their pilot's association. But they were temporary reserves of the Coast Guard and we had military authority over them. Every once in awhile that became rather important.

As time went on the requirements, particularly for beach patrol which had been so great, went down. We didn't need them any more.

#7 Capron - 315

So that specific problem that came up at that time was this: Here are maybe 100,000 Coast Guardsmen who've been in the Coast Guard ever since the war started. They are all able bodied. We don't need them anymore for the jobs they've been doing. What shall we do? Shall we retrain them as Coast Guardsmen to do other jobs, or shall we discharge them from the Coast Guard and pick them up in the Navy? The obvious answer at that time, and in my opinion the correct answer, was that the Coast Guard keep them. They've already shown their loyalty to the service. Let the Coast Guard retrain them and give the Coast Guard some jobs which as basically Navy jobs. That's how we got frigates, and how we got to manning LSTs, and how we got to manning all of those Navy ships which were doing specifically Navy jobs, by retraining the people that were no longer needed who had originally had the Coast Guard jobs.

Does that answer it?

Q: That's the answer I was looking for.

Interview # 8

Captain Walter C. Capron, USCG, Ret.   by Peter Spectre
Arlington, Virginia   April 11, 1970

Mr. Spectre: Captain, the last time we spoke, we were talking about your assignment on the U. S. Coast Guard Cutter SPENCER on North Atlantic convoy duty during the second World War. We got pretty well through it. I was wondering if you might have some other details you might like to add.

Captain Capron: One or two incidents that took place more or less stand out in my memory. They're the type of incidents, when I meet one of the officers that was on there with me, we talk about.

One of them was in the Caribbean, where I was escort commander on the run between Port au Spain, Trinidad and Guantanamo Bay, Cuba. This particular time, a German submarine had been reported loose in the Caribbean. We were directed take the convoy, which was probably in the neighborhood of 40 ships, and six other escorts beside the SPENCER and go inside the line of islands which more or less fringes the north coast of South America.

#8 Capron - 317

Q: Is this the Windward Islands?

Capron: No, this would not be the Windward Islands.

These would be the islands like Aruba and Curacao, and several others whose names I've forgotten. They actually lie anywhere from 5 to 10 miles off the north coast of South America, particularly at Venezuela. Aruba and Curacao both had, and still do, large refineries where the crude oil was brought from Venezuela in small tankers, there refined and taken by tanker from there to both the United States and other parts of the world.

We received orders to go between those islands and the mainland. It was about noon time, as I remember, that we went inside. At that point, we had plenty of room.

As I said before we had our escort group, all except the SPENCER were PCs, with relatively primitive radar and not PPI scope (remote scope that we had at that time, that all the ships nowadays have). So that if the officer of the deck wanted to look at a scope he actually had to leave the bridge and go down into the radar room. Not only that, it was in relative rather than true bearings. So that for relatively inexperienced officers, it was somewhat of a difficult deal. The upshot of it was that we on the SPENCER, with a lot of experienced people and very good radar, had to do the navigating for the whole outfit.

The distance between Aruba and the mainland is somewhere around 3 or 4 miles, with reefs stretching out particularly from the South American side. There were no navigational lights either on the beach or on the islands. These small tankers were crossing ahead of us between Venezuela, taking on a cargo, and Aruba. Our PCs just didn't have much speed to send out ahead as pickets to warn these ships, "Get out of the way."

The SPENCER, being the only one that had any decent speed, had to get out well ahead, acting both as picket and escort commander. None of the merchant ships had radar so we also had to be navigator. The distance between Aruba and the mainland there was such that we probably didn't have more than a half a mile to spare on either side of the convoy.

Q: This was the full convoy, the 40 ships?

Capron: This was the full convoy, front. We had to navigate the convoy, using voice radio to the convoy Commodore, who in turn used light signals to change course and so on. We ourselves would tell him a course to steer, at the same time we would be plotting all of these small tankers that were crossing in front of us. When we found one that was getting in the way of the convoy, we had to more or less speed up and warn him out of the way. This took several hours of that night. I think all of us picked up quite a few grey hairs going through it.

As an after thought, I think that probably we took more risks when we came through there than we ever would have with a German submarine by going outside. It was a hairy experience. I wouldn't dare try it now.

The other incident, which is a little more than an incident maybe, took place about March of 1944 when a German submarine had been sighted trying to go through the Straits of Gilbraltar. We had already dropped our convoy. The rest of the escort group, which at this time was made up of destroyers and DEs, had gone to Casablanca.

We went into Gilbraltar with the Commodore to pay an official visit on the British Admiral there. As we came out, possibly six o'clock in the evening, we picked up sonar contact. It's the kind, when you're on ASW duty, that you love to get. It was a good solid one; it wasn't any fish or whale or anything else.

So we made an attack and nothing happened. That is, no explosions or anything. At that time we were not using depth charges; we were using the hedgehog, which only explodes on contact.

We circled around and made another attack, and nothing happened. Then one of us, either my navigator or myself, had the thought to check the steering repeater of the gyrocompass with the wind repeater. We found, for some reason or another,

8   Capron - 320

that they were 10 or 15 degrees different. Which meant that the repeater on the sonar gear was also out. So we had just been missing the course that we wanted by some 10 or 15 degrees.

The upshot of that was that, not being able to trust and not knowing which one was right, we made that attack - the same way you con a ship coming into a harbor really. Bring the helm right ~~degree~~, so many degrees rudder, ~~easy~~ ease your rudder steady, and then finding out what course he's steering. We did that.

Then we fired and got two explosions from the hedgehog projectiles, followed by a larger explosion and considerable oil. We lost him for awhile, then followed him, and lost him, and so on. We made some depth charge attacks, which apparently never did anything.

We spent all night with a number of other escorts, a Polish escort and a couple of British, all from Gilbraltar, with us. We swept up and down and so forth and never regained contact. I was personally of the opinion that we had sunk her, and I still am.

We got the evaluation given us by the Commander in Chief, who happened to be a Britisher, in the Mediterrancean that it was a class D attack - which is seriously damaged enough to require the submarine to return to port.

8 Capron - 321

After the war, they found that there was a submarine that was missing in the Straits at that time. But also, an American Air Force plane had bombed a submarine that same day. They got the credit for the kill, rather than us. Naturally every one of us aboard were sure that we were the ones that had the kill.

That was the one real experience that we had while I was on there, an actual attack of any success at all on a known submarine. We had other times when we attacked. We were pretty sure it was a submarine, but we couldn't prove it. The attacks were not successful as far as getting any kind of an explosion.

Those two items are particularly ones that those of us who were on the SPENCER at the time always talk about since. The rest of it, most of it, was routine. After you had a week of it, it wasn't much change.

Q: That's probably like weather patrol.

What happened to you after you left the SPENCER? What was your next assignment?

Capron: I left the Spencer in August in 1944, as she was in the shipyard at Norfolk being converted to an AGC, an amphibious command and communications ship.

8 Capron - 322

I came to headquarters and reported as one of the operations officer in the Chief Operation's Officer of the Coast Guard at headquarters.

Q: What did Coast Guard headquarters operations do during the war? I imagine it was quite a bit different --

Capron: Actually as far as operations in the sense of operating ships and so on, they didn't do much. Let's face it, because all of the ships were under Navy command.

Q: The Navy was controlling Coast Guard ships through their own operations?

Capron: Through their own operations. As an exception of course to that, there was a certain number of buoy tenders and some of the smaller vessels and the Port Security and beach patrol and things like that. Which were still in existance, although in a much lesser degree than in the early part of the war. Those came directly under the Coast Guard and under our operation.

Our operations, to a great extent, were liaison work with the Navy, with the CNO's office, and so on, but very definitely liaison work.

I was in that office from August, 1944 until around February of 1946.

Q: Do you know how many Coast Guardsmen were on duty, other than wartime duty, in the United States. For instance, tending buoys, lighthouses, and beach patrols.

Capron: I don't think there would be any records anywhere that would indicate that. Furthermore, I don't believe that you could make that kind of breakdown.

For instance - the lightships were all taken in. They did use some as examination vessels, but they were not operating as lightships.

Q: Examinations for what?

Capron: You had torpedo nets, submarine nets, at every port. Before a vessel was permitted to come through, unless it was a vessel that was in a convoy or something like that, somebody would have to go aboard and check them. An examinations vessel was a vessel that would house the people that did that boarding and so forth.

Q: It was like a mother ship for the pilot boats?

Capron: You might say that, yes. Every port had an examination vessel. The lightships were very good for that purpose, because they didn't have to move, they anchored. Being designed the way they were, they were relatively comfortable in bad weather. They were designed to be comfortable, as much as a small ship can be.

Most of the lighthouses were turned off. There were no lights on the Atlantic coast at all.

The buoy tenders — a lot of their work was taking care of buoys marking the swept channels. It was right up the alley of being buoy work, but it was strictly a wartime proposition.

I don't believe it would be possible to come up with any kind of a breakdown, other than make a wild guess that about the same were involved as were involved before any wartime expansion. Let's say 8 or 10,000. That's a wild guess.

Q: You were operations officer and you were also in the Chief of the Enlisted Personnel Division.

Capron: After I'd been in operations there for a year and 8 months, after both V-E day and V-J day, I was transferred from operations down into personnel as Chief of the Enlisted Personnel Division in headquarters. That was somewhere around the middle of March.

In between I did have some temporary duty directly under then Captain Richmond, wherein in a special section which I headed we came up with the recommended post war complement of the Coast Guard by unit. I say recommended, because we never got anywhere near what we thought we should have gotten. From there, I went down, sometime in March, to Enlisted Personnel.

Q: So you were deeply involved in demobilization of the Coast Guard?

Capron: I was painfully involved, yes.

Q: Before we get into that, there's one other question I'd like to ask you. It has to do with demobilization as well.

During the second World War, the Coast Guard established two new organizations. One of them continues now, but one of them was done away with after the war, the Coast Guard Auxiliary and the temporary Reserve.

The temporary Reserve, I understand, did a lot of the functions that the Coast Guard would normally do in peacetime. Can you elaborate some on that?

Capron: I'll see if I can; I'm going to have to correct you a little bit.

The Auxiliary was originally established as a Coast Guard Reserve about 1939 or '40. Admiral O'Neil ~~Neal~~, incidentally, had a lot to do with it. The Reserve of that day was actually what later became the Auxiliary.

About the time that we got into the war, possibly 3 or 4 months before that, legislation was passed establishing a Coast Guard Reserve and changing the name of the old Coast Guard Reserve to Auxiliary.

The temporary Reserve was actually not any kind of an organization. The people were really temporary members of the Reserve. As such, they did a lot of the duties which regular Coast Guard (I use regular here in the broad sense) had been doing in guarding docks on Port Security, in doing some of the inshore patrol work with small boats, and so forth. The temporary members of the Reserve were never paid. They were all volunteers and they did this on their own time.

Many members of the Auxiliary also served as temporary members of the Reserve. All these small boats I'm speaking of, which were civilian boats to begin with, were manned by Auxiliary people who were temporary members of the Reserve. The boat itself would have a number, CGR something or other.

The temporary members of the Reserve, in many cases, were the reason that we in the regular Coast Guard were able to release men from beach patrol and from Port Security duties to man ships and so forth. Their duties were being taken over, partially at least, by these temporary members of the Reserve.

Q: Were temporary members of the Reserve eligible for the draft? Or was this something that you would use instead?

Capron: They were very much eligible for the draft. The only thing was that most of them were of an age that they were not susceptible to being drafted. Most of them were older men, and many of them were people who were not physically qualified for the draft. So that, it was not a haven for draft dodgers. I doubt if there were one in a hundred of those people that could have been drafted anyway.

They were strictly a volunteer outfit. In fact, the first group of them were in Philadelphia. Strictly volunteers doing all this work on their own time. The only remuneration they got was if they were on duty, they were fed and if they used their own vehicles or boats, Uncle Sam furnished the gasoline.

Q: Sounded like it was a lucky asset to have.

Capron: It was. It was a lucky asset for the whole United States to have, because it released thousands of able-bodied young men that otherwise would have been still tied up.

8 Capron - 328

Q: Going back to demobilization. I imagine the temporary members of the Reserve were also involved in demobilization. Could you tell me how you went about the whole process, what considerations you gave to who was going to stay and where they were going to go - this type of thing?

Capron: In the first place, V-J day as you remember was in late summer of '45, August. Immediately before that, Congress had passed these enormous appropriation bills and so on. They begin to consider what they called recission bills. These would take away money that had already been appropriated but not spent. We went through the same kind of headaches on hearings on those as you would normally go through on appropriations.

At this time, bear in mind, we were still in the Navy. But it wasn't any question that pretty soon we would be going back to Treasury.

We got word that part of the appropriation committee, which considered Treasury Department appropriations, expected us to come down in size to reach our final level and they didn't tell us what the final level would be, on July 1st, '46, at the rate of 10% per month.

Q: 10% of the total amount that was there --

8 Capron - 329

Capron: No, 10% of the decrease. In other words, if we were going to end up with 20,000 men then it would be 10% of the difference between 20,000 and 176,000.

Q: How could you figure that out, if they didn't tell you what your final level would be?

Capron: Reach up in the clouds and come up with an answer, or hopefully an answer. That of course, was one reason why I was on this special detail to come up with the recommended post war complement.

Q: What they were trying to do was make you pick the figure, and see if they could pin you down before they would pin themselves down?

Capron: Practically, yes.

So, we went into demobilization. In the early part of demobilization, it was not too hard. Of course, we had to follow Navy practice to a great extent. But at the same time, we didn't get all the cooperation that we might have gotten.

The mad cry at that time was - "Bring the boys home." Every ship that could float was used to bring them home - aircraft carriers, transports, and everything else.

8 Capron 330

We had a lot of transports that were Coast Guard manned. The committee told us that they would approve our keeping extra people provided that they were defined as essential duty. We tried to get the Navy to make a statement that transports were essential, and they wouldn't do it. Why I don't know, there was a lack of communication somewhere.

So the end result was that we discharged people, we would finally end up with a transport at anchor without enough people to run it. Then the CNO and MSTS, at that time it was NTS, would scream that the Coast Guard wasn't running the ship it was supposed to run. There wasn't any one to run it.

To more or less really compound the difficulty, about January 1st of '46, the Coast Guard was returned to the Treasury Department.

During the time we'd been in the Navy, there was a brand new crowd in the Treasury. Not only that, but there was on the hill a completely new Merchant Marine and Fisheries Committee, and a completely new group of appropriations committee that would handle Coast Guard appropriations.

Q: The Merchant Marine and Fisheries Committee, just for the record, is the committee that considers Coast Guard appropriations

Capron: No, Coast Guard affairs, which might include that.

The appropriations committee itself is broken down into a lot of sub-committees. So we went before a new sub-committee that didn't know anything about us. All they were interested in was you cut back to what you were pre-war.

In the meantime, we had taken on and been given a lot more duties. It was almost impossible to cut back. So we had our troubles there.

We started out by, first of all, selectively releasing people on points. The point system, I don't remember too many of the details, basically it was how long a man had been in, how much time he'd had overseas in combat areas, and so forth. He would be out on points. Our point system was just about the same as the Navy's.

After that, we were still at the point where we had a lot more people than we were going to be able to keep for post war duties. Unfortunately, though, these were all bodies. We had a lot of boatswain's mates, and a lot of quartermasters. We were horribly short of radiomen and ended up by being very short of enginemen. As always, we had all kinds of cooks.

Meanwhile, we still didn't know what the post war Coast Guard was going to be. We started out with 25,000 as a figure. That was reduced to 20,000.

Q: Who reduced it, the Coast Guard or the Congress?

Capron: Congress inferentially reduced it. I say inferentially, because they never did come out until we had our final appropriation wherein, if I remember correctly, they came up with money for 17,000 people. Each time that they changed something, we had to discharge more men.

I mentioned here some time ago in one of the early interviews the 'big bust' we had had in the Coast Guard in 1933, '34. I was determined that we weren't going to have anything, as far as enlisted men were concerned, like that. That it was going to be a general bust, and that we would control it from headquarters. So that it was strictly on the basis of going by the numbers, what day did you make it, and so on, with no attempt to determine whether one man was better than the other one or anything like that.

So we selectively offered discharge to various ratings, to bring them down to what we thought we would need for post war service.

Q: What happened to a person who wanted to stay in the service?

Capron: If he was regular, there wasn't any question. If he was a reservist, he could only stay in if he took a bust to seaman. Unfair, admittedly unfair, but what could we do.

Q: I can see where it would be a problem.

Capron: Yes. Another big problem too was that Congress, in the attempt to build up volunteer and recruiting as opposed to the draft, passed in October what was called the Red Apple Bill, which had a lot of inducements in there to get people to reenlist.

One of those inducements was that anybody who reenlisted within 90 days of the passing of that act, reenlisted permanently in his grade and couldn't be reduced from that grade, except for court martial or something like that. So anybody who was lucky to have his discharge come up during that 90 days and reenlisted was guaranteed the rate that he reenlisted.

Actually, we had to bust back almost everybody. Almost everybody was busted back one grade. We also put into effect the rule that if it became necessary for a man to go back more than one grade, we'd give him his discharge.

We couldn't bust the so-called "Red Apple Boys." Here we had this special group, many of them Chief Petty Officers.

Q: It was just because they were in that 90 day period.

Capron: Yes, just because they were in that 90 day period.

So we were in the position of busting people who would maybe have had 5 or 10 years more service in the ~~Navy.~~ Coast Guard.

Q: You must have had a lot of people knocking on your door.

Capron: We did. The best thing that every happened to me was, in the first place, I insisted and got away with, that the bust for enlisted and officers take place on the same day.

What we did, on about the 25th of June, we sent out and made everybody permanent in all the grades. Not the grade they were holding, but told them what their permannent grade was. Then on the 30th of June, with an ALCOAST, we busted everybody back to his permanent grade. The thing I insisted on was that officers all be busted on the same day as the enlisted.

It so happened that I was busted from Captain to Commander.

We did a lot of things. We let the Chiefs, for instance, that were busted work for a year wearing their Chief's uniform with a first class insignia. As a matter of fact, we let them wear it longer than that. Of course, they were the ones that felt they were hurt the most.

I had two signs on my desk. I had one that said "Captain," and one that said, "Commander."

When one of these busted Chiefs would come in and tell me what a sad story it was and how his neighbors wondered what was wrong with him and everything else, I just pointed to those signs and said, "I know, Chief, exactly how you feel. I got busted too."

Q: I guess it was good that everybody got it.

Capron: We ended up with a strength of 17,000 at that point. Then, when all of a sudden, the Congressmen found out that their favorite lifeboat stations were also going to take a cut to be within this 17,000, then a big hullaboo was raised. And they passed a supplemental appropriation bill to give us 500 additional men, who must be stationed at lifeboat stations. So, for one year, we had to work in that kind of a framework. That wasn't easy either.

Q: Were you the one that was involved in determining where these people were going to go, as well? For instance - A seaman was stationed on a transport or a destroyer, he was then transferred to his peacetime station.

Capron: Actually, no. We did this: People who came from units that had been a long long way from home, the Far East and so forth, we did give those individuals an opportunity to give their first, second, and third choice of districts. When you could, you'd send him there.

Unfortunately the word would get around that a certain district would be the best district, so everybody would want to go there. Quite often it didn't turn out to be as nice as they thought it was going to be.

The same thing applies now, or it did ten years ago when people were coming back from Loran Station. They'd ask for either the St. Louis district or the 7th district or maybe the 11th. There was a lot of unpleasant duty down in the 7th district, even though it was warm.

Those lighthouses out on the keys for instance: take a guy who's been out in the Philippines, let's say, on Loran Station that's not isolated and you put him out on Alligator Reef right down in Florida. He isn't going to be very happy.

Q: He isn't any better off than he was before.

Capron: Worse.

We did give those people as much a choice as we could. But as far as all the rest, it was a question of directing a district to transfer so many people of such and such a rating to another district. The districts themselves made the selections.

Q: Since you were involved in enlisted personnel and probably were aware of the officers as well, how would you characterize the personnel situation of the Coast Guard as far as quality goes, between just prior to the second World War and post second World War? Did you have better men?

Capron: I don't know, quality wise I don't think there was too much of a change. There were certain things that took place after the war; we had some pretty rough periods. We had ships that didn't move for 5 or 6 months, didn't have enough men.

We had one ship for instance that was stuck up in Argentia about 6 months, it was PONTCHARTRAIN. I know several regular officers on there were Academy graduates, who were not war time graduates. In other words they had entered the Academy before war time, so they were essentially career men. One of them was a young cousin of mine. They were on the PONTCHARTRAIN up there. They finally got so fed up that they just resigned and got out. So we lost some very good officers that way.

At that time, it was pretty difficult to retain many of our reserve officers. We had some very outstanding ones. All of the promotions during the war were temporary. We had promoted a lot of former Warrant Officers up as high as 2½ or 3 stripes. Where educationally they might not be up to the standards of regular officers, the college graduate type, in many ways they couldn't approach them. When it came to certain types of jobs, they were outstanding.

We, the Coast Guard, had to make some determinations then as to how many reserve officers could be integrated. And how many of the former Warrant Officers could be retained in commission grades. Then balance that all with the number of regularly commissioned officers that we had that we couldn't fire.

I had nothing to do with those determinations, but they were made at the Chief of Staff level. At that time, they had a division up there they called Program Planning that worked all of that out.

All of this, of course, was in terms of money. As far as the rank structure's concerned, that was before Title 14 as it is now was enacted, we used the Navy's percentages as a guide. Later on, it was enacted into law so there was no difficulty.

Q: You mean percentages of people in --

Capron: The number of flag officers, Captains, Commanders, and so on down. That's all contained in the law.

Within those limits, we had to determine what and how we would retain our officers. They had a number of boards, selection boards, retention boards, and so on.

In some case, there'd be a former Warrant Officer that was just too old to be a Lieutenant. You couldn't give him 2½ or 3, so you'd offer him Chief Warrant, even though you might know that he had the competency to fill this higher grade. But you weren't about to make a 50 year old man a Lieutenant; that was kind of an insult. Those were the type of problems that we had.

After that, then came the education of the committees in Congress as well as Treasury. At that time, Admiral O'Neill was Assistant Commandant and Admiral Farley the Commandant. There was a lot of education that had to be done.

I would say by 1950, we'd reached the point where they were pretty well educated. They knew what the Coast Guard was, and what the Coast Guard was supposed to do. They had also come to the conclusion that instead of us being very *prodigal* in our use of men, we were very economical. So, we began to get pretty nearly what we asked for in the way of men. We never did have a numerical ceiling on enlisted; all we had was money. We had to tailor everything within the money limits.

Q: We're talking about excess people now. I would guess that by the late forties people would be leaving the service and the Coast Guard would have to go back into recruiting.

Capron: We went into a heavy recruiting during demobilization. We had to get apprentice seamen. There weren't any; we had to go out and recruit. We had to do a lot of our heavy recruiting. That was one of the things that caused us so much trouble later on.

Q: That must have been tough to explain.

Capron: You can take any given crisis, and we were always having them, in personnel. If you had a three year enlistment at that time, you knew that three years from now you were going to have another hump when all the boys that you get to enlist now, that their three years are going to be up. Anybody that knew anything about personnel would realize that. You try, if possible, to smooth that curve out.

Meanwhile, every commanding officer and every district commander was yelling for more men and he didn't give a darn what happened three years from now. He needed the men right now. Those of us that were trying to do the planning, we were in betwixt and between. We knew we were just fixing ourselves up for the future.

So we had that, yes. That period we were frantically recruiting apprentice seamen, at the same time that we were letting many go in droves.

Q: I can understand why you did it. I can see the necessity for it. But I would also imagine that there were people who were being released who might not have wanted to be released.

Capron: There were a lot of people who didn't want to be, but they were all in the upper grades. We had to have the seamen, the firemen. The second class Petty Officers: we were lousy with good ones. But the man wouldn't have stayed as a seaman; many of them were married. So on the one hand you had experienced men going out because they were too experienced and on the other hand we were out beating the bushes for enlisting more. We had that difficulty all the time I was down there.

It wasn't until the draft was reinstituted, which was around 1947 or '48, that we began to have reasonable success in recruiting people.

I had four years in that job that were probably as interesting as any four years I ever had, and probably one of the toughest that I ever had.

Q: I can appreciate it. Tell me about your next assignment, how it came about.

8 Capron - 342

Capron: I wanted to go to sea again. I talked it over with the then chief personnel officer. He told me, "You ought to go out on the district. You've had enough sea duty, so you don't have to worry about it." I still wanted some. So being in the position I was, my relief was already ordered in, I asked to go back to the SPENCER again. I went back to her in August of 1950.

Q: What was the SPENCER's duty then?

Capron: Ocean station.

Q: That's something else we haven't talked about.
Did the Coast Guard go right back to weather patrols after the war?

Capron: In a way, yes. We discussed here one or two times before.
The Coast Guard got into this weather patrol business, first of all, prior to World War II when they had a couple vessels that were sending in weather reports for trans-Atlantic flying. Then, during the war, we got into it in a big way.
After the war, it looked as if we were going to get out of it. And I guess an awful lot of people hoped we'd get out of it. There was a pretty general demand from the flying

public that the Coast Guard should maintain weather stations.

At about the same time as a result of World War II, this group which was PICAO, which was the Provisional International Committee on Air Operations, was set up. Later on, they dropped the P and it was no longer Provisional.

Later on they operated under the United Nations Under that, all these nations agreed to establish certain weather stations. The United States agreed to set up some, and the English, the Dutch, Canada, and I believe Japan. As far as the international agreement was concerned, the United States would establish these stations.

Within the United States, it was determined the Coast Guard was the one that would do it. So we got into that business soon after the war. Whether there was an actual period when we didn't have any or not, I don't remember. It might have been a period of several months, but I don't think so.

Q: When you were on the SPENCER, how many weather stations were there?

Capron: There was A, which was up off of Greenland. There was B up there, and a C, D, and E. So there would have been five at that time. These were U. S. manned, in the Atlantic.

Q: Were there any in the Pacific?

Capron: At that time, yes. Most of the time we had two. However there was one period, during Korea, that we had about half a dozen out there.

That's when we took a bunch of Navy DE's back; the ones we had during World War II. We put them back in commission and used them out there on weather stations. They were strictly a Korean War deal. As soon as things folded up on that, they were done away with.

For awhile there was only one station; that was the one between Honolulu and San Francisco. There was another station out there that was manned by Canadians, off the west coast of Canada, that actually is half and half as far as responsibility is concerned.

There was one on the Atlantic that was the same way. We manned the one in the Atlantic for both Candad and U. S. They manned the one in the Pacific full time for the two countries.

Q: I don't think the machine knows what's involved in a weather patrol. Could you tell me a little bit about what it's like and what you do?

Capron: I think it's best to start out by saying that the vessels on ocean stations, which is the real name for them, have a dual mission. One: to collect and obtain weather data from not only the surface of the ocean, which is very simple, but from the upper air, all the way up to 30 or 40,000 feet, which is done by balloons, which have instruments attached, and a radio transmitter.

As the balloon rises, the transmitter signals back to the ship. You get the temperature, the barometric pressure, and the humidity that way. By tracking them with either theodolite, range finder, and radar, you get the rate at which they are going both up and out. By triangulations, determine from that the wind strength at any give height of the balloon.

Those basically are normally released every four hours. All that information is then transmitted back to the weather bureau in the United States. It is from that information that the various air routes are laid out, changed sometimes, and so on for trans-Atlantic flying.

As additional missions, you also provide a beacon service for planes. You've got a radio beacon there that is transmitting most of the time. You've got to maintain your position within a ten mile square on the ocean. You're supposed to be in the center of it. If you're in the center of it, your radio beacon sends one signal. As you drift off, it will be a different signal. So the pilot then can, from the beacon, determine exactly what part of your ten mile square you're in, and thereby position himself accurately.

At the same time, at his request, you give him weather conditions and a few of the other things he might need. For instance, he has no way usually of telling whether he's bucking a head wind or tail winds or what he's up against.

As a further thing and probably the most romantic about it, fortunately it doesn't happen very often. If there is a vessel on station in the event of aircraft who either has to ditch or does ditch - we had two or three occasions where aircraft did have to ditch. They ditched alongside of the ocean station ship and all hands were saved.

Q: Were you involved in any of these?

Capron: I was involved later on from a shore position with the Pan American Boeing Stratocruiser that went down between Honolulu and San Francisco. That was some years later.

There have been probably as many as half a dozen times when commercial airlines had, for one reason or another, to ditch. Whenever they've been able to ditch near one of the ocean station vessels, all hands have been saved.

Q: What about search and rescue to ships?

Capron: You are always available. If there is a case that comes up, in which you are the closest vessel, you're always authorized to leave to handle the job. There again once you got out of your circle, you had to shut off that beacon. There were a number of other things you had to go through.

Let's face it, the commanding officer is the one who usually has to make the final decision. He has to weigh maybe the advantages and disadvantages relatively of leaving his station for a vessel that may not be truly in distress. There may be airplanes without anybody to look after them navigationally.

Q: When you were out there, storms must have come up periodically. How does the weather ship maintain it's position in storms, or is it necessary?

Capron: You've got two problems. One is staying on station. The other one is determining, from the navigational standpoint, when you aren't on station.

Most stations are so located that you could use loran. You do use loran plus celestial sights, stars, and so forth.

There are some stations where your loran is only partially good.

In 1950, '51 I was involved in Station Echo, which was then called Easy. We could only get one loran line. If you could get a fix and you had to one way or another, you had to get some kind of a celestial observation. Sometimes of the year, you don't see the sun very often. You sounded as well. They had pretty well charted those stations, with getting soundings by echo ranging and so forth. That is a help.

As far as the actual staying on station in a storm is concerned, there again that's up to the seamanship of the people that are on board.

I know of one case where a ship was blown off. They got a couple of hundred miles off, staying in the middle of the storm all the way. If they had steamed through it, they could have been back on the station in a few hours when the storm had gone past. That didn't reflect very highly of the commanding officer. There again, there was some kind of technicality.

The old Secretary Class, the 327s, were not too long-legged as modern ships go. So that on one of the distant stations, you would conserve your fuel very carefully because you knew for sure that if you didn't and you were on the way home, there'd be a distress case and you'd be stuck without enough fuel to handle it. So you arrived at an arbitrary figure of percentage of fuel that you would not let yourself get below.

For that reason I used to, for instance, once every four to eight hours, after you knew what the wind direction was and you knew what some of the currents were doing, would go up to the extreme corner of your ten mile square. Then shut everything down and drift. You have some 10 or 15 miles that you'd drift, and then you'd go back and do it all over again.

The AVPs, diesel and very long-legged, didn't have to worry about things like that. They had enough that they could get underway.

Of course lots of times we had to get underway to provide artificial wind for the weather observors, if you didn't have any wind. A baloon going straight up was no good; it had to go off at a certain angle. So in order to buy that angle, you had to provide the artificial wind by getting underway and maybe steaming up to 15 knots. That, of course, would be completely independent of any station. Or you tried, if you could, to combine the two.

I was on the SPENCER that time somewhere around 6 to 8 months. While I was on there, incidentially, Korea was really breaking.

I remember we felt awfully alone on patrol because we got no kind of instructions from the beach or anything else. All we knew about the Korean War was what we'd heard on the radio, most on BBC (British Broadcasting Corporation). When the Chinese crossed the Yalu, we were sure that that was the outbreak of general war.

I guess every ship took different steps. I just put into effect all the wartime buttoning up that we did during the war – watertight doors, darkening the ship, and everything else. But we still had running lights. I operated just as if we were in a war zone.

Apropos of the outbreak, that was the marked increase in the Port Security problem. So I was detached rather suddenly and ordered up to the 3rd district office in New York.

Q: Did you want to get transferred?

Capron: No, I did every thing I could. The district commander said finally, "I guess you don't want to come up here and work for me." That kind of pinned my ears back a little bit and I said, "Oh, it isn't anything like that." I ended up by being transferred.

We were setting up then the Port Security for the 3rd district. I was in charge of that, which included New York and Philadelphia. Those were our main ports.

I stayed there until about the middle of August, at which time I was transferred to the National War College here in Washington.

Q: Had you requested that?

Capron: I had requested that a year previous, and had been given unofficial assurance that I probably would be the one selected.

Q: How many are selected each year?

Capron: One.

The National War College had 120 students, which are broken down into 30 Army, 30 Air Force, and 30 Navy. Of the 30 Navy, six are Marines and one is Coast Guard. There were 30 civilians, who came from various departments - state department, CIA, Treasury, and various departments that have jobs that call for that type of training.

Q: Why did you want to go to the Nataional War College?

Capron: Why does anybody want to go to school? In the first place, there is a lot of prestige involved, but that wasn't the real reason. Two very good friends of mine had attended in earlier classes and told me exactly what it was like and everything else. I just really wanted to go. It's 10 months that is pretty rough.

Very satisfying, that's how I feel. You wouldn't take a million for the one you had, but you wouldn't have another one for a million. I don't know that I'd ever want to go through that same 10 months again.

Q: Can you tell me something about what you studied?

Capron: Basically the course there is broken down in two semesters. The fall semester is strictly what you might call broadly educational. You study the economics of practically every country in the world, and all the political angles of various countries. You study their geography. It's very broad in the studies that you have to carry out. They're laid out pretty carefully. There is no such thing as reciting; there is no such thing as marks. You either graduate with honors, or you're kicked out.

Q: Are people kicked out?

Capron: I've heard of one or two.

If you stop and figure out, that is the highest school under the military service. It's directly ~~in with~~ under the Joint Chiefs. With the numberof people who might like to go, you can see the service is going to be pretty doggone careful in it's selection. So you don't have to ride herd on anybody that goes.

Also you study various strategies, not military strategy, but various strategies that are possible to attain political ends and so forth of our own country and so forth.

The second half of the year is all military, military strategy in making various studies and so on. Again this is in the highest strategy angle; it's not how you fight a battle or anything like that.

During that period they have two weeks that everybody goes on an orientation trip to some part of the world that you haven't been to too much. In my case, I went to Japan, Korea, Okinawa, and generally the Far East.

They had one group that went to northern Europe and one group that went to southern Europe.

At the time I went, MacArthur was still in Tokyo. His headquarters was one of our points that we had to visit.

That basically is what the War College is. As I say, there are no instructors as such. There are instructors there.

8 Capron - 354

Everyone gives a lecture, followed by a question period. Then you would break up into committees. You'd hash over everything you had heard that morning and so forth. You'd also hash over the problem that you'd been given.

The committees were rotated about once every two weeks, so you finally ended up by having served on a committee with every member of the student body. A committee would be given some kind of a problem to study. They would spend their afternoon studying that, looking up various details and so on, and fainally coming up with a committee solution to this problem. Then you had a chairman of that committee, the chairmen would rotate during these periods, he had to get up in front of the entire student body and present a paper on how they analyzed the problem, all the pros and cons, and their answer.

Q: Was it a problem a day?

Capron: No, at that time it was about one every two weeks. You do have a problem a day that you kick around in that hour's discussion in the morning. But the big one, they usually give out every two weeks. Some occasionally would be one week, and once in a while three weeks.

Q: What does the Coast Guard hope to gain by sending a Coast Guardsman to the National War College?

Capron: In the first place, you gain knowledge from knowing an awful lot of people. People that later on are valuable to know, not to you as an individual but to the Coast Guard.

For instance, just the other day there was an Alumni Association luncheon over here at Fort Meyer. President of the Washington chapter is a four striper who is a recent graduate of the National War College. The speaker was General Lemnitzer, formerly Supreme Commander of NATO and formerly Army Chief of Staff. He also, at one time, was Superintendent over there at the War College.

In my job, later on, as Deputy Chief of Staff, when I had to have so many contacts to go over with the Army, with the Navy, and with the various civilian branches, the fact that I had gone to school or the fact that I had been there. I'd meet somebody who had been there the year before I had been there, or the year after I had. The mere fact that I had been there; let's say I belonged to the club, if you will. The result was that it made it very easy to talk to somebody. You talked the same language and understood each other. Lots of times there'd be things that you'd want to put across that would be much easier under those circumstances.

The Coast Guard sends an officer to the Naval War College, one to the National here, and several to the Armed Forces Staff College in Norfolk. At the moment, I don't know whether they send anybody over to the Industrial College over here in Washington or not. They didn't when I was on active duty.

Q: Captain, what was your next assignment after the National War College?

Capron: I came back to Coast Guard headquarters as Chief of the Programs Analysis Division.

Q: Is this the normal thing to happen? In other words, people who go to the National War College have a particular assignment that they go through afterwords?

Capron: Yes, there are certain assignments that are usually used. Not only that, as an economical measure, and convenient for the individual rather than upsetting them by sending them another place after only a year, they give them another tour in headquarters.

In my case I went to the Programs Analysis Division, under which was the War Plans Section of the Coast Guard. There again, that's where having been to the War College helped me.

The three officers that were in that War Plans Section, the requirements were that one of them had to be an aviator, one had to be a War College graduate, and one had to be an Armed Forces Staff College graduate. As a general rule, when an officer was sent to one of those schools, he was more or less pegged where he was going when he finished.

I was in that job from 1952 until about February of 1955.

Q: What did the job involve?

Capron: For one thing it involved preparation of all the necessary data for our budget, supporting arguments and so on. We were supposed to do a lot of the advanced planning for the whole Coast Guard.

The War Plans Section was a specialists group. That planning of course consisted of making plans for the budget for future years, working up the arguements and working very closely with what was called the Budget Division.

Then supposedly an analysis, at the end of a period of time, every year or what have you, as to how close to your goals you had come. I say supposedly because we never had enough people to do that part of the job. That part of the job was a part that was more or less glossed over. We just didn't have enough people to do it. It just happened to be something you could get away with.

Q: How far in advance did you plan?

Capron: In general, it would be five years.

Again, on that one, on your general planning for construction, what the Coast Guard call AC&I, for your appropriations on that and plans and everything else, that's at least five years.

For your operating, I would say that you can't do much more than a couple of years in advance on that one. Conditions are changing and everything else.

Q: I guess in every period in the service there's one particular thing that totally dominates everything around it. What dominated your planning while you were Chief of the Division?

Capron: This was during Korea. It was also during a great period of expansion of the Loran system. This was still Loran-A, not Loran-C. Loran-C was still four or five years off.

One of the biggest things we had to do in our planning was to catch up with many years of neglect, you might say, of our physical planting. Our Coast Guard physical plant was pretty well run down, ashore and afloat.

Q: Why did this happen?

Capron: If you don't get money from Congress, you don't spend it. It isn't always Congress either, it's the particular administration you're with and their policies, and the Bureau of the Budget, and occasionally the Treasury, and so on.

I'm not sure if my figure is right at the moment, but I believe that last year for instance the Coast Guard got somewhere in the neighborhood of $75,000,000 for what they call AC&I, which is Acquisition Construction and Improvement. That money was appropriated and always available. It was different from operating money. That's what they used to build ships, build new stations, imporve the stations, or things like that, other than routine maintenance.

The first year of the Eisenhower administration, we got $500,000.

Out of that also comes the cost of new buoys and their appendages and so on, out of their AC&I. Actually the $500,000 we got that one year didn't quite pay for all the buoys we had. Those are the two very great extremes.

In the first place, in about 1950 or '51 there was a committee set up at the direction of the appropriation committee in Congress. This *Committee* was set up to study the needs of Coast Guard aviation and determine what they needed.

What they needed, how many aircraft, a partial survey of the conditions of what we already had, and come up with a recommended procurement schedule.

That went in, and for awhile there was a lot of pulling and tugging between the Administration and the Hill on it. Finally, there was a show down one year when the appropriations committee just slashed everything. They said, "No when you come in with that plan, then we'll put the money back in."

That started us on our aviation procurement program. That worked very very well.

There is one thing about airplanes. If a ship breaks down, it will still float. You may have to tow it in, but it will still float. If the roof on a lifeboat station leaks, you can always put a bucket under it to catch the water. But if an airplane quits, it doesn't stay up in the air, it comes down. So automatically, the air people and the aviation part of the Coast Guard had a much better argument than anybody else had. That seemed to work pretty well.

Several years later, this is after I ceased to be in CPA, I'd gone to the west coast and was back as Deputy Chief of Staff, there was another committee set up on ships and shore stations. I was made the chairman of that committee.

We came up with, after some two years of study and so on, our ship plan. (Bear in mind that all of this is additional work for members of one of those committees.) Which was adopted and finally approved by the Secretary of the Treasury.

That's the one these new cutters are under, the MELLON and those ships. New buoy tenders, in fact everything that's been built since the 95 footers was under that particular plan.

We never did, as a group, find ourselves able to handle all the shore stations. So we dissolved and another group was set up that did the same thing for all the shore stations. I believe that master plan was, more or less, accepted.

Of course they outgrew our plans. They were too specific, they had to broaden.

I think generally that's the kind of planning the Coast Guard had to do. Most of it was forced on us by years and years of not getting any money, or not enough money to do anything with. Our poor old ships finally wore out. After all of the AVPs that were still running, most of those were wartime built ships. They're being replaced now, after all this time. The 327s were built in '35 and '36; they were a much better-built ship, but that's still pretty old for a ship.

8 Capron - 362

Q: What was the Coast Guard's role in the Korean War?

Capron: Combat wise, practically none.

We did have one loran station that was established on the outskirts of Pusan. That was continually raided by bandits. They actually had to have barbed wire all around them, and everything else.

There were several areas in there, in the non-combat phases, that we did a lot. Loran of course was one of the big ones. We established a whole lot of new loran stations. Everything in the western Pacific was brand new, set up for Korea. They provided the navigation system for both the Air Force and the Navy in all their planes and so forth that were going out to the westward. I've forgotten exactly how many loran stations were set up, probably in the neighborhood of 20 or 25.

In addition, with all those aircraft flying, we had to set up search and rescue outfits. We set them up at Guam, with a couple of planes. We had one at Manila and Sangley Point. We had a number of ships that were designed for search and rescue purposes and RCCs set up throughout the Pacific, all of which were designed to facilitate the passage of aircraft. And also rescue, if they had to ditch or anything like that.

I would say basically that. Plus back in the states, the grealy increased emphasis on Port Security.

Q: I know this is a touchy subject for everybody.

Was the increased Port Security in the United States, during the Korean War, a case of crying wolf?

Capron: I don't know. I don't think that anyone could answer that unless he could read Stalin's mind.

Q: How did you fell about it at that time? Not how you feel about it now.

Capron: There wasn't any question in my mind, at that time that we were extremely vulnerable to any kind of infiltration, either with atomic weapons or chemical or biological. We were wide open. If Russia had wanted to they could have wiped out New York without any trouble.

We did have actual cases where some things were smuggled in. I don't think there was ever any case of anything even remotely resembling an atomic weapon that way. But we did have the *things* smuggled in that were weapons, without any question.

We had the case of the BATORY, which came in over here. That was the one that that east German communist escaped on.

So that, as things were going at that time, I felt that there wasn't any question we needed Port Security.

To get back to your 'crying wolf'. I do not think that we were. But you've got to be in the position in order to really answer that, you have to be able to either have access to Russian files of those days and be able to read them

The Russians had the capability to do all these things. We did not have the capability of preventing it. So what it boils down to is, 'did they want to or didn't they'.

I don't doubt but what the McCarthyism of that day -- I won't say it caused all of this. I don't think it had anything to do with it, in that sense. I think the Port Security did. Except that in each case, it represented a national thinking and a fear of what might happen.

Right now, I think the country is going the other way. I'm getting into politics now.

Q: Those are very political questions.

What was your next assignment after headquarters?

Capron: After that headquarters, I was ordered to the 12th district, San Francisco, as Operations Officer. That was about March, 1955.

8 Capron - 365

I remained there as Operations Officer until the 1st of July, 1957. During that period, we had one Chief of Staff transferred and change in district commanders. Finally the new Chief of Staff arrived there and had a stroke the day he got there.

I ended up my last years as being both Operations Officer and Chief of Staff of the 12th district. I found that very very intersting work. I enjoyed it very much.

It was during that period that I had the contact which we mentioned here sometime back with one of the airplanes that had to ditch.

Q: What was that?

Capron: That was a Pan American Boeing Stratocruiser, which was bound from Honolulu to San Francisco. It lost an engine about half way over, between Honolulu and the continent. Another one began running rough. There wasn't any question in the pilot's mind that he wouldn't have enough fuel left to make San Francisco. He was quite close to our ocean station vessel, the PONTCHARTRAIN, which was on station November.

So he called the station and told them his problems and everything else. He and the Captain, whose name was

Earl, of the PONTCHARTRAIN, talked things over and they decided that the thing to do would be to wait until daylight. Circling all the time, deliberately using up fuel for one thing. Soon after dawn, they would then ditch.

During the long night, which was several hours, Earl personally carried on conversation with the pilot. They decided which would be the best course for dtiching. There were a lot of technicalities to that - like which way the seas were running, which way the swelling were running, the wind, try to land with controlling swells. It's quite a technical proposition. They arrived at all of that.

At a given signal early in the morning the PONTCHARTRAIN steamed down, this was standard procedure for ditching, and made a slick. The Pan American plane came in and landed on that slick and ditched.

Q: Were they in touch with you during this?

Capron: Yes, we were sweating it out on the beach.
I was at this time the acting district commander of the 12th district, who was also commander of the western area. He and the deputy area commander were both in Bangkok. So, I was wearing about five hats.

The people called me from the comm center, the RRC, along about seven o'clock and told me everything that was happening. They were now waiting to find out how things were going. So I told them I'd stay home and would not pester them with telephone calls or anything else. They had plenty to do. But they were to let me know the minute anything happened and somebody was available to call me up.

Of course I knew very well that every newspaper in California would have his reporter up there pestering him and all that stuff.

That's what happened. They set down. All the time they were flying around, everybody in the United States were beginning to hear about this. It made every kind of news service, wire service, and everything there was.

They had picked up everybody. The plane went down very shortly thereafter. Then we had a problem.

I was acting area deputy commander. Here we had the PONTCHARTRAIN out there 1,000 miles out with all these people aboard. I've forgotten how many there were, 50 or 60 people. Although the PONTCHARTRAIN is a fairly good sized ship, they don't carry food for all those extra people for weeks at a time. There were women and children too.

I gave orders that the standby ship, which was supposed to get underway in six hours from Seattle, was to get out there in a hurry.

We tried to find some ship that could bring all those survivors in and there wasn't anything. The best thing was a Navy reserve destroyer on a reserve cruise bound for Honolulu. They agreed that they would do it, but pointed out just what it would mean to this reserve cruise alone. Plus the fact that a destroyers couldn't take care of these people even as well as the PONTCHARTRAIN could.

It became quite evident that the only thing to do was to bring that ship in. So I did. I ordered them in.

I called up Richmond, who was the Commandant here in Washington, and told him I'd ordered them in. In fact, I called him up first and asked him, "Should I order them in?" He said, "That's your problem." He was right. I told him everything that happened and he said, "I'm glad that you've called me because in a few minutes I'm going up on the Hill to testify for our appropriation. This will be first hand news for the Congressmen."

We ordered them in, and we had to leave the station unattended for about two days until the other ship got out. We brought them into San Francisco.

From then on, it became quite a deal. Newspaper men from all over the country were flocking in, television people and everybody.

Meanwhile, the people out on the PONTCHARTRAIN, as far as they were concerned, it was a routine job.

I called a conference of all my officers there to determine what should we do. Here we had all these people coming in. Fortunately two of my officers had been in Boston when the Bermuda SKY QUEEN, which was another plane that had to ditch, was brought in by the BIBB a number of years ago. Public relations wise, that was one of the most horribly mismanaged things there has ever been. I mean completely mismanaged.

I had these two officers, one was the comptroller and the other was a chief engineer of the district, that had been in Boston. I asked them, "Let's figure out now. What did they do wrong in Boston that we won't do now?" We had three or four days to do our planning in. There was an awful lot of planning to do.

They told me all the things that happened in Boston. Among other things, they took newspapermen out to meet the BIBB outside the harbor. All these survivors had put in a pretty rough time and weren't too happy to have all these photographers and newspapermen climbing all over them right in the beginning. When they got into the pier, all of the friends and relatives that had been waiting for them were so engulfted again by the television and newspapermen that they couldn't even talk to each other. The whole thing was a mess.

We made our plans pretty carefully. One thing, the PONTCHARTRAIN was going to need fuel. We were bringing her into a city dock. One of the city's regulations are that you can't fuel a ship alongside of the dock. We went to all the right people and got a waiver on that. We knew very well the ship was going to be out of supplies, so we had to radio the men and find out what stores they wanted. They had to go back within 10 or 12 hours, and go back to their home station, which was down in Long Beach. We did all of that.

The television was going to go on national hookup. I knew that Captain Earl didn't know too much about San Francisco. San Francisco is just about as tricky as the Narrows in New York. If you don't know the currents, you can really wreck a ship just trying to dock. Furthermore, San Francisco fogs are famous. The TV people had everything cleared for time and all that.

I sent a message to Earl, "Suggest you take a pilot." He came back, "I don't need a pilot." I sent one finally and made it as strong as I could, without ordering. That's one thing you don't usually do, order a skipper to take a pilot. So, he finally agreed to take one.

Pam Am was very interested in all of this, vitally interested. One of the things we were avoiding was the use of the word 'survivors'. After all, you don't kill off your prospects of future flights with that. And yet, there wasn't any question, it was a big big thing. Pam Am were doing their best to prove, and they did, that the reason it went off so successfully was the fact that that very plane crew within the last week had been over to our air station and trained in this ditching drill. We had a fuselage anchored out in the water, they knew how to get out of the thing and all that. Pam Am blew that up and that didn't make us mad either.

We talked it over with them, and Pam Am decided that it would be a very smart idea, and asked if we'd help them on it, to get new clothes out to everybody. Most of these people had been in the water, and had been living in the same clothes for four or five days. None of them had shoes. In that particular procedure, the first thing you do is take off your shoes.

Pam Am sent out a long list of questions, getting sizes on every passenger and crew member. They finally got all the dope. They had about a dozen of their hostesses out shopping around San Francisco. They made everything up into suitcases and tagged them for whoever it was for. Somebody was smart enought to realize that the exchange on the PONTCHARTRAIN would not be carrying rouge and lipstick and all that stuff. So we even got some of that to send down.

They were due early in the morning at the lightship. So we had the GRESHAM go out and carry all these packages out and transfer them by boat over to the PONTCHARTRAIN, out at the lightship to the same place they took the pilot. There was about two hours run from the lightship into the dock, so those people had plenty of time to change clothes and get spruced up.

When they came in, I think it was about 10 o'clock when they hit the dock, sure enough there was television grinding away. I saw the PONTCHARTRAIN coming in, and I hoped the commercial pilot on there was a good ship handler. He was; he put her right in there exactly where she should be. We had a tug standing by when he came in.

That's another thing that happened in Boston. When they came in, they smacked the dock.

We had made arrangements on the dock. We had one area set aside for the friends and relative of the survivors. We had another area set aside for all the newsmen and photographers. We had gotten ahold of them and told them, "You've got to stay away from that area until the survivors have a chance to speak to their friends and relatives who've been waiting. Once they do that, then you're on your own." With one or two exceptions, they accepted that okay.

So the whole thing went off pretty well I think, and everybody else seemed to think so.

We picked up the pictures that had been taken on the PONTCHARTRAIN by the helicopter on the lightship. By the time the PONTCHARTRAIN was in, some of those were on the front page of the newspapers being sold on the street.

Q: That's a pretty famous rescue. I hear a lot about it; one of the more spectacular ones.

Captain your next assignment, you went from Chief of Staff of the district to Deputy Chief of Staff at headquarers. Did you ask for this duty?

Capron: I did not ask for it. I was very much surprised when I got it at that time, specifically at that time because there was no Chief of Staff as such in the Coast Guard. The Assistant Commandant wore two hats. So that the Deputy Chief of Staff was damn near the Chief of Staff.

Q: It's what the Chief of Staff is right now.

Capron: Practically what the Chief of Staff is right now. As a matter of fact, that was my office.

So it was a decided promotion, as far as responsibility was concerned. I felt pretty good about it. I came somewhere around the middle of July, 1957. I remained in that job until I retired the 1st of September, 1962.

Q: What were some of the highlights during that period of time? What would you list as your greatest accomplishments?

Capron: Probably what I have already mentioned. Our Committee on Ship requirements and replacement was probably the one single one.

However our Loran-C program, which in some areas was quite highly classified, was highly urgent and extremely urgent at that time.

We set up kind of a system, you might say, quite similar to the Navy system on their Polaris submarines, of expediting and building of these various Loran-C stations. Most of those Loran-C stations, at that time, were budgeted entirely by the Navy. They turned the funds over to us.

The extreme urgency of that system was such that we had to streamline everything. This included the system in the Mediterranean, the system in the North Atlantic, and also a system in the Pacific including Alaska and Honolulu and so forth. So I was given an assistant to be expediter for the Loran-C construction.

When we started that first chain, the one on the Mediterranean, the final transmitter hadn't even been designed yet. All we had was a laboratory model. We had a dead line in about 12 months, to get the whole system on the air. It required then an awful lot of expediting, chasing, and so on. Right within the Coast Guard alone we had aides to navigation people, we had electronic engineers, we had the civil engineers, and so on. All of which had their own parts to play. But somebody had to keep them together.

In addition, we were going into foreign countries. We had to have State Department concurrence. We had to have somebody working with the State Department and in many cases going over to these foreign countries and working deals. Some of the diplomatic deals we had to work were really something. France was one of the toughest ones we had to deal with, so was Great Britain. Denmark and Norway were wonderful.

We got that chain on the air in the time that it had to be done.

I had nothing to do with the actual building. The thing of coordinating that construction was done from the top, apportioning the money out and so forth.

One of the hardest things was getting somebody to design a tower that we could build in Alaska, 1300 feet high, without knowing what the winds and icing conditions had ever been there before, that would stand up. Everything had to be designed in pieces, so that it could be hauled up there on barges and be constructed in about the only three months of the year that they could build it.

Q: Did it work?

Capron: It hasn't blown down yet.

Then the usual thing of fighting off Congressmen who wanted the contract for one of their constituents, or their particular area. Senator Magnuson was the guy who saved us many many headaches. We were able to tellhim the whole story and some of his committeemen would start embarrassing questions. We could call the Senator, and he could just shut them up.

That was a one single thing. Among the other ones, I felt when I'd got all through that I'd accomplished an awful lot in the job. I was the last Deputy without a Chief of Staff.

Q: Who was the Commandant at that time?

Capron: Richmond.

Q: Were you under Richmond the whole time?

Capron: The last six months, I was under Eddie Roland.

Q: Did you notice any difference in the way the two handled --

Capron: I wouldn't say that I noticed any particular difference, no.

Eddie Roland was the class behind me at the Academy. I knew Eddie Roland personally as a contemporary. Richmond had been an instructor at the Academy when I was a Cadet. He was some 3 or 4 years ahead of me. Whereas I knew him quite well, it had never been as a contemporary. There were those differences.

Althouth I will say this of Admiral Richmond. I could go in and if I disagreed with some of his ideas, I could argue and many times win. But he never held it against me as far as I know. Once a decision was made, you stuck by it, that's the way you do business. Once a decision is made, it's all over. But until he'd made it, he was perfectly willing to hear all my arguøments. I think several times he went along with me, when maybe his better judgement said no.

In 1960, I'd reached the point where I was so pooped, I'd come home around eight, beaten down all the time. I talked with Admiral Richmond; I was going to retire right then.

My annual physical came up and much to my pain my annual physical showed that I had diabetes. My mother died as a result of diabetes. It threw a couple of fears in me anyway. I spent some time in the hospital and they straightened it out with medicine and all that.

Of course that meant the end of any promotion career as far as I was concerned, because I couldn't pass any physical. They did give me a waiver for two years on the physical.

That waiver is really based on as long as you're in one particular job. As long as I was in that job, where I could be near medical attention and get my medicine and everything else, I was as good as anybody else.

In fact I made trips to San Juan, and quite a few trips. I don't think I ever did make a trip out to the Far East again.

So I was on a waiver there for my last two years that I served. Then finally when retirement came, I'd had 34 years and 3 or 4 months active duty. That's not counting Academy time. It was, in a way, a physical disability retirement.

One of the last things that happened to me was the day beofre I legally retired, in a complete surprise move, I was called into the Commandant's office to find an awful lot of people in there. I was presented the Legion of Merit.

Q: Can we read that into the record?

"The President of the United States takes pleasure in presenting the Legion of Merit to Captain Walter Clark Capron, United States Coast Guard for services set forth in the following citation: For exceptionally meritorious conduct in the performance of outstanding service as Deputy Chief of Staff, United States Coast Guard from July 1957 to August 1962. During this period, Captain Capron demonstrated the highest levels of professional skill and resourcefulness in the planning and coordinating of the day to day operations of the Coast Guard by his success in resolving and executing difficult and complex problems in the field of administrative planning and management. He has been closely associated with the guiding of the present day Coast Guard to a position of increasing importance to the United States. His outstanding ability to foster harmonious relationships with other governments and private agencies has resulted in the exceptional high spirited cooperation now existing between them and the Coast Guard. Through his constant interest, broad vision, and skillful interpretation in maritime, legislative, and military trends and with unsparing personal diligence, he has been able to produce accomplishments of great value to the service and the American people. Captain Capron's skill, diplomacy and zealous devotion to duty reflect great credit upon himself and the United States Coast Guard."

For the President,

Douglas Dillon.

INDEX

for Interviews with

WALTER C. CAPRON
Captain, U. S. Coast Guard (Ret.)

Abel, Comdr. Carl H., C. G. officer, 230-232

Acacia (Lighthouse tender), 104

Alexander Hamilton (ex-VICKSBURG), barkentine, 10; 37-38

Algonquin, ice breaker, 177, 192

Antietam, C. G. cutter, 147

Apache, C. G. cutter, 201

Argo, C. G. cutter, 147

Azores, 247

Barnett, C. G. cutter, 258, 284

Batory, 363

Berdine, Harold S., Comdr., 294

Berengaria, 88-89

Bibb, C. G. cutter, 297, 303

Black Duck, rum runner, 68

Bluenose, participant in Fisherman's Race, 73

Bolero, proposed U. S. Army operation across the Channel, 260-264

Calumet, C. G. tug, 218

Calypso, C. G. cutter, 198, 200, 207, 230ff

Camp Bradford, Amphibious Force Base, 279

Camp Devens, CMTC 5-6

Camp Edwards, 260-261

Campbell, C. G. cutter, 293, 303

Capron, Capt. Walter C., Interest in Coast Guard, 3; Coast Guard exams, 8-9; summer practice cruise, 11-13, 18-21; line cadet vs engineer cadet, 15-17; 1st year academy,

22-26; hazing, 27; discipline, 28-29; courses of study, 33-37; last 2 years in academy, 45-48; communications officer, 129; public relations officer, 148-150; command of COMANCHE, 186-187; Baltimore Port captain, 205-210; 215; take over of Italian vessels, 217-220; visit to Puerto Rico, 96-99, 107; Fleet Training leaflet, Norfolk, 287; National War College, 351ff; War Plans Section, 357-358; Legion of Merit, 379

CCC - Rescue Incident, 152-154

Chesapeake Regattas, 201-202

Cloud, Capt. - (Furness-Withy Agency in Baltimore), 232

Comanche, Ice breaker, 177, 178, 197

Communications, 129-130; 132-134; calling and distress frequencies, 140-141; call signals, 141; New York Division of Communications, 143; Navy experimental effort to take over Coast Guard communications, 158-159

Connecticut River flood in 1936, 160 ff

Convoys, organization of, 297-301

Convoy escorts, discussion of Allied vulnerability, 306-307

Conyngham, DD, 53-54, 56, 63

Cuyahoga, Escort vessel, 230

Danish ships, Baltimore port, 222, 226

Decentralization, policy of 1934, 146

Destroyers, derelict, 91-94

Dexter, Dwight, C. G. officer, 246

Dimmock, Prof. Chester H., 25

Dione, C. G. cutter, 203, 293

Duane, C. G. cutter, 303, 304

Enterprise, Cup Race, 71

Ericcson, C. G. cutter, 38-40

Escanaba, ice breaker, 177

Fisherman's Race, 1931, 73-76

Frederick Lee, C. G. cutter, 147

Fuller, transport, 257

Gertrude L. Thibaud, participant in Fisherman's Race, 73

Golden Mountain (freighter), 105

Harmon, Major Gen. Ernest, 284

Harriet Lane, C. G. cutter, 147, 152-153

Harris, transport, 283

Hekla, fishing trawler, 141

Hewitt, Admiral H. K., 266

Hudson River, C. G. problems in winter, 184-186; convoys on, 188

Ice breaking for commercial purposes, 126-127

Ingham, C. G. cutter, 302

Kickapoo, 126, 147

Kirk, Admiral Alan G., 290

League of Women of Coast Guard, 169

Lemburg, Canadian trawler, 143

Leonard Wood, transport, 241, 258

Lifeboat radio receivers, 136-138

Lighthouse Service, integrated into Coast Guard, 233-234, 235, 236

Loran stations, 374-376

Lynhaven Roads, maneuvers, 251

Machias, telephone communication line, 131

Merchant Marine Inspection Service, 314

Mohawk, ice breaker, 177, 190

Mojave, C. G. cutter, 38, 43

Morganthau, Henry L., 193-194

Morris, Ev, reporter, N. Y. Herald Tribune, 71-73

Narada, sea-going yacht, 4-5

New Jersey (tanker), 104

New River, proposed maneuvers, 250-251

Ossippee, 126, 147

Pamlico, C. G. cutter, 204

Park, RADM Charles A., 236

Philadelphia, First and Second Battles of, 42

Pt. Allerton Station, 139, 163, voice traffic station

Pontchartrain, C. G. cutter, 195, 337, 365, 373

Porto Rico (steamship), incident involving, 102-103

Port security measures (Korean War), 350

Potomac, yacht (ex-ELECTRA), 230

Reinburg, Capt., 221, 223, 225

Roosevelt (FDR), intention to put Coast Guard under Navy, 30-31, 113-116; Presidential proclamation, 244

Rum runners, 54-55, 58, 62, 68-70; description of 165-footers, designed against rum runners, 174-175, 179

Safi, landing at, 283-284

Seneca, C. G. cutter, 79-80, 82-83, 90-93, 95

Shamrock V, America's Cup Race, 71

Smuggling, 171

Spencer, C. G. cutter, 291-292, 294, 303, 316-319, 342

Star, Lt. Comdr. Jerry, 65-66, 128

Steele, Erwin B., C. G. officer, 168, 195

Thetis, C. G. cutter, 147, 171-173

Torch, operation - training for, 265-271, 272 ff

Training radio men, 155-157

U. S. Coast Guard: State of, 1933, 109 ff; Alumni Association, 31, 115; personnel policy, 117-120; aviation, 47, 120, 122-124, 308-309; building program, 1920-30, 176-177; responsibility for keeping rivers open, 180-181; mans army transports, 238-241; rationale for World War II expansion, 312-315; examination vessels, 323-324; temporary reserve, 325; auxiliary, 326; demobilization, 328-329 ff; post war 'busting,' 334-335

Vieques, Joint Amphibious Maneuvers, 237

War Memorial, Arlington, 49-50

Waesche, Admiral Russell, C. G. Commandant, 197-199, 200, 222-223

Wakefield (ex-MANHATTAN), transport, 238, 241

Weather stations, 343, 349

WHDH, radio station, 142

www.ingramcontent.com/pod-product-compliance
Lightning Source LLC
Chambersburg PA
CBHW080621170426
43209CB00007B/1486